PORTFOLIO
MANAGEMENT FORMULAS

PORTFOLIO MANAGEMENT FORMULAS

Mathematical Trading Methods
for the Futures, Options,
and Stock Markets

Ralph Vince

Wiley Finance Editions
JOHN WILEY & SONS
New York • Chichester • Brisbane • Toronto • Singapore

IBM® and IBM PC® are registered trademarks of International Business Machines Corp.
   MS DOS is a registered trademark of Microsoft Corp.
   Lotus 1–2–3 is a trademark of Lotus Development Corp.

Copyright © 1990 by Ralph Vince

Published by John Wiley & Sons, Inc.

Library of Congress Cataloging in Publication Data

Vince, Ralph. 1958–
      Portfolio management formulas : mathematical trading methods for the futures, options, and stock markets / Ralph Vince.
            p.   cm.
      Includes bibliographical references.
      ISBN 0-471-52756-4
      1. Commodity futures.   2. Futures.   3. Options (Finance)
      I. Title.
      HG6046.V56 1990
      332.64′5—dc20   90-12145
                                                                              CIP

Printed in the United States of America

10 9 8 7 6

For Arlene

Preface

This is a book about mathematical tools. So important are these tools to a trader, from a mathematical perspective, that it is my contention that they will change the way a trader views the markets.

The subject matter applies to participants in any of the markets, although it is expressed primarily for traders of the commodities markets. Whatever market the reader participates in, he or she most likely lacks one or more of the tools that will be discussed here. As we shall see, an enormous price is paid for neglecting any of these tools.

The first tool is simply trade selection, or, for system traders, system selection. This is the area where most traders concentrate their energies, and this is the area on which volumes have been written. This book does not concentrate on trade or system selection, other than to show remedies to many system problems and pitfalls. These problems and pitfalls are primarily the tradeoff of using the computer in the process of building the trading system.

Now we come to the neglected tools, which are the focus of this text. The first of these is quantity. This book shows the trader the proper quantity to trade in for a given market for a given system. Here the reader's understanding of trading the markets will be changed as the reader comes to realize that quantity is every bit as important as trade selection. One does not dominate the other. Readers will begin to see that the aspect of their trading that they should be monitoring is not whether they won or lost on the last trade, but whether or not they had the right quantity on. Incorrect quantity is one of the main reasons so many fund managers cannot beat the S&P 500 Index. An index does not have the problem of reinvesting returns, whereas a fund manager does.

The third tool a trader needs, after a good tool for trade selection and the proper tool for determining quantity, is the important concept of intercorrelation of returns. This, the second neglected tool, is also referred to as diversification and is just as important as the first two tools. This book quantifies the diversification process, showing the reader not only what markets and systems to trade, but how to diversify with respect to trading the right quantities for each market. Diversification is neglected in the sense that most traders view diversification solely as a function of eliminating risk. However, diversification can do a great deal more than simply eliminate some of the risk involved in trading. If done properly, diversification provides for improved performance. It is possible, as will be demonstrated, to take a market that made money, and one that lost money over the same period, and have the composite of the two show greater returns than simply the one that made money.

The two neglected tools, quantity and intercorrelation of returns, are little understood in regard to the power they give the trader as well as in regard to the penalty a trader pays for neglecting either of these tools. Together with proper trade and/or system selection, they comprise what is known as money management. All three of these tools are required for any successful trading campaign in the markets. This book shows mathematically how any success achieved in the markets without using all three of these tools is purely incidental.

The reader will also be affected in a more conceptual way than that presented by the money-management tools. The reader is introduced to the idea of looking at the stream of profits and losses generated by a trading system as a non-stationary distribution. This explains why systems tend to run hot and cold. Prices of any items traded on a free market also display this characteristic, which is why the charts of any freely traded item seem to show periods where the prices appear to be generated randomly, as well as periods where a strong nonrandom element is definitely present (such as ten days in a row that are locked-limit). I hope that this concept of a non-stationary distribution will inspire the reader in a different and more productive direction than simply looking at better ways to enter and exit trades.

Lastly, the reader will be conditioned to expect substantial drawdowns as part of the longer-term growth of an account utilizing the techniques explained in this book. These substantial drawdowns are, unfortunately, a fact of life if a trader is managing an account in the mathematically optimal fashion. Unlike most traders, readers of this text will be mentally prepared for these drawdowns, recognizing them when they occur as a part of the process. The reader will notice that any successful trading program must cover a time period where the trader of that program will be very tempted to stop trading it. If the program is any good, then to quit trading it is not a wise choice. As a result of the treatment of this subject in this book, I hope the reader will not be throwing in the towel when most traders would be most tempted to. Pulling punches requires more skill than throwing them.

Chagrin Falls, Ohio   R.V.
June 1990

Contents

INTRODUCTION
About This Book

You have traded the markets before. You have what you believe to be a winning approach. Now what?

This book will change the way you look at trading the markets. You may have some preconceived notions about money management or risk and reward. Some of the topics presented in this book may be enlightening, some boring, and others frustrating in what they imply. Regardless of how you find these topics, they are paramount to making your winning approach work. This book shows you why this is so from a mathematical standpoint.

This book concerns itself with the problem of maximizing geometric growth in an environment of *favorable uncertainty*.[1] In other words, an environment of risk on each individual event where the sum of the events is favorable. This implies that there is a broad spectrum of applications to this material, even though it is presented in the rather narrow field of trading the markets.

Much of the math described in this book is applicable to other geometric growth functions, such as:

- Cellular growth or the development of physical strength

- Growth of sales due to advertising

- Decay of a radioactive substance

[1] This is a term coined by R. C. Wentworth, private correspondence, 1989.

- Pharmaceutical half-lives

- Change of a chemical reaction

- The cooling of a body

- The growth of a population of people, animals, plants, bacteria, or virus, or the spread of infectious disease through such a population.

The list can go on and on.

However, this book concerns itself only with the geometric function of the growth of capital. We look at the mathematics involved and develop rules to maximize that growth with respect to other criteria. In the vocabulary of market participants, this is called "money management." But bear in mind that we are only covering a sliver of the spectrum of applications of this material.

Many people involved in the markets have false ideas regarding money management. Fortunately there are mathematically correct ideas in this regard. This book presents the mathematically correct concepts so that you will not be lost in the same sea of ignorance as are so many other traders and fund managers.

Many of the ideas presented are original and grew out of my programming experience with people in the futures industry. Around the middle of 1988, a disturbing anomaly occurred with one of the computer programs I had created for a certain trader. Late one Friday afternoon it was brought to my attention that my program was showing us to be making profits during this period, but the accounts being managed with this computer program were not. What was disturbing was that there was nothing wrong with the computer program, and we were taking all of the trades it had signaled. I didn't understand. For the rest of that day I could not get my mind off this problem.

That Saturday morning I awoke just percolating with all kinds of ideas and formulas to account for what was really happening. That trail of ideas has culminated in this book. What I have tried to do is paint a complete, unified picture of how traders or fund managers should manage their accounts for the highest mathematical performance in the future. So, most of what you read here is not original; rather, it is needed to fill in the voids in order to create the complete picture. Nor is it the purpose of this book to usurp other books on this or similar topics, but rather to embellish them, as well as to present new and pertinent topics.

I had no intention of writing a book on this subject. What actually happened was that, as I went to work on the mathematics of this project, I ended up with solutions that simply couldn't be explained in a five-minute conversation. Furthermore, the nature of the solutions was such that it led to a book (in that the solutions build upon each other in sequential fashion). So you see, this book is the inevitable outgrowth of what I at first thought was a simple bug in a computer program.

When many people hear the phrase "money management" they think you are alluding to eliminating or reducing drawdown. That is not what is meant in this book. Often you will have to endure great drawdowns to make the highest and best use of your money in the markets.

The ideas presented herein won't guarantee that you will make money. They are not foolproof formulas that create dollars from nothing. Rather, the ideas presented herein will show you *mathematically* how to maximize the *ratio* of potential reward to potential risk for a given situation *where you have the advantage*. Finding that advantage is your responsibility. This book assumes you are already capable of making money in the markets. This book assumes you are already operating in an environment of favorable uncertainty.

THE QUANTS ARE HERE

Computerized analysis of the markets has led us to a point today where we have beaten to death all of the oscillators, averages, trading systems, and other number-crunching techniques of trading the markets. After all the computerized optimizations and simulations, we find that the Holy Grail still eludes us.

Enter the quants, the strategy-game champions of today with a new definition of quality control: "Put a number on it." If you can put a number on something then you at least have some kind of understanding of the process. The quants' posture towards the markets is one of understanding *risk-management strategies* as a foundation for trading the markets.

This is the direction of today's market analysis, an approach that is mathematical rather than magical, an approach characterized by computers rather than the hunches of aged "high priests." This book falls into the category of a quant approach, yet it is not the alpha and omega of the approach.

Do not confuse the heading of risk-management strategies as necessarily meaning low risk. Often just the opposite is true. The approaches described here are concerned with maximizing the *ratio* of potential profits to potential losses; often the potential losses may be uncomfortably high.

Generally, this flies in the face of most people's levels of risk aversion. For instance, traders employing the tools discussed in this book may find that their optimal level of trading should be to trade twice as much as they are now. This may be more risk than they can tolerate; so instead they stay trading the same quantity as at present. In doing so, they have only half the risk that they would if they were trading the optimal quantities. However, they don't have half the potential profits; they have *less* than half the potential profits.

Finally, the approaches described in this book pertain to asymptotic dominance, meaning that the ratio of potential profits to potential losses is maximized in the *long-run* sense. In other words, the conclusions drawn are generally drawn with the proviso of performing something an infinite number of times.

WHAT YOU WON'T FIND IN THIS BOOK

None of the material is complicated, although it may be tricky to grasp at first. Each chapter builds upon the last in a textbook format. Therefore, you must progress through the book one chapter at a time in the order presented.

I have tried to be as concise and to the point as possible. I have tried to find that happy medium of providing complete explanations of complex phenomena without writing a treatise. As a result, some of the "further reaches" have not been probed completely. This happens when both of the following reasons occur together:

1. We do not yet have what we consider to be a complete understanding of the phenomenon.

2. Even to paint an incomplete (and, as a result, possibly inaccurate) picture of this phenomenon would require a lengthy, involved, and often technical dissertation.

Here is an example of just this type of thing. Most often we use what is known in statistics as the Normal Probability Distribution. We can use statistical tools based on this type of distribution. We often use these tools on futures prices, yet futures prices do not conform to the Normal Probability Distribution. Some people contend they conform to the stable paretian family of distributions, some contend futures prices conform to the Student's Distribution, and so on. We can prove that prices do not conform to the Student's Distribution because the Student's Distribution is symmetrical and the distribution of futures prices is not. The stable paretian family, on the other hand, is hardly understood at all. We can delve into the reasons why it is hardly understood, we can delve into other types of distributions; from here, we can explore many paths of reasoning. To do so would be pointless, however, since we do not yet have exact answers to these questions and the discussion would get lengthy and involved. It doesn't mean that these aren't material and important questions, though. They just belong in a different book, not this one.

For similar reasons, we will not touch upon certain related concepts such as the study of nonlinearity and chaos in the markets, expert systems for money management, and so forth. It is not that these topics aren't worthy of much discussion, rather that they (and others) are better suited as topics for entire books in and of themselves.

Another thing you will not find in this book are Greek letters as variables. Thank God! I grew up learning how to program computers in the 1970's using FORTRAN. The computer keyboards then did not have Greek letters on them. They don't today and hopefully never will. Greek letters do nothing to aid in the clarity of a mathematical expression and are therefore counterproductive.

SEQUENCE OF CHAPTERS

In Chapter 1 we explore the random process and gambling theory. The purpose here is to lay a foundation for looking at trading systems from the quantitative approach. Chapter 2 looks at trading systems, and how to make them perform reliably in the future. Chapter 3 builds upon what we have covered in the prior chapters by looking at characteristics of reinvestment of returns. It is in this chapter that we begin discussing geometric growth concepts.

Chapter 4 is the heart of the entire book; here, optimal f is introduced. Optimal f is a technique for generating the maximum geometric growth possible from a discrete stream of outcomes of any probability distribution (assuming the summation of those discrete outcomes is profitable). Assume we have a thermometer measuring the temperatures in downtown Los Angeles. The temperature change throughout the day is continuous, yet we only record the temperature, say, every hour. Those hourly readings are what we call discrete readings. They are individual little "packets," often taken as samplings from an otherwise continuous function. The trades generated from a trading system are also discrete (although they do not come from a continuous function), as are the outcomes of a game of roulette.

Chapter 5 concerns risk of ruin calculations. Chapter 6 shows how to combine the optimal fs in an optimal diversification. It quantifies what the optimal systems and markets to trade those systems on are. Then, Chapter 7 discusses some loose ends and closing thoughts that are pertinent. Finally, there are appendixes that cover many of the equations in the book, as well as computer code for performing some interesting tasks, and some ready-to-run programs.

THE OBVIOUS USUALLY GOES UNNOTICED

When you are through with this book, all of the concepts presented should seem obvious. So obvious that you may wonder why in your trading you have placed excessive emphasis on trade selection and not enough emphasis on these "money management" concepts. You will see mathematically how these concepts must be the core of a sound trading program.

There is a reason why these techniques are not given the proper weighting by traders. Most people can never see the mathematically obvious. For example, here in America, and everywhere else I presume except Great Britain, if a car wants to make a left turn the turning car must yield to oncoming traffic.

Now let's examine that. Every car behind the turning car in that lane, as well as the turning car, must wait until all the other cars in the oncoming lane have passed. Mathematically, the "car wait units" in the status-quo left-turn setup is roughly equal to A times B, where A is the left-turn car as well as all the cars behind him, and B is the number of cars in the oncoming lane.

Now let's look at what would happen if the left-turn car were given the right of way (we are only considering the case of a two-lane road, where we are starting out from a red light and the car turning left is the first car back from the light. It is also assumed that the car turning left has its signal on!). Now if the car turning left were allowed to turn before the oncoming traffic, the equation for car wait units would be roughly 1 times B, where B is the number of cars in the oncoming lane.

Suppose there are 5 cars in the oncoming lane and 5 cars in the lane turning left, including the car turning left. Under the status quo, the net wait to traffic is 25 car units. Under the alternate approach, it is 1/5 of that, or 5 units. Clearly, the second scenario would greatly expedite traffic. The more traffic, the greater the amount it would be expedited by, since this is an exponential function.

Yet has this idea ever been demonstrated to you before? The point is that there are still better ways of doing things that have not been presented to you before, are workable, and make good sense.

A BOOK FOR BEGINNERS

One other thing a trader will need to begin this book is a profitable technique of trading the markets. On that note I might end by saying that this is not a book for beginners. But it is my hope that when you are through with this book you will see that it should be.

CONVENTIONS USED IN THIS BOOK

An effort has been made to keep the mathematical symbols to a minimum throughout the text, even though the text is laden with equations. Furthermore, an effort has been made to make the symbols consistent throughout the text. As a result, division (fractions) is almost always expressed with a slash (/). This is more "keyboard-like" than if division were expressed any other way. Most computer languages express division this way.

Likewise, multiplication is always expressed with an asterisk (*). There are four reasons for this. The first, again, is that most computer languages express this operation this way. Second, by using the asterisk, we won't be confusing an X as the symbol for multiplication with a variable named X. The third reason for using the asterisk as opposed to another means of expressing multiplication, the dot, is that the dot is not on all keyboards, and is usually not so universally accepted. Fourth and finally, the other alternative, no operator, can be confusing, too, as the following example illustrates.

Assume we have two variables, A and B. Now if we introduce the statement:

AB = C

We have to ask if this means:

A * B = C

Or is there a new variable, AB, being introduced here that is independent of variable A and variable B?

Throughout the text, exponentiation is denoted with a raised caret (^). For example, the expression 10^3 means ten to the third power, or 1000. Roots are simply fractional exponents. Therefore the cube root of 1000 would be denoted as 1000^(1/3), which of course equals 10. Exponentiation deserves an operator, not simply a superscription of the exponent. So, our notation is more consistent. Further consistency is achieved when we take the root of a number. By using the caret as an operator, we express taking the root of something in a way that relates it to what it mathematically does, raises a number to a fractional power (in effect lowering a number that is greater than 1).

But the main reason exponentiation is being presented this way is that many readers will want to program much of the material in this book. Using this format for exponentiation, will make that programming quicker, easier, and less prone to error.

By expressing exponentiation this way, we also do away with using the radical sign. In so doing we have made exponentiation more "keyboard-like" as well as making it easier to parse a formula by the rules of mathematical precedence (more on mathematical precedence shortly). Moreover, paralleling the evolution of the computer has been a trend toward expressing exponentiation this way. (I am not trying to establish a trend here, but rather to follow one that is already in progress and that improves our understanding.)

We tend to think that our system of numbers and mathematical symbols is constant and universal. Rather, it is extremely dynamic. Consider for a moment that it wasn't until the 11th century that the base-10 system reached Europe, where it wasn't readily accepted because it had no way to express fractions. It wasn't until 1617 that the decimal point was introduced by John Napier. Consider that during the 15th century the symbols p and m were used for plus and minus. The earliest use we find of the symbols + and − is in the year 1481. Only recently did mathematical symbols gain some semblance of universality. For instance, Leibniz, a 17th-century German mathematician, used a symbol that resembles an upside down lowercase letter u to denote multiplication. René Descartes used what looks to us like the lowercase letters o and c, connected "back to back" to represent equality. Incidentally, it was Descartes who introduced the square root radical, which we are attempting to overturn here with ^(1/2). The early Romans used a symbol we now use to denote infinity to denote the number 1000 prior to using the letter M. In 1713, Bernoulli began using this symbol to represent infinity and it has been accepted as such ever since.

The evolution of mathematical symbols has mostly occurred in recent centuries. With the advent of the computer this evolutionary rate is now increased manyfold. So we can be keeping with tradition in this book and still express exponentiation with a raised caret, as the tradition of mathematical symbols has hardly been static!

I am most curious to see what the accepted mathematical symbols will be 100 years from now! I would imagine our descendants will use some sort of a multi-based number system rather than our primitive single-base, base-ten system. Perhaps with such a system they will be better able to express irrational numbers as well as numerical concepts that we have difficulty expressing today.

Many conventions we take for granted will be replaced by better ones. For instance, when you are on the North Pole everything is south of you! From the North Pole, whichever direction you take your first step in, you are stepping south. That is because our system of longitude and latitude uses polar coordinates. Polar coordinates try to force-fit a two-dimensional system (for mapping on a plane) to the surface of a three-dimensional object—the earth. Obviously, this is foolish and frustrating. We should have a better system in use for specifying points on the surface of a three-dimensional object.

Long before Columbus rediscovered America, everyone knew the earth was round except for a few imbeciles. How else could one have explained the disappearance of a ship over the horizon when it had returned? The point is that a better system doesn't come into everyday usage just because time has elapsed until an effort is put forth to use the new system. This is part of the reason why an effort is being made to express mathematical operations this way in this text. Our hope is that the operations will be clearer and the equations easier to parse by the rules of mathematical precedence (and as a result, easier to take from the text to the computer keyboard).

It is assumed that the reader has at least a marginal understanding of algebra and basic statistics (or at least once had). One area worth going over at this time is that of mathematical precedence. There will be numerous equations throughout this text. Many readers cannot adequately understand an equation unless all elements are completely parenthesized (otherwise they feel the writer of the equation is being vague and allowing the reader to interpret the equation in more than one way). An example might make this clear. Consider:

$$1 + 2 * 3$$

Some people might think this means $(1 + 2) * 3$, which would equal 9. But that is not correct. The correct answer is $1 + (2 * 3)$ or 7.

Now consider the equation:

$$-6 + 7^2$$

This is the same as $-6 + 49$, or 43. It is not the same as:

$$(-6 + 7)^2$$

which is equal to 1. You should know this by the rules of mathematical precedence, which state that *unless parenthesized to the contrary* (and in pureness parentheses should be used only if the equation is to be performed contrary to mathematical precedence), you perform an equation in the following manner:

1. All exponentiation is performed first (including radical signs).

2. All unary minus is performed second.

3. All multiplication and division are performed third.

4. All addition and subtraction are then performed.

5. If there is equal precedence, perform from left to right.

Unary minus simply means a minus sign with only one operand. Normally subtraction takes 2 operands:

Operand – Operand

as opposed to unary minus which has only one operand:

– Operand

Unary minus means literally "a negative number." If you do not understand mathematical precedence, learn it now or you will have trouble with the equations in this text.

Repeatedly throughout the text you will encounter the term "market system." A market system is a particular trading system on a particular market. System A on Bonds is a different market system than System B on Bonds or System A on Silver. Please make note also that at no other point than this in the book will pyramiding be discussed. That should keep things simple. We will be discussing systems that do not pyramid once they are in a trade, with "pyramiding" defined as adding more contracts to a trade already in progress. This simplification should aid understanding. The concepts to be presented will be complicated enough without adding pyramiding into the picture. Which is not to say that we ignore pyramiding altogether. Rather, the contracts that are added once a trade is already in progress should be treated by futures researchers as a separate system, apart from the system that initiated the position. In doing so we can compare apples to apples with respect to different systems and with respect to comparing the initial entry and the additional (pyramid) entries. When we discuss optimal f in Chapter 4 you will learn what the optimal number of contracts to trade for a given market system are for your initial entry system. By segregating your initial entry system and the rules for pyramiding it into separate systems, you will be able to know exactly how many contracts to pyramid with as well.

Often, the concepts presented will be in terms of a bet or will use gambling terminology. The main difference between gambling and speculation is that gambling creates risk (and hence is considered morally wrong in most societies) whereas speculation is a transference of an already existing risk to a speculator. The gambling references and examples are all used to illustrate the points involved in as clear a manner as possible. Often the gambling illustrations are easier to grasp than trading illustrations would be, since the gambling illustrations tend to be simpler. However, this is *not* a book about gambling.

Throughout the text certain sentences, phrases, or paragraphs are italicized. These are not italicized simply for emphasis. Rather, when an idea is an axiom or principle it will be in italics. Therefore, as you read the text make certain you always understand completely something that is italicized.

1

The Random Process and Gambling Theory

Toss a coin in the air. For an instant you experience one of the most fascinating paradoxes of nature—the random process. While the coin is in the air there is no way to tell for certain whether it will land heads or tails. Yet over many tosses the outcome can be reasonably predicted.

Oddly enough, though, there is a great deal of misconception and misinformation regarding the random process. Our ancestors tried to explain the random process and in so doing created what we now call superstitions. Most people have never been taught anything about the random process in school aside from a brief glossing over in probability and statistics classes. Is it any wonder that the random process is still mostly misunderstood?

This, then, is where we begin our discussion.

Certain axioms will be developed as we discuss the random process. The first of these is that *the outcome of an individual event in a random process cannot be predicted. However, we can reduce the possible outcomes to a probability statement.*

Pierre Simone Laplace (1749–1827) defined the probability of an event as the ratio of the number of ways in which the event can happen to the total possible number of events. Therefore, when a coin is tossed, the probability of getting tails is 1 (the number of tails on a coin) divided by 2 (the number of possible events), for a probability of .5. In our coin-toss example, we do not know whether the result will be heads or tails, but we do know that the probability that it will be heads is .5 and the probability it will be tails is .5. So, *a probability statement is a number between 0 (there is no chance of the event in question occurring) and 1 (the occurrence of the event is certain).*

Often you will have to convert from a probability statement to odds and vice versa. The two are interchangeable, as the odds imply a probability, and a probability likewise implies the odds. These conversions are given now. The formula to convert to a probability statement, when you know the given odds is:

Probability = (odds for/(odds for + odds against))

If the odds on a horse, for example, are 4 to 1 (4:1), then the probability of that horse winning, as implied by the odds, is:

Probability = $(1/(1 + 4))$

$\qquad$ = $(1/5)$

$\qquad$ = .2

So a horse that is 4:1 can also be said to have a probability of winning of .2. What if the odds were 5 to 2 (5:2)? In such a case the probability is:

Probability = $(2/(2 + 5))$

$\qquad$ = $(2/7)$

$\qquad$ = .2857142857

The formula to convert from probability to odds is:

Odds (against, to one) = (1/probability) − 1

So, for our coin-toss example, when there is a .5 probability of the coin coming up heads, the odds on it coming up heads are given as:

Odds = $(1/.5) − 1$

$\qquad$ = $2 − 1$

$\qquad$ = 1

This formula always gives you the odds "to one." In this example, we would say the odds on a coin coming up heads are 1 to 1.

How about our previous example, where we converted from odds of 5:2 to a probability of .2857142857? Let's work the probability statement back to the odds and see if it works out.

$$Odds = (1/.2857142857) - 1$$

$$= 3.5 - 1$$

$$= 2.5$$

Here we can say that the odds in this case are 2.5 to 1, which is the same as saying that the odds are 5 to 2. So when someone speaks of odds, they are speaking of a probability statement as well.

Most people can't handle the uncertainty of a probability statement; it just doesn't sit well with them. We live in a world of exact sciences, and human beings have an innate tendency to believe they do not understand an event if it can only be reduced to a probability statement. The domain of physics seemed to be such a solid one prior to the emergence of quantum physics. We had equations to account for most processes we had observed. These equations were real and provable. They repeated themselves over and over and the outcome could be exactly calculated before the event took place. With the emergence of quantum physics, suddenly a theretofore exact science could only reduce a physical phenomenon to a probability statement. Understandably, this disturbed many people.

I am not espousing the random walk concept of price action nor am I asking you to accept anything about the markets as random. Not yet, anyway. Like quantum physics, the idea that there is or is not randomness in the markets is an emotional one. At this stage, let us simply concentrate on the random process as it pertains to something we are certain is random, such as coin tossing or casino gambling. In so doing, we can understand the process first, and later look at its applications. Whether the random process is applicable to other areas such as the markets is an issue that can be developed later.

Logically, the question must arise, "When does a random sequence begin and when does it end?" It really doesn't end. The blackjack table continues running even after you leave it. As you move from table to table in a casino, the random process can be said to follow you around. If you take a day off from the tables the random process may be interrupted, but it continues upon your return. So, when we speak of a random process of X events in length we are arbitrarily choosing some finite length in order to study the process.

INDEPENDENT VERSUS DEPENDENT
TRIALS PROCESSES

We can subdivide the random process into two categories. First are those events for which the probability statement is constant from one event to the next. These we will call independent trials processes or sampling with replacement. A coin toss is an example of just such a process. Each toss has a 50/50 probability regardless of the outcome of the prior toss. Even if the last five flips of a coin were heads, the probability of this flip being heads is unaffected, and remains .5.

Naturally, the other type of random process is one where the outcome of prior events *does* affect the probability statement and, naturally, the probability statement is not constant from one event to the next. These types of events are called dependent trials processes or sampling without replacement. Blackjack is an example of just such a process. Once a card is played, the composition of the deck for the next draw of a card is different from what it was for the previous draw. Suppose a new deck is shuffled and a card removed. Say it was the ace of diamonds. Prior to removing this card the probability of drawing an ace was 4/52 or .07692307692. Now that an ace has been drawn from the deck, and not replaced, the probability of drawing an ace on the next draw is 3/51 or .05882352941.

Some people argue that dependent trials processes such as this are really not random events. For the purposes of our discussion, though, we will assume they are—since the outcome still cannot be known beforehand. The best that can be done is to reduce the outcome to a probability statement. Try to think of the difference between independent and dependent trials processes as simply whether the probability statement is *fixed* (independent trials) or *variable* (dependent trials) from one event to the next based on prior outcomes. This is in fact the only difference.

Everything can be reduced to a probability statement. Events where the outcomes can be known prior to the fact differ from random events mathematically only in that their probability statements equal 1. For example, suppose that 51 cards have been removed from a deck of 52 cards and you know what the cards are. Therefore you know what the one remaining card is with a probability of 1 (certainty). For the time being, we will deal with the independent trials process, particularly the simple coin toss.

MATHEMATICAL EXPECTATION

At this point it is necessary to understand the concept of mathematical expectation, sometimes known as the player's edge (if positive to the player) or the house's advantage (if negative to the player):

Mathematical Expectation $= (1 + A) * P - 1$

where: P = Probability of winning.

A = Amount you can win/Amount you can lose.

So, if you are going to flip a coin and you will win $2 if it comes up heads, but you will lose $1 if it comes up tails, the mathematical expectation per flip is:

Mathematical Expectation = (1 + 2) * .5 − 1

$$= 3 * .5 − 1$$

$$= 1.5 − 1$$

$$= .5$$

In other words, you would expect to make 50 cents on average each flip.

This formula just described will give us the mathematical expectation for an event that can have two possible outcomes. What about situations where there are more than two possible outcomes? The next formula will give us the mathematical expectation for an unlimited number of outcomes. It will also give us the mathematical expectation for an event with only two possible outcomes such as the 2 for 1 coin toss just described. Hence it is the preferred formula.

$$\text{Mathematical Expectation} = \sum_{i=1}^{N} (P_i * A_i)$$

where: P = Probability of winning or losing.

A = Amount won or lost.

N = Number of possible outcomes.

The mathematical expectation is computed by multiplying each possible gain or loss by the probability of that gain or loss, and then summing those products together.

Now look at the mathematical expectation for our 2 for 1 coin toss under the newer, more complete formula:

Mathematical Expectation = (.5 * 2) + (.5 * (− 1))

$$= 1 + (− .5)$$

$$= .5$$

In such an instance, of course, your mathematical expectation is to win 50 cents per toss on average.

Suppose you are playing a game in which you must guess one of three different numbers. Each number has the same probability of occurring (.33), but if you guess one of the numbers you will lose $1, if you guess another number you will lose $2, and if you guess the right number you will win $3. Given such a case, the mathematical expectation (ME) is:

$$ME = (.33 * (-1)) + (.33 * (-2)) + (.33 * 3)$$
$$= -.33 - .66 + .99$$
$$= 0$$

Consider betting on one number in roulette, where your mathematical expectation is:

$$ME = ((1/38) * 35) + ((37/38) * (-1))$$
$$= (.02631578947 * 35) + (.9736842105 * (-1))$$
$$= (.9210526315) + (-.9736842105)$$
$$= -.05263157903$$

If you bet $1 on one number in roulette (American double-zero) you would expect to lose, on average, 5.26 cents per roll. If you bet $5, you would expect to lose, on average, 26.3 cents per roll. Notice how *different amounts bet have different mathematical expectations in terms of* amounts, *but the expectation as a* percent *of the amount bet is always the same.*

The player's expectation for a series of bets is the total of the expectations for the individual bets. So if you go play $1 on a number in roulette, then $10 on a number, then $5 on a number, your total expectation is:

$$ME = (-.0526 * 1) + (-.0526 * 10) + (-.0526 * 5)$$
$$= -.0526 - .526 - .263$$
$$= -.8416$$

You would therefore expect to lose on average 84.16 cents.

This principle explains why systems that try to change the size of their bets relative to how many wins or losses have been seen (assuming an independent trials process) are doomed to fail. The sum of negative-expectation bets is always a negative expectation!

EXACT SEQUENCES, POSSIBLE OUTCOMES, AND THE NORMAL DISTRIBUTION

We have seen how flipping one coin gives us a probability statement with two possible outcomes—heads or tails. Our mathematical expectation would be the sum of these possible outcomes. Now let's flip two coins. Here the possible outcomes are:

Coin 1	Coin 2	Probability
H	H	.25
H	T	.25
T	H	.25
T	T	.25

This can also be expressed as there being a 25% chance of getting both heads, a 25% chance of getting both tails, and a 50% chance of getting a head and a tail. In tabular format:

Combination	Probability	
H2	.25	*
T1H1	.50	**
T2	.25	*

The asterisks to the right show how many different ways the combination can be made. For example in the above two-coin flip there are two asterisks for T1H1, since there are two different ways to get this combination. Coin A could be heads and coin B tails, or the reverse, coin A tails and coin B heads. The total number of asterisks in the table (four) is the total number of different combinations you can get when flipping that many coins (two).

If we were to flip three coins, we would have:

Combination	Probability	
H3	.125	*
H2T1	.375	***
T2H1	.375	***
T3	.125	*

for four coins:

Combination	Probability	
H4	.0625	★
H3T1	.25	★★★★
H2T2	.375	★★★★★★
T3H1	.25	★★★★
T4	.0625	★

and for six coins:

Combination	Probability	
H6	.0156	★
H5T1	.0937	★★★★★★
H4T2	.2344	★★★★★★★★★★★★★★★
H3T3	.3125	★★★★★★★★★★★★★★★★★★★★★★
T4H2	.2344	★★★★★★★★★★★★★★★
T5H1	.0937	★★★★★★
T6	.0156	★

Notice here that if we were to plot the asterisks vertically we would be developing into the familiar bell-shaped curve, also called the Normal or Gaussian Distribution (see Figure 1-1).[1]

Finally, for ten coins:

Combination	Probability	
H10	.001	★
H9T1	.01	★★★★★★★★★★
H8T2	.044	★★★★(45 different ways)
H7T3	.117	★★★★(120 different ways)
H6T4	.205	★★★★(210 different ways)
H5T5	.246	★★★★(252 different ways)
T6H4	.205	★★★★(210 different ways)
T7H3	.117	★★★★(120 different ways)
T8H2	.044	★★★★(45 different ways)
T9H1	.01	★★★★★★★★★★
T10	.001	★

---

[1] Actually, the coin toss does not conform to the Normal Probability Function in a pure statistical sense, but rather belongs to a class of distributions called the Binomial Distribu-

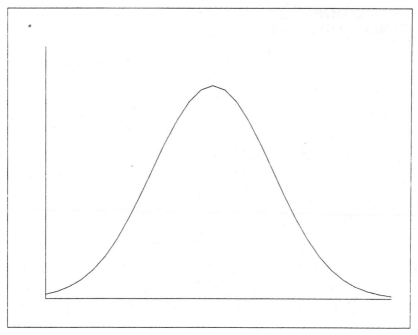

Figure 1-1   Normal probability function.

Notice that *as the number of coins increases, the probability of getting all heads or all tails decreases.* When we were using two coins, the probability of getting all heads or all tails was .25. For three coins it was .125, for four coins .0625; for six coins .0156, and for 10 coins it was .001.

---

tion (a.k.a. Bernoulli or Coin-Toss Distributions). However, as N becomes large, the Binomial approaches the Normal Distribution as a limit (provided the probabilities involved are not close to 0 or 1). This is so because the Normal Distribution is continuous from left to right, whereas the Binomial is not, and the Normal is always symmetrical whereas the Binomial needn't be. Since we are treating a finite number of coin tosses and trying to make them representative of the universe of coin tosses, and since the probabilities are always equal to .5, we will treat the distributions of tosses as though they were Normal. As a further note, the Normal Distribution can be used as an approximation of the Binomial if both N times the probability of an event occurring and N times the complement of the probability occurring are both greater than 5. In our coin-toss example, since the probability of the event is .5 (for either heads or tails) and the complement is .5, then so long as we are dealing with N of 11 or more we can use the Normal Distribution as an approximation for the Binomial.

POSSIBLE OUTCOMES AND
STANDARD DEVIATIONS

So a coin flipped 4 times has a total of 16 possible exact sequences:

1.	H	H	H	H
2.	H	H	H	T
3.	H	H	T	H
4.	H	H	T	T
5.	H	T	H	H
6.	H	T	H	T
7.	H	T	T	H
8.	H	T	T	T
9.	T	H	H	H
10.	T	H	H	T
11.	T	H	T	H
12.	T	H	T	T
13.	T	T	H	H
14.	T	T	H	T
15.	T	T	T	H
16.	T	T	T	T

The term "exact sequence" here means the exact outcome of a random process. The set of all possible exact sequences for a given situation is called the *sample space*. Note that the four-coin flip just depicted can be four coins all flipped at once, or it can be one coin flipped four times (i.e., it can be a chronological sequence).

If we examine the exact sequence T H H T and the sequence H H T T the outcome would be the same for a person flat-betting (i.e., betting 1 unit on each instance). However, to a person not flat-betting, the end result of these two exact sequences can be far different. To a flat bettor there are only five possible outcomes to a four-flip sequence:

4 Heads

3 Heads and 1 Tail

2 Heads and 2 Tails

1 Head and 3 Tails

4 Tails

As we have seen, there are 16 possible exact sequences for a 4-coin flip. This fact would concern a person who is not flat-betting. We will refer to people who are not flat-betting as "system" players, since that is most likely what they are doing—betting variable amounts based on some scheme they think they have worked out.

If you flip a coin 4 times you will of course see only one of the 16 possible exact sequences. If you flip the coin another 4 times you will see another exact sequence (although you could, with a probability of $1/16 = .0625$, see the exact same sequence). If you go up to a gaming table and watch a series of 4 plays, you will see only one of the 16 exact sequences. You will also see one of the 5 possible end results. *Each exact sequence has the same probability of occurring*, that being .0625. *But each end result does not have equal probability of occurring:*

End Result	Probability
4 Heads	.0625
3 Heads and 1 Tail	.25
2 Heads and 2 Tails	.375
1 Head and 3 Tails	.25
4 Tails	.0625

Most people do not understand the difference between exact sequences and end results and as a result falsely conclude that exact sequences and end results are the same thing. This is a common misconception that can lead to a great deal of trouble. It is the end results (not the exact sequences) that conform to the bell curve—the Normal Distribution, which is a particular type of probability distribution. An interesting characteristic of all probability distributions is a statistic known as the *standard deviation.*

For the Normal Probability Distribution on a simple binomial game, such as the one being used here for the end results of coin flips, the standard deviation (SD) is:

$$SD = N * (((P * (1 - P))/N)^\wedge(1/2))$$

where: P = Probability of the event (e.g., result of heads).

N = Number of trials.

For 10 coin tosses (i.e., N = 10):

$$SD = 10 * (((.5 * (1 - .5))/10)^{\wedge}(1/2))$$

$$= 10 * (((.5 * .5)/10)^{\wedge}(1/2))$$

$$= 10 * ((.25/10)^{\wedge}(1/2))$$

$$= 10 * (.025^{\wedge}(1/2))$$

$$= 10 * .158113883$$

$$= 1.58113883$$

The center line of a distribution is the peak of the distribution. In the case of the coin toss the peak is at an even number of heads and tails. So for a 10-toss sequence the center line would be at 5 heads and 5 tails. For the Normal Probability Distribution, approximately 68.26% of the events will be + or − 1 standard deviation from the center line, 95.45% between + and − 2 standard deviations from the center line, and 99.73% between + and − 3 standard deviations from the center line (see Figure 1-2). Continuing with our 10-flip coin toss, 1 standard deviation equals approximately 1.58. We can therefore say of our 10-coin flip that 68% of the time we can expect to have our end result be composed of 3.42 (5 − 1.58) to 6.58 (5 + 1.58) being heads (or tails). So if we have 7 heads (or tails) we would be beyond 1 standard deviation of the expected outcome (the expected outcome being 5 heads and 5 tails).

Here is another interesting phenomenon. Notice in our coin-toss examples that as the number of coins tossed increases, the probability of getting an even number of heads and tails decreases. With two coins the probability of getting H1T1 was .5. At four coins the probability of getting 50% heads and 50% tails dropped to .375. At six coins it was .3125, and at ten coins .246. Therefore we can state that *as the number of events increases, the probability of the end result exactly equaling the expected value decreases.*

The mathematical expectation is what we expect to gain or lose, on average, each bet. However, it does not explain the fluctuations from bet to bet. In our coin-toss example we know that there is a 50/50 probability of a toss coming up heads or tails. We expect that after N trials approximately (1/2) * N of the tosses will be heads, and (1/2) * N of the tosses will be tails. Assuming that we lose the same amount when we lose as we make when we win, we can say we have a mathematical expectation of 0, regardless of how large N is.

We also know that approximately 68% of the time we will be + or − 1 standard deviation away from our expected value. For 10 trials

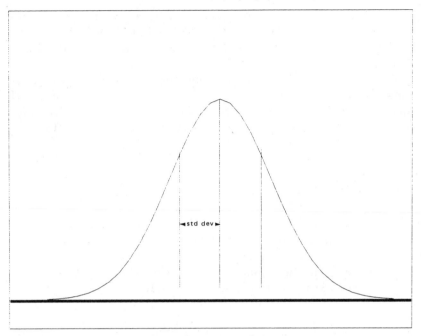

Figure 1-2　Normal probability function: center line and 1 standard deviation in either direction.

(N = 10) this means our standard deviation is 1.58. For 100 trials (N = 100) this means we have a standard deviation size of 5. At 1,000 (N = 1,000) trials the standard deviation is approximately 15.81. For 10,000 trials (N = 10,000) the standard deviation is 50.

N	Std Dev	Std Dev/N as %
10	1.58	15.8%
100	5	5.0%
1,000	15.81	1.581%
10,000	50	0.5%

Notice that as N increases, the standard deviation increases as well. This means that contrary to popular belief, *the longer you play, the further you will be from your expected value (in terms of units won or lost)*. However, as N increases the standard deviation as a percent of N decreases. This means that *the longer you play the closer to your expected value you will be as a percent of the total action (N)*. This is the "Law of Averages" presented in its mathematically correct form. In other words, if you make a long series of bets, N, where T equals your total profit or loss and E equals your expected profit or loss, then T/N tends towards E/N as N increases. Also, the difference between E and T increases as N increases.

In Figure 1-3 we will observe the random process in action with a 60-coin-toss game. Also on this chart you will see the lines for + and − 1 and 2 standard deviations. Notice how they bend in, yet continue outward forever. This conforms with what was just said about the Law of Averages.

THE HOUSE ADVANTAGE

Now let us examine what happens when there is a house advantage involved. Again, refer to our coin-toss example. We last saw 60 trials at an even or "fair" game. Let's now see what happens if the house has a 5% advantage. An example of such a game would be a coin toss where if we win we win $1.00 but if we lose we lose $1.10.

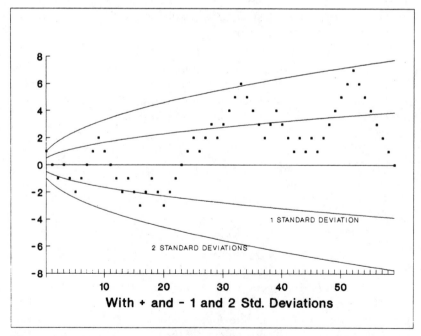

Figure 1-3 The random process: results of 60 coin tosses, with 1 and 2 standard deviations in either direction.

Figure 1-4 shows the same 60-coin-toss game as we previously saw, only this time there is the 5% house advantage involved. Notice how, in this scenario, ruin is inevitable—as the upper standard deviations begin to bend down (to eventually cross below zero).

Let's examine what happens when we continue to play a game with a negative mathematical expectation.

N	Std Dev	Expectation	+ or − 1 SD
10	1.58	− .5	+ 1.08 to − 2.08
100	5	− 5	0 to − 10
1,000	15.81	− 50	− 34.19 to − 65.81
10,000	50	− 500	− 450 to − 550
100,000	158.11	− 5000	− 4,842 to − 5,158
1,000,000	500	− 50000	− 49,500 to − 50,500

The principle of ergodicity is at work here. It doesn't matter if one person goes to a casino and bets one dollar one million times in succession or if one million people come and bet one dollar each all at once. The numbers are the same. At one million bets, it would take more than

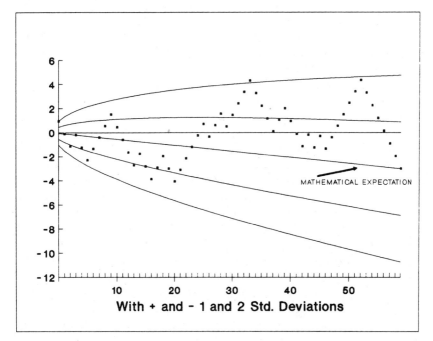

Figure 1-4   Results of 60 coin tosses with a 5% house advantage.

100 standard deviations away from the expectation before the casino started to lose money! Here is the Law of Averages at work. By the same account, if you were to make one million $1 bets at a 5% house advantage, it would be equally unlikely for you to make money. Many casino games have more than a 5% house advantage, as does most sports betting. Trading the markets is a zero sum game. However, there is a small drain involved in the way of commissions, fees, and floor slippage. Often these costs can run in excess of 5%.

Next, let's examine the statistics of a 100-coin-toss game with and without a 5% house advantage:

Std. Deviations from Center	Fair 50/50 Game	5% House Advantage Game
+3	+15	+10
+2	+10	+5
+1	+5	0
0	0	-5
-1	-5	-10
-2	-10	-15
-3	-15	-20

As can be seen, at 3 standard deviations, which we can expect to be the outcome 99.73% of the time, we will win or lose between +15 and -15 units in a fair game. At a house advantage of 5%, we can expect our final outcome to be between +10 and -20 units at the end of 100 trials. At 2 standard deviations, which we can expect to occur 95% of the time, we win or lose within + or - 10 in a fair game. At a 5% house advantage this is +5 and -15 units. At 1 standard deviation, where we can expect the final outcome to be with 68% probability, we win or lose up to 5 units in a fair game. Yet in the game where the house has the 5% advantage we can expect the final outcome to be between winning nothing and losing 10 units! Note that at a 5% house advantage it is not impossible to win money after 100 trials, but you would have to do better than 1 whole standard deviation to do so. In the Normal Distribution, the probability of doing better than 1 whole standard deviation, you will be surprised to learn, is only .1587!

Notice in the previous example that at 0 standard deviations from the center line (that is, at the center line itself), the amount lost is equal to the house advantage. For the fair 50/50 game, this is equal to 0. You would expect neither to win nor to lose anything. In the game where the house has the 5% edge, you would expect to lose 5%, 5 units for every 100 trials, at 0 standard deviations from the center line. So you can say that *in flat-betting situations involving an independent process you will lose at the rate of the house advantage.*

MATHEMATICAL EXPECTATION LESS THAN ZERO SPELLS DISASTER!

This brings us to another axiom, which can be stated as follows: *In a negative expectancy game, there is no money management scheme that will make you a winner. If you continue to bet, regardless of how you manage your money, it is almost certain that you will be a loser, losing your entire stake regardless of how large it was to start.*

This sounds like something to think about. Negative mathematical expectations (regardless of how negative) have broken apart families, caused suicides and murders and all sorts of other things the bettors weren't bargaining for. I hope you can see what an incredibly losing proposition it is to make bets where there is a negative expectancy, for even a small negative expectancy will eventually take every cent you have. All attempts to outsmart this process are mathematically futile. Don't get this idea confused with whether or not there is a dependent or independent trials process involved; it doesn't matter. If the sum of your bets is a negative expectancy you are in a losing proposition.

As an example, if you are in a dependent trials process where you have an edge in 1 bet out of 10, then you must bet enough on the bet for which you have an edge so that the sum of all 10 bets is a positive expectancy situation. If you expect to lose 10 cents on average for 9 of the 10 bets, but you expect to make 10 cents on the 1 out of 10 bets where you know you have the edge, then you must bet more than 9 times as much on the bet where you know you have the edge, just to have a net expectation of coming out even. If you bet less than that, you are still in a negative expectancy situation, and complete ruin is all but certain if you continue to play.

Many people have the mistaken impression that if they play a negative expectancy game they will lose a percentage of their capital relative to the negative expectancy. For example, when most people realize that the mathematical expectation in roulette is 5.26% they seem to think this means that if they go to a casino and play roulette they can expect to lose, on average, 5.26% of their stake. This is a dangerous misconception. The truth is that they can expect to lose 5.26% of their *total action*, not of their entire stake. Suppose they take $500 to play roulette. If they make 500 bets of $20 each, their total action is $10,000, of which they can expect to lose 5.26%, or $526, more than their entire stake.

The only smart thing to do is only bet when you have a positive expectancy. This is not so easily a winning proposition as negative expectancy betting is a losing proposition, as we shall see in a later chapter. You must bet specific quantities, which will be discussed at length. For the time being, though, resolve to bet only on positive expectancy situations. In the next chapter we will discuss finding positive expectancy situations in the markets.

When it comes to casino gambling, though, the only time you can find a positive expectancy situation is if you keep track of the cards in blackjack, and then only if you are a very good player, and only if you bet your money correctly. There are many good blackjack books available, so we won't delve any further into blackjack here.

BACCARAT

If you want to gamble at a casino but do not want to learn to play blackjack correctly, then baccarat has the smallest negative expectancy of any other casino game. In other words you'll lose your money at a slower rate. Here are the probabilities in baccarat:

Banker wins 45.842% of the time.

Player wins 44.683% of the time.

A tie occurs 9.547% of the time.

Since a tie is treated as a push in baccarat (no money changes hands, the net effect is the same as if the hand were never played) the probabilities, when ties are eliminated become:

Banker wins 50.68% of the time.

Player wins 49.32% of the time.

Now let's look at the mathematical expectations. For the player side:

$$ME = (.4932 * 1) + ((1 - .4932) * (-1))$$
$$= (.4932 * 1) + (.5068 * (-1))$$
$$= .4932 - .5068$$
$$= -.0136$$

In other words, the house advantage over the player is 1.36%.

Now for the banker side, bearing in mind that the banker side is charged a 5% commission on wins only, the mathematical expectation is:

$$ME = (.5068 * .95) + ((1 - .5068) * (-1))$$

$$= (.5068 * .95) + (.4932 * (-1))$$

$$= .48146 - .4932$$

$$= -.01174$$

In other words the house has an advantage, once commissions on the banker's wins are accounted for, of 1.174%.

As you can see, it makes no sense to bet on the player since the player's negative expectancy is worse than the banker's:

Player's disadvantage	$-.0136$
Banker's disadvantage	$-.01174$
Banker's edge over Player	$.00186$

In other words, after about 538 hands (1/.00186) the banker will be 1 unit ahead of the player. Again, the more hands that are played, the more certain this edge is.

This is not to imply that the banker has a positive mathematical expectation—he doesn't. Both banker and player have negative expectations, but the banker's is not as negative as the player's. Betting 1 unit on the banker on each hand, you can expect to lose 1 unit for approximately every 85 hands (1/.01174); whereas betting 1 unit on the player on each hand, you would expect to lose 1 unit every 74 hands (1/.0136). You will lose your money at a slower *rate*, but not necessarily a slower *pace*. Most baccarat tables have a $25 minimum bet. If you are betting banker, 1 unit per hand, after 85 hands you can expect to be down $25.

Let's compare this to betting red/black at roulette, where you have a mathematical expectation of $-.0526$, but a minimum bet size of $2. After 85 spins you would expect to be down about $9 ($2 * 85 * .0526). As you can see, mathematical expectation is also a function of the total amount bet, the action. If, as in baccarat, we were betting $25 per spin in red/black roulette, we would expect to be down $112 after 85 spins, compared with baccarat's expected loss of $25.

NUMBERS

Finally, let's take a look at the probabilities involved in numbers. If baccarat is the game of the rich, numbers is the game of the poor. The probabilities in the numbers game are absolutely pathetic. Here is a game where a player chooses a 3-digit number between 0 and 999 and bets $1 that this number will be selected. The number that gets chosen as that day's number is usually some number that (a) cannot be rigged and (b) is well publicized. An example would be to take the first 3 of the last 5 digits of the daily stock market volume. If the player loses, then the $1 he bet is lost. If the player should happen to win then $700 is returned, for a net profit of $699. For numbers, the mathematical expectation is:

$$ME = (699 * (1/1000)) + ((-1) * (1 - (1/1000)))$$

$$= (699 * .001) + ((-1) * (1 - .001))$$

$$= (699 * .001) + ((-1) * .999)$$

$$= .699 + (-.999)$$

$$= -.3$$

In other words your mathematical expectation is to lose 30 cents for every dollar of action. This is far worse than any casino game, including Keno. Bad as the probabilities are in a game like roulette, the mathematical expectation in numbers is almost six times worse. The only gambling situations that are worse than this in terms of mathematical expectation are most football pools and many of the state lotteries.

PARI-MUTUEL BETTING

The games that offer seemingly the worst mathematical expectation belong to a family of what are called pari-mutuel games. Pari-mutuel means literally "to bet among ourselves." Pari-mutuel betting was originated in the 1700s by a French perfume manufacturer named Oller. Monsieur Oller, doubling as a bookie, used his perfume bottles as ticket stubs for his patrons while he booked their bets. Oller would take the bets, from this total pool he would take his cut, then he would distribute the remainder to the winners. Today we have different types of games built on this same pari-mutuel scheme, from state lotteries to football pools, from numbers to horse racing. As you have seen, the mathematical expectations on most pari-mutuel games are atrocious. Yet these very games also offer many situations that have a positive mathematical expectancy.

Let's take numbers again, for example. We can approximate how much money is bet in total by taking the average winning purse size and dividing it by 1 minus the take. In numbers, as we have said, the take is 30%, so we have $1 - .3$, or .7. Dividing 1 by .7 yields 1.42857. If the average payout is, say, $1,400, then we can approximate the total purse as 1,400 times 1.42857, or roughly $2,000. So step one in finding positive mathematical expectations in pari-mutuel situations is to know or at least closely approximate the total amount in the pool.

The next step is to take this total amount and divide it by the total number of possible combinations. This gives the average amount bet per combination. In numbers there are 1,000 possible combinations, so in our example we divide the approximate total pool of $2,000 by 1,000, the total number of combinations, to obtain an average bet per combination of $2.

Now to figure the total amount bet on the number we want to play. Here we would need inside information. The purpose here is not to show how to win at numbers or any other gambling situation, but rather to show how to think correctly in approaching a given risk/reward situation. This will be made clearer as we continue with the illustration. For now, let's just assume we can get this information. Now, if we know what the average dollar bet is on any number, and we know the total amount bet on the number we want to play, we simply divide the average bet by the amount bet on our number. This gives us the ratio of what our bet size is relative to the average bet size.

Since the pool can be won by any number, and since the pool is really the average bet times all possible combinations, it stands to reason that naturally we want our bet to be relatively small compared to the average bet. Therefore, if this ratio is 1.5, it means simply that the average bet on a number is 1.5 times the amount bet on our number.

Now this can be converted into an actual mathematical expectation. We take this ratio and multiply it by the quantity $(1 - \text{takeout})$ where the takeout is the pari-mutuel vigorish (also known as the takeout, or the amount that the house skims off the top, and out of the total pool). In the case of numbers, where the takeout is 30%, then 1 minus the takeout equals .7. Multiplying our ratio in our example of 1.5 times .7 gives us 1.05. As a final step, subtracting 1 from the previous step's answer will give us the mathematical expectation, in percent. Since $1.05 - 1$ is 5%, we can expect in our example situation to make 5% on our money on average if we make this play over and over.

Which brings us to an interesting proviso here. In numbers, we have probabilities of 1/1000 or .001 of winning. So, in our example, if we bet one dollar for each of 1,000 plays we would expect to be ahead by 5%, or $50, if the given parameters as we just described were always present. Since it is possible to play the number 1,000 times, the mathematical expectation is possible, too.

But let's say you try to do this on a state lottery with over 7 million possible winning combinations. Unless you have a pool together or a lot of money to cover more than one number on each drawing it is unlikely you will see over 7 million drawings in your lifetime. Since it will take (on average) 7 million drawings until you can mathematically expect your number to have come up, your positive mathematical expectation as we described it in the numbers example is meaningless. You most likely won't be around to collect!

In order for the mathematical expectation to be meaningful (provided it is positive) you must be able to get enough trials off in your lifetime (or the pertinent time period you are considering) to have a fair mathematical chance of winning. The average number of trials needed is the total number of possible combinations divided by the number of combinations you are playing. Call this answer N. Now, if you multiply N by the length of time it takes for 1 trial to occur, you can determine the average length of time needed for you to be able to expect the mathematical expectation to manifest itself. If your chances are 1 in 7 million and the drawing is once a week, you must stick around for 7 million weeks (about 134,615 years) to expect the mathematical expectation to come into play. If you bet 10,000 of those 7 million combinations, you must stick around about 700 weeks (7 million divided by 10,000, or about 13½ years) to expect the mathematical expectation to kick in, since that is about how long, on average, it would take until one of those 10,000 numbers won.

The procedure just explained can be applied to other pari-mutuel gambling situations in a similar manner. There is really no need for inside information on certain games. Consider horse racing, another classic pari-mutuel situation. We must make one assumption here. We must assume that the money bet on a horse to win divided by the total win pool is an accurate reflection of the true probabilities of that horse winning. For instance, if the total win pool is $25,000 and there is $2,500 bet on our horse to win, we must assume that the probabilities of our horse winning are .10. We must assume that if the same race were run 100 times with the same horses on the same track conditions with the same jockeys, and so on, our horse would win 10% of the time.

From that assumption we look now for opportunity by finding a situation where the horse's proportion of the show or place pools is much less than its proportion of the win pool. The opportunity is that if a horse has a probability of X of winning the race, then the probability of the horse coming in second or third should not be less than X (provided, as we already stated, that X is the real probability of that horse winning). If the probability of the horse coming in second or third is less than the probability of the horse winning the race, an anomaly is created that we can perhaps capitalize on.

The following formula reduces what we have spoken of here to a mathematical expectation for betting a particular horse to place or show, and incorporates the track takeout. Theoretically, all we need to do is bet only on racing situations that have a positive mathematical expectation. The mathematical expectation of a show (or place) bet is given as:

$$(((W_i/\Sigma W)/(S_i/\Sigma S)) * (1 - \text{takeout})) - 1$$

where: W_i = Dollars bet on the i'th horse to win.

ΣW = Total dollars in the win pool—i.e., total dollars bet on all horses to win.

S_i = Dollars bet on the i'th horse to show (or place).

ΣS = Total dollars in the show (or place) pool—i.e., total dollars on all horses to show (or place).

i = The horse of your choice.

If you've truly learned what is in this book you will use the Kelly formula (more on this in Chapter 4) to maximize the rate of your money's growth. How much to bet, however, becomes an iterative problem, in that the more you bet a particular horse to show, the more you will change the mathematical expectation and payout—but not the probabilities, since they are dictated by $(W_i/\Sigma W)$. Therefore, when you bet on the horse to place, you alter the mathematical expectation of the bet and you also alter the payout on that horse to place. Since the Kelly formula is affected by the payout, you must be able to iterate to the correct amount to bet.

As in all winning gambling or trading systems, employing the winning formula just shown is far more difficult than you would think. Go to the racetrack and try to apply this method, with the pools changing every 60 seconds or so while you try to figure your formula and stand in line to make your bet and do it within seconds of the start of the race. The real-time employment of any winning system is always more difficult than you would think after seeing it on paper.

DECISION ORIENTATION VERSUS
SELECTION ORIENTATION

As previously stated, the purpose in bringing up pari-mutuel betting anomalies here is to show you how you should be thinking in order to get to the true mathematics involved. Most gambling is a shell game; you are bound to be a loser, there's no way around it. However, there are anomalies that can be exploited. An anomaly in risk/reward situations (be it gambling, trading, etc.) is any situation where you can find a positive mathematical expectation. Step one then must be to *find positive mathematical expectations*. This is the foundation to mathematically sound money management.

Most people play numbers by hunch, or find some other reason to pick the number they do. Go to the racetrack and watch the characters. They're looking at their programs, reading the racing form, all to select horses they think will finish in the money. Similarly, most stock fund managers pick the stocks they do for some reason that they believe is important—earnings, management, or any of the other "high priest" criteria. All of these actions are *selection* oriented. Those who are selection oriented, and their criteria for selection, create anomalies. This happens when "the crowd" perceives the probability of an event occurring, expressed as the odds, and is not equal to the *actual* probability of such an event occuring. It is these anomalies that create positive mathematical expectations for those who are *decision* oriented.

These are concepts that permeate life; they are not concepts that are restricted to gambling, even though they are being presented in the arena of gambling for the sake of illustration. As an example, consider a cat in the wild chasing down its prey. The cat must continually decide whether to continue the pursuit of its prey or abandon the chase. Although we consider this "instinctual" in animals, or a "right-brain" process if we are discussing human behavior, the situation can be dissected to a mathematical decision. If the cat can get (by way of an estimate) 10 times the fuel value from the prey, that it estimates it will have to expend in order to catch the prey, plus the expended fuel, then it must estimate the probability of actually catching the prey to be greater than .0909 in order for it to continue the chase.

The odds in this case are 10 to 1. Converting these odds to a probability statement yields .0909. If the probability of the cat catching its prey in this instance is greater than the odds imply (i.e., if the probability is greater than .0909), then for the moment there is an anomaly in nature, which the cat can exploit. For the moment, this is a positive mathematical expectation to the cat. Of course, all this depends upon the estimates being accurate. Of course, the cat isn't doing the math in its head as the chase goes on; nonetheless, the math describes the situation. To the extent that the cat can arrive at these answers, be it instinctually or however, and to the extent that the estimates used are accurate, the cat will survive. Otherwise, the cat will perish. It can be argued that decision orientation has played a major role in evolution.

The same abilities are called upon in almost all aspects of life where decisions are required. This is very true in the arena of trading the markets. *Being decision oriented means you are only looking to take action when you have a positive mathematical expectation.* Whenever the odds of an event occurring do not equal the probability of an event occurring, an anomaly is created which can possibly be exploited. Usually the odds are dictated by "the crowd" and the probability is estimated by you, the player. The closer your estimations are to the true probabilities involved, the better you will be able to discern anomalistic situations.

WINNING AND LOSING STREAKS IN THE RANDOM PROCESS

We have already seen that in flat-betting situations involving an independent trials process you will lose at the rate of the house advantage. To get around this rule, many gamblers then try various betting schemes that will allow them to win more during hot streaks than during losing streaks, or will allow them to bet more when they think a losing streak is likely to end and bet less when they think a winning streak is about to end. Yet another important axiom comes into play here, which is that *streaks are no more predictable than the outcome of the next event* (this is true whether we are discussing dependent or independent events). In the long run, we can predict approximately how many streaks of a given length can be expected from a given number of chances.

Imagine that we flip a coin and it lands tails. We now have a streak of one. If we flip the coin a second time, there is a 50% chance it will come up tails again, extending the streak to two events. There is also a 50% chance it will come up heads, ending the streak at one. Going into the third flip we face the same possibilities. Continuing with this logic we can construct the following table, assuming we are going to flip a coin 4,096 times:

Length of Streak	No. of Streaks Occurring	How Often Compared to Streak of One	Probability
1	512	1	.50
2	256	1/2	.25
3	128	1/4	.125
4	64	1/8	.0625
5	32	1/16	.03125
6	16	1/32	.015625
7	8	1/64	.0078125
8	4	1/128	.00390625
9	2	1/256	.001953125
10	1	1/512	.0009765625
11 +	1	1/1024	.00048828125

The real pattern does not end at this point; rather it continues with smaller and smaller numbers.

Remember that this is the expected pattern. The real-life pattern, should you go out and record 4,096 coin flips, will resemble this, but most likely it won't resemble this exactly. This pattern of 4,096 coin tosses is for a fair 50/50 game. In a game where the house has the edge, you can expect the streaks to be skewed by the amount of the house advantage.

DETERMINING DEPENDENCY

As we have already explained, the coin toss is an independent trials process. This can be deduced by inspection, in that we can calculate the exact probability statement prior to each toss and it is always the same from one toss to the next. There are other events, such as blackjack, that are dependent trials processes. These, too, can be deduced by inspection, in that we can calculate the exact probability statement prior to each draw of a card, and it is not always the same from one draw to the next. For still other events, dependence on prior outcomes cannot be determined upon inspection. Such an event is the profit and loss stream of trades generated by a trading system. For these types of problems we need more tools.

Assume the following stream of coin flips where a plus (+) stands for a win and a minus (−) stands for a loss:

+ + − − − − − − + − + − + − − − + + + − + + + − + + +

There are 28 trades, 14 wins and 14 losses. Say there is $1 won on a win and $1 lost on a losing flip. Hence the net for this series is $0.

Now assume you possess the infant's mind. You do not know if there is dependency or not in the coin toss situation (although there isn't). Upon seeing such a stream of outcomes you deduce the following rule which says "Don't bet after 2 losers, go to the sidelines and wait for a winner to resume betting." With this new rule, the previous sequence would have been:

+ + − − − + − + − − + + − + + + − + + +

So, with this new rule the old sequence would have produced 12 winners and 8 losers for a net of $4. You're quite confident of your new rule. You haven't learned to differentiate an exact sequence (which is all that this stream of trades is) from an end result (the end result being that this is a break-even game).

There is a major problem here, though, and that is that you do not know if there is dependency in the sequence of flips. *Unless dependency is proven no attempt to improve performance based on the stream of profits and losses alone is of any value, and quite possibly you may do more harm than good.*[2] Let us continue with the illustration and we will see why.

Since this was a coin toss there was in fact no dependency in the trials—i.e., the outcome of each successive flip was independent of (unaffected by) the previous flips. Therefore, this exact sequence of 28 flips was totally random. (Remember, each exact sequence has an equal

---

[2] A distinction must be drawn between a stationary and a non-stationary distribution. A stationary distribution is one where the probability distribution does not change. An example would be a casino game such as roulette, where you are always at a .0526 disadvantage. A non-stationary distribution is one where the expectation changes over time (in fact, the entire probability distribution may change over time). Trading is just such a case. Trading is analogous in this respect to a drunk wandering through a casino, going from game to game. First he plays roulette with $5 chips (for a − .0526 mathematical expectation), then he wanders to a blackjack table, where the deck happens to be running favorable to the player by 2%. His distribution of outcomes curve moves around as he does; the mathematical expectation and distribution of outcomes is dynamic. Contrast this to staying at one table, at one game. In such a case the distribution of outcomes is static. We say it is *stationary*. The outcomes of systems trading appear to be a non-stationary distribution, which would imply that there is perhaps some technique that may be employed to allow the trader to advantageously "trade his equity curve." Such techniques are, however, beyond the mathematical scope of this book and will not be treated here. Therefore, we will not treat non-stationary distributions any differently than stationary ones in the text, but be advised that the two are profoundly different.

probability of occurring. It is the end results that follow the Normal Distribution, with the peak of the distribution occurring at the mathematical expectation. The end result in this case, the mathematical expectation, is a net profit/loss of zero). The next exact sequence of 28 flips is going to appear randomly, and there is an equal probability of the following sequence appearing as any other:

$$- - + - - + - - + - - + - - + - - + - - + + + + + + +$$

Once again, the net of this sequence is nothing won and nothing lost. Applying your rule here, the outcome is:

$$- - - - - - - - - - - - - - + + + + + + +$$

Fourteen losses and 7 wins for a net loss of $7.

As you can see, unless dependency is proven (in a stationary process) no attempt to improve performance based on the stream of profits and losses alone is of any value, and you may do more harm than good.

THE RUNS TEST, Z SCORES, AND CONFIDENCE LIMITS

For certain events, such as the profit and loss stream of a system's trades, where dependency cannot be determined upon inspection, we have the runs test. The runs test is essentially a matter of obtaining the Z scores for the win and loss streaks of a system's trades. Here's how to do it. First, you will need a minimum of 30 closed trades. There is a very valid statistical reason for this. Z scores assume a Normal Probability Distribution (of streaks of wins and losses in this instance). Certain characteristics of the Normal Distribution are no longer valid when the number of trials is less than 30. This is because a minimum of 30 trials are necessary in order to resolve the shape of the Normal Probability Distribution clearly enough to make certain statistical measures valid.

The Z score is simply the number of standard deviations the data is from the mean of the Normal Probability Distribution. For example, a Z score of 1.00 would mean that the data you are testing is within 1 standard deviation from the mean. (Incidentally, this is perfectly normal.) The Z score is then converted into a confidence limit, sometimes also called a degree of certainty. We have seen that the area under the curve of the Normal Probability Function at 1 standard deviation on either side of the mean equals 68% of the total area under the curve. So we take our Z score and convert it to a confidence limit, the relationship being that the Z score is how many standard deviations and the confidence limit is the percentage of area under the curve occupied at so many standard deviations.

Confidence Limit	Z Score
99.73%	3.00
99%	2.58
98%	2.33
97%	2.17
96%	2.05
95.45%	2.00
95%	1.96
90%	1.64
85%	1.44
80%	1.28
75%	1.15
70%	1.04
68.27%	1.00
65%	.94
60%	.84
50%	.67

With a minimum of 30 closed trades we can now compute our Z scores. We are trying to determine how many streaks of wins/losses we can expect from a given system. Are the win/loss streaks of the system we are testing in line with what we could expect? If not, is there a high enough confidence limit that we can assume dependency exists between trades, i.e., is the outcome of a trade dependent on the outcome of previous trades?

Here then is how to perform the runs test, how to find a system's Z score:

1. You will need to compile the following data from your run of trades:
   A. The total number of trades, hereafter called N.
   B. The total number of winning trades and the total number of losing trades. Now compute what we will call X. X = 2 * Total Number of Wins * Total Number of Losses.
   C. The total number of runs in a sequence. We'll call this R.
   Let's construct an example to follow along with. Assume the following trades:

$$-3 \quad +2 \quad +7 \quad -4 \quad +1 \quad -1 \quad +1 \quad +6 \quad -1 \quad 0 \quad -2 \quad +1$$

The net profit is + 7. The total number of trades is 12; therefore, N = 12 (we are violating the rule that there must be at least 30 trades only to keep the example simple). Now we are not concerned here with how big the wins and losses are, but rather how many wins and losses there are and how many streaks. Therefore, we can reduce our run of trades to a simple sequence of pluses and minuses. Note that a trade with a P&L of 0 is regarded as a loss. We now have:

$$- + + - + - + + - - - +$$

As can be seen there are 6 profits and 6 losses. Therefore, X = 2 * 6 * 6 = 72. As can also be seen there are 8 runs in this sequence, so R = 8. We will define a *run* as any time we encounter a sign change when reading the sequence as shown above from left to right (i.e., chronologically). Assume also that we start at 1. Therefore we would count this sequence as follows:

$$
\begin{array}{ccccccccccc}
- & + & + & - & + & - & + & + & - & - & - & + \\
1 & 2 & & 3 & 4 & 5 & 6 & & 7 & & & 8
\end{array}
$$

2. Solve for the equation:

N * (R − .5) − X

For our example this would be:

12 * (8 − .5) − 72

12 * 7.5 − 72

90 − 72

18

3. Solve for the equation:

(X * (X − N))/(N − 1)

So for our example this would be:

(72 * (72 − 12))/(12 − 1)

(72 * 60)/11

4,320/11

392.727272

4. Take the square root of the answer in number 3. For our example this would be:

$392.727272^{(1/2)} = 19.81734777$

5. Divide the answer in number 2 by the answer in number 4. This is the Z score. For our example this would be:

18/19.81734777 = .9082951063

6. Now convert the Z score to a confidence limit from the table. In our example this equals somewhere between 60 and 65% as a confidence limit, or just shy of 1 standard deviation.

If the Z score is negative, simply convert it to positive (take the absolute value) when finding your confidence limit. A negative Z score implies positive dependency, meaning fewer streaks than the Normal Probability Function would imply, and hence that wins beget wins and losses beget losses. A positive Z score implies negative dependency, meaning more streaks than the Normal Probability Function would imply, and hence that wins beget losses and losses beget wins.

As long as the dependency is at an acceptable confidence limit, you can alter your behavior accordingly to make better trading decisions, even though you do not understand the underlying cause of the dependency. Now, if you could know the cause you could then better estimate when the dependency was in effect and when it was not, as well as when a change in the degree of dependency could be expected.

The runs test will tell you if your sequence of wins and losses contains more or less streaks (of wins or losses) than would ordinarily be expected in a truly random sequence, which has no dependence between trials. Since we are at such a relatively low confidence limit we can assume that there is no dependence between trials in this particular sequence.

What would be an acceptable confidence limit then? Dependency can never be proved nor disproved beyond a shadow of a doubt in this test; therefore, what constitutes an acceptable confidence limit is a personal choice. Statisticians generally recommend selecting a confidence limit at least in the high nineties. Some statisticians recommend a confidence limit in excess of 99% in order to assume dependency; some recommend a less stringent minimum of 95.45% (2 standard deviations).

Rarely if ever will you find a system that shows confidence limits in excess of 95.45%. Most frequently the confidence limits encountered are less than 90%. Even if you find one between 90 and 95.45%, this is not exactly a nugget of gold, either. You really need to exceed 95.45% as a bare minimum to assume that there is dependency involved that can be capitalized upon to make a substantial difference.

For example, some time ago a broker friend of mine asked me to program up a money management idea of his that incorporated changes in the equity curve. Before I even attempted to satisfy his request, I looked for dependency between trades, since we all know now that unless dependency is proven (in a stationary process) to a very high confidence limit, all attempts to change your trading behavior based on changes in the equity curve are futile and may even be harmful.

Well the Z score for this system (of 423 trades) clocked in at -1.9739! This means that there is a confidence limit in excess of 95%, a very high reading compared to most trading systems, but hardly an acceptable reading for dependency in a statistical sense. The negative number meant that wins beget wins and losses beget losses in this system. Now this was a great system to start with. I immediately went to work having the system pass all trades after a loss, and continue to pass trades until it passed what would have been a winning trade, then to resume trading. Here are the results:

	Before Rule	After Rule
Total Profits	$71,800	$71,890
Total Trades	423	360
Winning Trades	358	310
Winning Percentage	84.63%	86.11%
Average Trade	$169.74	$199.69
Maximum Drawdown	$4,194	$2,880
Max. Losers in Succession	4	2
4 losers in a row	2	0
3 losers in a row	1	0
2 losers in a row	7	4

All of the above is calculated with $50 commissions and slippage taken off of each trade. As you can see, this was a terrific system before this rule. So good, in fact, that it was difficult to improve upon it in any way. Yet, once the dependency was found and exploited, the system was materially improved. It was with a confidence limit of slightly over 95%. It is rare to find a confidence limit this high in futures trading systems. However, from a statistical point of view, it is hardly high enough to assume that dependency exists. Ideally, you will find systems that have confidence limits in the high nineties.

So far we have only looked at dependency from the point of view of whether the last trade was a winner or a loser. We are trying to determine if the sequence of wins and losses exhibit dependency or not. The runs test for dependency automatically takes the percentage of wins and losses into account. However, in performing the runs test on runs of wins and losses we have accounted for the sequence of wins and losses, but not their size. For the system to be truly independent, not only must the sequence of wins and losses be independent; the sizes of the wins and losses within the sequence must also be independent. It is possible for the wins and losses to be independent, while their sizes are dependent (or vice versa).

One possible solution is to run the runs test on only the winning trades, segregating the runs in some way (e.g., those that are greater than the median win versus those that are less). Then look for dependency among the size of the winning trades; then do the same for the losing trades.

THE LINEAR CORRELATION COEFFICIENT

There is, however, a different, possibly better way to quantify this possible dependency between the size of the wins and losses. The technique to be discussed next looks at the sizes of wins and losses from an entirely different mathematical perspective than does the runs test, and when used in conjunction with the latter, measures the relationship of trades with more depth than the runs test alone could provide. This technique utilizes the linear correlation coefficient, r, sometimes called Pearson's r, to quantify the dependency/independence relationship.

Look at Figure 1-5. It depicts two sequences that are perfectly correlated with each other. We call this effect "positive" correlation.

Now look at Figure 1-6. It shows two sequences that are perfectly uncorrelated with each other. When one line is zigging the other is zagging. We call this effect "negative" correlation.

The formula for finding the linear correlation coefficient (r) between two sequences, X and Y, follows. (A bar over the variable means the mean of the variables; for example, $\overline{X} = ((X_1 + X_2 + \ldots X_n)/n.)$

$$r = \frac{\sum_a (X_a - \overline{X}) * (Y_a - \overline{Y})}{\left(\left(\sum_a (X_a - \overline{X})^{\wedge}2 \right)^{\wedge}(1/2) \right) * \left(\left(\sum_a (Y_a - \overline{Y})^{\wedge}2 \right)^{\wedge}(1/2) \right)}$$

Here is how to perform the calculation:

1. Average the Xs and the Ys.

2. For each period find the difference between each X and the average X and each Y and the average Y.

3. Now calculate the numerator. To do this, for each period, multiply the answers from step 2. In other words, for each period multiply the

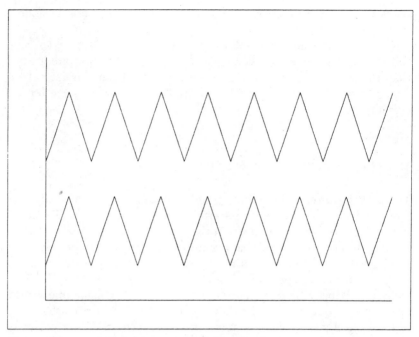

Figure 1-5 Perfect positive correlation (r = + 1.00).

difference between that period's X and the average X times the difference between that period's Y and the average Y.

4. Total up all of the answers to step 3 for all of the periods. This is the numerator.

5. Now find the denominator. To do this, take the answers to step 2 for each period, for both the X differences and the Y differences, and square them (they will now all be positive numbers).

6. Sum up the squared X differences for all periods into one final total. Do the same with the squared Y differences.

7. Take the square root of the sum of the squared X differences you just found in step 7. Now do the same with the Ys by taking the square root of the sum of the squared Y differences.

8. Multiply together the two answers you just found in step 7. That is, multiply the square root of the sum of the squared X differences by the square root of the sum of the squared Y differences. This product is your denominator.

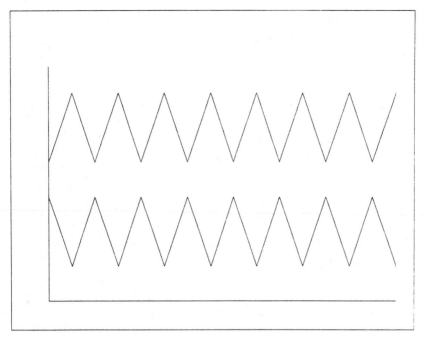

Figure 1-6   Perfect negative correlation (r = − 1.00).

9. Divide the numerator you found in step 4 by the denominator you found in step 8. This is your linear correlation coefficient, r.

The value for r will always be between + 1.00 and − 1.00. A value of 0 indicates no correlation whatsoever.

Look at Figure 1-7. It represents the following sequence of 21 trades:

1, 2, 1, − 1, 3, 2, − 1, − 2, − 3, 1, − 2, 3, 1, 1, 2, 3, 3, − 1, 2, − 1, 3

Now, here is how we use the linear correlation coefficient to see if there is any correlation between the previous trade and the current trade. The idea is to treat the trade P&Ls as the X values in the formula for r. Superimposed over that, we duplicate the same trade P&Ls, only this time we skew them by one trade, and use these as the Y values in the formula for r. In other words the Y value is the previous X value (see Figure 1-8).

A	B	C	D	E	F	G
X	Y	X – X avg	Y – Y avg	col C times col D	col C squared	col D squared
1						
2	1	1.2	0.3	0.36	1.44	0.09
1	2	0.2	1.3	0.26	0.04	1.69
– 1	1	– 1.8	0.3	– 0.54	3.24	0.09
3	– 1	2.2	– 1.7	– 3.74	4.84	2.89
2	3	1.2	2.3	2.76	1.44	5.29
– 1	2	– 1.8	1.3	– 2.34	3.24	1.69
– 2	– 1	– 2.8	– 1.7	4.76	7.84	2.89
– 3	– 2	– 3.8	– 2.7	10.26	14.44	7.29
1	– 3	0.2	– 3.7	– 0.74	0.04	13.69
– 2	1	– 2.8	0.3	– 0.84	7.84	0.09
3	– 2	2.2	– 2.7	– 5.94	4.84	7.29
1	3	0.2	2.3	0.46	0.04	5.29
1	1	0.2	0.3	0.06	0.04	0.09
2	1	1.2	0.3	0.36	1.44	0.09
3	2	2.2	1.3	2.86	4.84	1.69
3	3	2.2	2.3	5.06	4.84	5.29
– 1	3	– 1.8	2.3	– 4.14	3.24	5.29
2	– 1	1.2	– 1.7	– 2.04	1.44	2.89
– 1	2	– 1.8	1.3	– 2.34	3.24	1.69
3	– 1	2.2	– 1.7	– 3.74	4.84	2.89
	3					
avg = .8	avg = .7	Totals =		0.8	73.2	68.2

   The averages are different because you only average those Xs and Ys that have a corresponding X or Y value—i.e., you only average those values that overlap, therefore the last Y value (3) is not figured in the Y average nor is the first X value (1) figured in the X average.
   The numerator is the total of all entries in column E (.8). To find the denominator we take the square root of the total in column F, which is 8.555699, and we take the square root of the total in column G, which is 8.258329, and multiply them together to obtain a denominator of 70.65578. Now we divide our numerator of .8 by our denominator of 70.65578 to obtain 0.011322. This is our linear correlation coefficient, r. If you're really on top of this you would also compute your Z score on

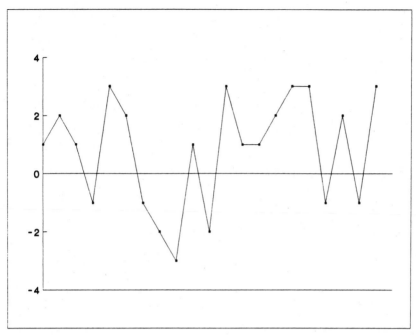

Figure 1-7   Individual outcomes of 21 bets/trades.

these trades, which (if you want to check your work) is .5916 to four
decimal places, or less than a 50% confidence limit that like begets
unlike (since the Z score was positive).

The linear correlation coefficient of .011322 in this case is hardly
indicative of anything, but it is pretty much in the range you can expect
for most trading systems. A high correlation coefficient in futures trading systems would be one that was greater than .25 to .30 on the positive
side, or less than − .25 to − .30 on the negative side. High positive
correlation generally suggests that big wins are seldom followed by big
losses and vice versa. Negative correlation readings below − .25 to − .30
imply that big losses tend to be followed by big wins and vice versa.

There are a couple of reasons why it is important to use both the runs
test and the linear correlation coefficient together in looking for
dependency/correlation between trades. The first is that futures trading
system trades (i.e., the profits and losses) do not necessarily conform to a
Normal Probability Distribution. Rather, they conform pretty much to
whatever the distribution is that futures prices conform to, which is as
yet undetermined. Since the runs test assumes a Normal Probability

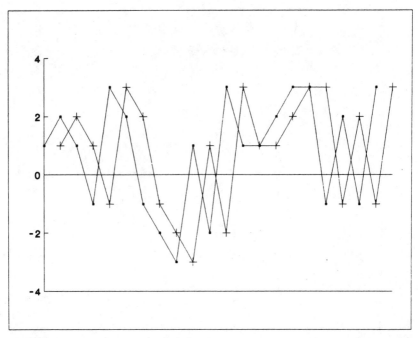

Figure 1-8   Individual outcomes of 21 bets/trades, skewed by 1 bet/trade.

Distribution, the runs test is only as accurate as the degree to which the system trade P&Ls conform to the Normal Probability Distribution.

The second reason for using the linear correlation coefficient in conjunction with the runs test is that the linear correlation coefficient is affected by the size of the trades. It not only interprets to what degree like begets like or like begets unlike, it also attempts to answer questions such as, "Are big winning trades generally followed by big losing trades?" "Are big losing trades generally followed by little losing trades?" And so on.

Negative correlation is just as helpful as positive correlation. For example, if there appears to be negative correlation, and the system has just suffered a large loss, we can expect a large win, and would therefore have more contracts on than ordinarily. Because of the negative correlation, if the trade proves to be a loss, the loss will most likely not be large.

Finally, in determining dependency you should also consider out-of-sample tests. That is, break your data segment into two or more parts. If you see dependency in the first part, then see if that dependency also exists in the second part, and so on. This will help eliminate cases where there appears to be dependency when in fact no dependency exists.

Using these two tools (the runs test and the linear correlation coefficient) can help answer many of these questions. However, they can only answer them if you have a high enough confidence limit and/or a high enough correlation coefficient (incidentally, the system we used earlier in this chapter, which had a confidence limit greater than 95%, had a correlation coefficient of only .0482). Most of the time, these tools are of little help, since all too often the universe of futures system trades is dominated by independence.

Recall the system mentioned in the discussion of Z scores that showed dependency to the 95% confidence limit. Based upon this statistic, we were able to improve this system by developing rules for passing trades. Now here is an interesting but disturbing fact. That system had one optimizeable parameter. When the system was run with a different value for that parameter, the dependency vanished! Was this saying that the appearance of dependency in our cited example was an illusion? Was it saying that only if you keep the value of this parameter within certain bounds can you have any dependency? If so, then isn't it possible that the appearance of dependency can be deceiving? To an extent this seems to be true.

Unfortunately, as traders we most often must assume that dependency does not exist in the marketplace for the majority of market systems. That is, when trading a given market system, we will usually be operating in an environment where the outcome of the next trade is not predicated upon the outcome(s) of the preceding trade(s). This is not to say that there is never dependency between trades for some market systems (because for some market systems dependency does exist), only that we should act as though dependency does not exist unless there is very strong evidence to the contrary. Such would be the case if the Z score and the linear correlation coefficient indicated dependency, and the dependency held up across markets and across optimizeable parameter values. If we act as though there is dependency when the evidence is not overwhelming, we may well just be fooling ourselves and cause more self-inflicted harm than good. Even if a system showed dependency to a 95% confidence limit for all values of a parameter, that confidence limit is hardly high enough for us to assume that dependency does in fact exist between the trades of a given market/system.

Yet the confidence limits and linear correlation coefficients are tools that should be used, because on rare occasions they may turn up a diamond in the rough, which can then possibly be exploited. Furthermore, and perhaps more importantly, they increase our understanding of the environment in which we are trying to operate.

On occasion, particularly in longer-term trading systems, you will encounter cases where the Z score and the linear correlation coefficient indicate dependency, and the dependency holds up across markets and across optimizeable parameter values. In such rare cases, you can take advantage of this dependency by either passing certain trades or altering your commitment on certain trades (more on this idea in Chapter 4).

To help you get a feel for the interplay between them, this chapter closes with examples of these two statistical measures. By studying the examples, you will better understand the subject matter.

$-10, 10, -1, 1$
Linear Correlation $= -.9172$
Z score $= 1.8371$ or 90 to 95% percent confidence limit that like begets unlike.

$10, -1, 1, -10$
Linear Correlation $= .1796$
Z score $= 1.8371$ or 90 to 95% percent confidence limit that like begets unlike.

$10, -10, 10, -10$
Linear Correlation $= -1.0000$
Z score $= 1.8371$ or 90 to 95% percent confidence limit that like begets unlike.

$-1, 1, -1, 1$
Linear Correlation $= -1.0000$
Z score $= 1.8371$ or 90 to 95% percent confidence limit that like begets unlike.

$1, 1, -1, -1$
Linear Correlation $= .5000$
Z score $= -.6124$ or less than 50% confidence limit that like begets like.

$100, -1, 50, -100, 1, -50$
Linear Correlation $= -.2542$
Z score $= 2.2822$ or more than 97% confidence limit that like begets unlike.

2

Systems and Optimization

Many traders eventually end up as "system" traders. Having been beaten by the markets they somewhere along the line realize they must take the emotion out of their trading decisions.

Not all systems are purely mechanical systems, but this chapter discusses only those systems that are in fact purely mechanical. The term "purely mechanical" means that two people following the same market with the same system always receive the same signals. There is never any need for judgment.

An example of a system that is not purely mechanical is: "Always buy on a stop an Elliott wave three up after you take out the high of a wave two down." This would not meet our criterion for a purely mechanical system; interpretation is required. Two people following this rule will not always get the same signals, because the signals depend on how the people interpret the wave structure.

As I said, the principles discussed in this chapter pertain only to purely mechanical systems. A tested, purely mechanical system is *absolutely essential*. The reasons for this will become more apparent after you understand the next two chapters.

From a purely mathematical standpoint, it is very unlikely that anyone can win for a long time without using a set of mechanical rules (a system) to decide what and when to buy and sell. Sure, some people have had some success in the markets without such rules, but if they keep doing what they are doing long enough they, too, will most likely self-destruct. If you don't believe me then read on in Chapter 4, which presents the mathematical evidence why a mechanical approach is necessary. Further, Chapter 6 will demonstrate that you also need a mathematical, quantitative method of diversification, or failure is all but assured. After reading all that, if you still think trading the markets is easy enough that you do not need a mechanical system to guide you, then perhaps "Tougher Than It Looks" in Chapter 7 will convince you. In that section you will find the formula showing how much of a percentage gain is required to obtain the percentage gain desired.

If, like so many people, you do not believe you can find a decent system for sale, you are sadly mistaken. True, most systems that are for sale are junk, yet there are some that are very good, and some that are terrific. If you think that anyone with a decent system isn't going to sell it, you are dead wrong. The old argument, "If it's so good why would that guy be selling it?" is a poor argument. There are two reasons to sell a system. The first is to make money. A good system is no good whatsoever if you don't have the capital to trade it. Many good systems come on the market this way. The second reason someone sells a system is for recognition. People attach their own name to something that is offered publicly will obviously want it to make them look good. Unfortunately, many names attached to systems as their authors' are really noms de plume. This is usually a tip-off that there is something wrong with the system.

This is not to say that you should rush out and buy every system on the market. Systems, like market ideas, are 99.73% junk. However, there are some good systems out there.

MONEY MANAGEMENT
AND TRADING SYSTEMS

Although this is a book on money management, the discussion of what constitutes a good system cannot be dodged. The two are mutually inclusive. You cannot have one without the other. You cannot have a good system without proper money management (you'll see in the next couple of chapters how a good system can lose money if it is not managed properly). On the other hand, all the money management concepts in the world won't help you if your system isn't profitable. Chapter 1 showed that you must have a positive mathematical expectation or ruin is certain. However, of the two, systems and money management, the money management is far and away more important in terms of your performance as a trader or fund manager.

Two guys go to the track with $100 each. They bet ten races, and they both make identical bets except in terms of how much they bet on what races. One guy comes back with $10,000. The other comes back a loser. Is this possible? Yes, not only is it possible, but the same principles are at work in the marketplace all the time. This is why so often you see new traders using a system that has worked in the past who seem to blow up when they begin trading it. It isn't that the system has blown up, it is the lack of money management knowledge on the part of the trader that has sabotaged the profits the system should have been generating.

If money management is so much more important than what system you are trading, why devote an entire chapter to systems? The answer is simply that you must have a winning system, a positive mathematical expectation, in order to apply the money management principles that will be covered in the following chapters—otherwise the principles are of no value whatsoever. Money management is predicated upon having a winning system.

So let's look at what constitutes a winning system. Perhaps you already have one. Perhaps you're testing other ideas in addition to a system you feel is already a winner. Perhaps you're tinkering with a system that is already good. If you are a system trader, you no doubt tinker with systems and ideas constantly. Here is what to look for when you look at systems in their proper light—as a prerequisite to a good money management program.

IT DOESN'T PAY TO FOOL YOURSELF

When it comes to testing out trading systems it doesn't pay to fool yourself. Many seemingly great systems don't hold up to computer testing. Many systems look great when you go through the charts, or they look great on the last two years of a market, but put them under the scrutiny of at least a five-year test on a computer. You will find that very few systems that you program up will be able to walk out of the laboratory on their own two feet.

When I was a programmer I was constantly approached by all kinds of people who thought they had the Holy Grail. In almost every single instance, when their whiz-bang system was crunched out on the computer, the results would be rather dismal. "Impossible," they would say. "There must be something wrong with your program" (which was often the case). I would work out the bugs, the performance would still be dismal, and again they would say, "Impossible. There must be something wrong with your program."

The reason people seem to be able to come up with useless systems that look great to them until they are computer tested is that human beings form mental structures of how things work and then create systems to fit the structure already in their mind. It's the old case of people seeing what they want to see. This is so true in the markets. People construct a mental structure of how the markets work, create a system to trade that structure successfully, then look at that system on the charts. At this stage they only see the good points of the system on their charts; they don't see how the system really performed. If you have ever spent much time programming up market trading ideas, especially other people's ideas, then you are no doubt familiar with this.

So if point number one was that you need a purely mechanical system, then point number two is that it must be computer tested and the results acceptable, with a fair and reasonable deduction on each trade for commissions and slippage. You will miss things testing out a system by hand that the computer doesn't miss. If you cannot program the system yourself, then it's probably too complicated to work real-time for any reasonable length of time.

You no longer need to be a programmer to computer test a trading system. There are products available now that allow you to program and test your ideas via a "natural language interface." If these programs won't do the job for you then go out and hire a programmer. Money you spend on computer testing a system is money you will probably save many times over by seeing the system's flaws on the computer runs instead of on your purchase and sales statements. That is why almost every single major money manager has at least one and usually a handful of programmers. In the markets it just doesn't pay to fool ourselves.

Which brings us to the main topic of this chapter—optimization. Just as the computer has allowed us to test out our systems, it has also given us the power to create systems that look great but won't work in the future. We must consider for starters why we are computer testing out the system. The answer is: to make certain that we are working with a system that has a *positive mathematical expectation in the future.*

It is very easy to make a program from the past look good. If you gave me the last X days of data I could create a system that created a prediction that ran through each and every point. It would be the perfect system—in hindsight. "Look," I would say to you, "my system correctly predicted the close on each and every X day of historical data." But there is no way the system would hold up going into tomorrow's close.

An analogy is the situation of a gambler watching the roulette wheel come up black, red, black, red, black, red. The gambler now says to himself, "Aha, the perfect system would be if I only bet black after a red." Since red was the last roll, the gambler bets black. Does he win? Is his system any good? I don't know. He seems to lose at a rate of the house advantage, though. Is there a causal relationship between the last roll being red and the next roll being black? Definitely not.

Anyone can make a system to work on past data. This is of no value to you as a trader. What is of value is that you have a system that will give you a positive mathematical expectation in the future.

IN DEFENSE OF OPTIMIZATION

Every system has certain constants. These constants can always be turned into variables and then optimized. The danger is that most systems created on past data get over-optimized, curve-fitted, to that past data, so that in hindsight the results look terrific. Yet in the real world tomorrow's optimal parameters are almost always not the same as yesterday's optimal parameters. The system that worked so well on past data falls apart in the real world.

Optimization is not the enemy—abuse of optimization is. In fact, optimization, like the technology to create nuclear weapons, cannot be eliminated once it is discovered. What can be done is that the technology not be abused. This is a process of de-optimizing, allowing the intelligent use of optimization so that a system can be optimized and relied upon in the future.

MEASURES OF PERFORMANCE— PESSIMISTIC RETURN RATIO

Let's begin by determining what is a good measure of performance of a system. When we optimize, we have certain criteria for determining if one parameter value is better than another. We need to find a numerical rating to measure the performance of a pass through the price data with one set of parameter values so that when we are optimizing (repeatedly passing through the data with different parameter values), we can determine which passes/parameter values are best. If we could use only one number to rank a pass through the data with given parameter values, what would be the best way to calculate that number?

Ideally, the number should incorporate the percentage of winning trades as well as the ratio of the size of the average win to the size of the average loss. The measure should also include how much money you made and how much money you lost. Finally, the system should adjust this figure so that the more trades there are the better the figure should be, since the more trades there are the more likely it is that the results can be duplicated in the future.

Although not set in stone, an ideal measure for ranking different passes through the data at different parameter values is the Pessimistic

Return Ratio (PRR). Before we get into the PRR, let's cover the forerunner of PRR, what is known as the profit factor. Essentially, the profit factor (PF) measures:

$$PF = \frac{(W\% * AW)}{(L\% * AL)}$$

where: W% = Percentage of winning trades.

L% = Percentage of losing trades (or 1 − W%).

AW = Average winning trade amount.

AL = Average losing trade amount.

The PF can also be expressed as:

PF = Total dollars won/total dollars lost.

Whichever way we calculate the figure we get the same answer, so we can say that the profit factor measure takes all six items into account.

The PRR is essentially the profit factor measure, only adjusted to give greater weight to more reliable passes (passes with more trades). The PRR is the profit factor with one fewer square root winner and one more square root loser. Mathematically:

$$PRR = \frac{(((W - (W^\wedge(1/2)))/T) * AW)}{(((L + (L^\wedge(1/2)))/T) * AL)}$$

where: W = The number of winning trades.

L = The number of losing trades.

T = The total number of trades (winning and losing).

AW = Average winning trade amount.

AL = Average losing trade amount.

Suppose we have a system that has 50% winning trades, and the ratio of the average profit to the average loss has been 2:1. Our profit factor is $(.5 * 2)/(.5 * 1) = 2$. Yet our PRR, assuming there are ten trades in all, is:

$$PRR = (((5 - (5^\wedge(1/2)))/10) * 2)/(((5 + (5^\wedge(1/2)))/10) * 1)$$

$$= (((5 - 2.236)/10) * 2)/(((5 + 2.236)/10) * 1)$$

$$= ((2.764/10) * 2)/((7.236/10) * 1)$$

$$= (.2764 * 2)/(.7236 * 1)$$

$$= .5528/.7236$$

$$= .7639$$

Now let's look at PRR again, only with 100 trades total:

$$PRR = (((50 - (50^{\wedge}(1/2)))/100) * 2)/(((50 + (50^{\wedge}(1/2)))/100) * 1)$$

$$= (((50 - 7.07)/100) * 2)/(((50 + 7.07)/100) * 1)$$

$$= ((42.93/100) * 2)/((57.07/100) * 1)$$

$$= (.4293 * 2)/(.5707 * 1)$$

$$= 8586/.5707$$

$$= 1.5045$$

We can state:

PRR = PF as N → infinity

where: N = The total number of trades.

In other words, the PRR is the profit factor weighted down inversely by the number of trades. PRR values greater than 2.00 are indicative of a very good system. Over 2.50 is excellent.

The PRR measure is perhaps the single best measure of system performance and can be used to compare runs at different parameter values. The run with the highest PRR is usually the best, or right up there in terms of other criteria (average trade, total dollars profit, and so on).

DE-OPTIMIZING

The validity of a system optimized on past data is directly proportional to how much data is used. Although there has been a great deal of discussion in recent years regarding how long a data segment to optimize over, the mathematically correct answer is to optimize over as much historical data as possible. Using those optimal parameters generally yields better results in the future than does using parameters obtained by optimizing over less data.

The rationale is consistent with what was presented in Chapter 1 as the correct interpretation of the law of averages: *The longer you play the closer you will be to your expected value as a percent of the total action (N).* In the case of optimization, the expected value is the relative performance at a given parameter value. In other words, *the more data you optimize over, the closer the relative performance of a given parameter value will be to its relative performance in the future.* Here future is an indeterminate period of time. Also, relative performance of a given parameter value means relative to other values for that parameter.

Stated another way, the actual outcomes in an independent trials process will tend towards the expected outcomes as the number of trials increases. Mathematically:

$A/N = E/N$ as $N \rightarrow$ infinity

where: A = The actual outcomes of N trials.

E = The expected outcomes of N trials.

An example may clarify. Suppose you are trading a channel breakout system. You find the highest high of the last X days and the lowest low of the last X days. You go long on a stop when the highest high is penetrated, and stop and reverse to short when the lowest low is penetrated. You want to optimize for X. This rule tells us that for an indeterminate time in the future, be it next week or for the next 50 years, we will obtain the most reliable value for X if we optimize X over as much past data as possible.

Consider for a moment that you know nothing of the game of roulette. You want to know what the probabilities of the ball falling on a red square are. You record a series of spins. As the number of spins you record increases, so too does the actual probability (of the spins you are recording) approach the expected probability of .4736842105 (American double zero).

This same logic carries over to finding the best parameter sets to use in the future by optimizing those parameter sets over as much past data as possible. If you only optimize over last week's data and use it to trade next week, your situation is like that of a person who records a few spins at roulette and determines how to play the game over the next few spins. Therefore, the first rule in de-optimization is to *optimize over as long a data set as possible.* Five years minimum per market and 30 trades minimum are the least you should demand.

The second rule is quite simple and straightforward. It is to *use as few parameters as possible.* Naturally, if a system is profitable without optimizing any of its parameters, and it is tested over a long period of time (5 years and 30 trades minimum), it can be considered more likely to perform in the future as it has in the past than if it had ten optimizeable parameters.

The purpose of historical testing is to get an approximation of what can be expected of the system in the future. This is contrary to optimizing a system. As will be made clear in Chapter 4, it is absolutely essential that you obtain as accurately as possible an approximation of what can be expected in the future. To the extent that you add more optimal parameters to a system you detract from how good your approximation is.

Not all parameters have the same degree of effect on detracting from your approximation. An example might help illustrate. Suppose we have a system that takes X percent of yesterday's daily range and adds it to the close to give us a buy stop point, and vice versa for a sell stop point. The system is always in the market. Here, X is our first optimizeable parameter. Now we will add a second optimizeable parameter, Y, which will be the largest amount of dollars we are willing to lose on any one trade. For instance, if we are long and our calculated sell stop is more than Y dollars away, we will go flat at the point that would be a Y-dollar loss. Notice now that parameter X comes into play every single day, yet parameter Y comes into play only under certain conditions. Clearly the X curve fits to the past more than Y does. Taking parameters like X out of a system, or at least minimizing the number of parameters that come into play under any given condition (X in our example) makes the system more reliable than does minimizing or eliminating conditional parameters (Y in our example). The flip side of this axiom is that adding parameters that always come into play (X in our example) detracts more from our approximation of the system's performance than does adding conditional parameters (Y in our example).

Ideally, the fewer parameters the better. The cruder the system is, the more it will tend to work in the future as it has in the past. Yet this is no guarantee. Generally when a system runs into a time period that gives it trouble, it is not so much because the parameters have changed as it is that the edge has changed, i.e., the probability distribution of the outcomes of a system has shifted to an unfavorable state. In other words, reoptimizing over the rough period and then comparing the new optimal parameters to the normal optimal parameters of the system prior to the rough period will reveal that the rough period was just that, a rough period—even if we had been trading at the optimal parameters over that period. We cannot control the fact that the edge moves around; we just have to learn to live with it. All told, it amounts to further reason why we should not over-optimize.

The third rule of de-optimization is to *bias yourself to systems that show robustness across parameters*. Look at Figure 2-1, which shows the relationship of the pessimistic return ratio to the different parameter values for two different systems. Notice how the curve of market system A is wider than that of market system B. This shows that market system B is more sensitive to changes in the value of its parameter. This is not what we want. We want market systems that are as insensitive to changes in the values of their parameter(s) as possible. In the case of Figure 2-1, then, we would pick market system A over market system B because the graph of the relationship of the pessimistic return ratio to the different parameter values is more "robust" for market system A than for market system B. By trading a market system that is relatively robust, we have a better probability that future performance will match past performance. If the optimal parameters in the future are not the same as those in the past (as is usually the case), the likelihood of the market system performing well (in terms of still having a relatively high pessimistic return ratio) is still good, because its graph of the pessimistic return ratio with respect to the different values of its parameters is a robust one.

Thus far we have discussed robustness in terms of how a market system performed over a given time period. It may be helpful to make sure that the robustness was also present over a different time period, as well as over different time periods within the time period we are looking at. For example, suppose we determine that a given market system shows robustness over a five-year test for market system A. It may now be helpful to run each year individually for each parameter value to be certain that the robustness existed each year within that five-year test. It may also be helpful to examine a different five-year period for that given market. Finally, if robustness for a given market system is determined, it may be a good idea to see that robustness exists also for a different market using the same system.

Robustness is not easy to describe in exact mathematical terms; it is purely relative to the shape of the curve of other market systems. Generally you should use the PRR versus the different parameter values in determining robustness, although you can use any measure of performance you like (average trade, total dollars, percentage of winners, and so on) versus the different parameter values to determine robustness. What we are looking for is robustness across parameter values across different time periods and different markets.

The fourth rule of de-optimization is to *forward test*. Some people refer to this as out-of-sample testing. Basically, forward testing involves optimizing your market system over a certain segment of time, then taking the optimal parameters you obtained and trading them in the

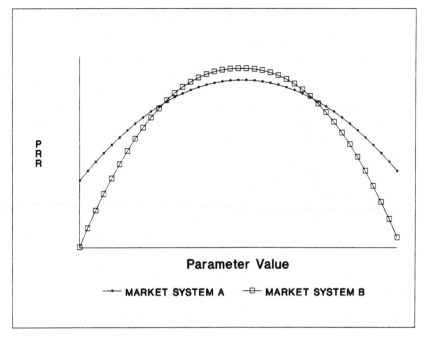

Figure 2-1   Robustness: Market system A is more robust than market
system B.

next segment of time to see how you would have fared. The idea is to
mimic the real-life process of optimizing, finding the optimal parameters, and trading them into the "future." If a system is in fact robust it
should prove itself out by being profitable on a forward-testing basis.

As to the specifics of forward testing, there are two periods that "roll"
through the data. The first of these is the optimization period, which, as
its name implies, is the data you use to optimize the parameter(s) over.
On the day immediately following the end of an optimization period
you begin the next period, the trading period. It is during the trading
period that you will actually record the system's performance, using the
optimal parameters from the optimization period. After the trading
period is complete, move everything forward by the number of days
that the trading period encompasses. Say the trading period is exactly
one year long. After the trading period, you would move the start date
and the end date of the optimization period ahead by one year and
repeat the whole process. When you are through all of the data, your
total results from the trading periods indicate how you would have done
in "real life."

You can use any length of data for the optimization period and the trading period. What's more, the optimization period and trading period need not be for the same length of time (although generally you don't want the trading period to be longer than the optimization period). What are the best lengths to use for the optimization and trading periods? That seems to be a function of the market system itself. This may not be a very definitive or comforting answer, but that is what the historical data crunches out and says. Different market systems perform differently, and you need to find out what periods work best for yours.

There are two different ways to treat the optimization period. One, the rolling type, is as we just described. In the other, the "anchored" type, the start date of the optimization period is fixed (it doesn't move forward). The rest of the dates do move forward each cycle (the end date of the optimization period as well as the start and end dates of the trading period move forward by the length of the trading period each cycle). Hence, the optimization period tends to grow each cycle by the length of the trading period. This is the preferred method of forward testing since it is consistent with de-optimization rule 1 in that we are optimizing over as much data as possible. The results from an anchored forward test will generally come out better than those from a rolling one. But remember, since you want to simulate reality, it is very important that you use realistic commissions and slippage when you forward test.

Next, you will see two computer runs showing the forward testing procedure with an optimization period of 30 days and a trading period of 15 days. These runs are done using a system that has only one optimizeable parameter, but you can do it on systems with more than one optimizeable parameter (you just have to make sure that you optimize over every possible combination for those parameter values).

Study the printouts carefully, especially the dates involved (a "record" is a market day). In doing so you will get a better understanding of how the forward testing process works.

```
---------------F O R W A R D   T E S T----------------
OPTIMIZED OVER 30 RECORDS AND TRADED OVER 15 RECORDS

OPTIMIZATION PERIOD        PARAMETERS              P & L
TRADING PERIOD             PARAMETERS              P & L
------------------------------------------------------------
860101   to   860213          1.2              $5,280.00
860214   to   860307          1.2              $4,350.00

860101   to   860310          .65             $11,062.51
860311   to   860401          .65               -$743.75
```

```
---------------F O R W A R D   T E S T------------------.
OPTIMIZED OVER 30 RECORDS AND TRADED OVER 15 RECORDS
```

| OPTIMIZATION PERIOD | | | PARAMETERS | P & L |
TRADING PERIOD			PARAMETERS	P & L
860101	to	860401	.85	$12,050.00
860402	to	860422	.85	$1,598.68
860101	to	860422	.65	$13,784.94
860423	to	860513	.65	$5,830.08
860101	to	860513	.65	$19,615.01
860514	to	860604	.65	$8,032.99
860101	to	860604	.65	$27,648.00
860605	to	860625	.65	$2,153.24
860101	to	860625	.65	$29,801.24
860626	to	860717	.65	$321.26
860101	to	860717	.65	$30,122.50
860718	to	860807	.65	$2,507.49
860101	to	860807	.65	$32,629.99
860808	to	860828	.65	-$435.00
860101	to	860828	.65	$32,194.99
860829	to	860919	.65	$6,726.26
860101	to	860919	.65	$38,921.25
860922	to	861010	.65	-$1,613.75
860101	to	861010	.65	$37,307.50
861013	to	861031	.65	$5,492.50
860101	to	861031	.65	$42,800.00
861103	to	861121	.65	$1,530.00
860101	to	861121	.65	$44,330.00
861124	to	861215	.65	$438.74
860101	to	861215	.65	$44,768.74
861216	to	870107	.65	$3,237.50
860101	to	870107	.65	$48,006.24
870108	to	870128	.65	$306.26
860101	to	870128	.65	$48,312.50
870129	to	870219	.65	$3,463.76
860101	to	870219	.65	$51,776.26
870220	to	870312	.65	$693.74

(continued)

```
---------------F O R W A R D   T E S T----------------
OPTIMIZED OVER 30 RECORDS AND TRADED OVER 15 RECORDS

OPTIMIZATION PERIOD          PARAMETERS            P & L
TRADING PERIOD               PARAMETERS            P & L
-----------------------------------------------------------
860101   to   870312             .65          $52,470.00
870313   to   870402             .65             $677.51

860101   to   870402             .65          $53,147.51
870403   to   870424             .65           $7,661.23

860101   to   870424             .65          $60,808.74
870427   to   870515             .65           $2,142.50

860101   to   870515             .65          $62,951.24
870518   to   870608             .65             $795.01

860101   to   870608             .65          $63,746.25
870609   to   870629             .65           $1,975.00

860101   to   870629             .65          $65,721.25
870630   to   870721             .65          -$1,776.25

860101   to   870721             .65          $63,945.00
870722   to   870811             .65             $735.00

860101   to   870811             .65          $64,680.00
870812   to   870901             .65            -$320.00

860101   to   870901             .65          $64,360.00
870902   to   870923             .65           $1,105.00

860101   to   870923             .65          $65,465.00
870924   to   871014             .65          -$2,510.02

860101   to   871014             .65          $62,944.98
871015   to   871104             .65           $6,895.02

860101   to   871104             .65          $69,830.00
871105   to   871125             .65           $2,050.00

Optimal Parameters Over the Entire Period...
  860101   to   871104             .65          $73,960.00
Versus Forward Test Results...
  860214   to   871125                          $63,320.00
                                          ===============
```

Now here is the same thing only with a rolling starting date of the optimization period.

```
--------------F O R W A R D   T E S T----------------
OPTIMIZED OVER 30 RECORDS AND TRADED OVER 15 RECORDS
```

OPTIMIZATION PERIOD			PARAMETERS	P & L
TRADING PERIOD			PARAMETERS	P & L
860102	to	860213	1.25	$5,280.00
860214	to	860307	1.25	$4,350.00
860124	to	860310	.65	$9,682.51
860311	to	860401	.65	-$743.75
860214	to	860401	.7	$8,571.24
860402	to	860422	.7	$2,896.20
860310	to	860422	.75	$4,479.94
860423	to	860513	.75	$4,930.04
860401	to	860513	.75	$7,073.74
860514	to	860604	.75	$7,285.51
860422	to	860604	.65	$15,844.19
860605	to	860625	.65	$2,153.24
860513	to	860625	.65	$11,561.24
860626	to	860717	.65	$321.26
860604	to	860717	.9	$6,409.50
860718	to	860807	.9	$2,898.74
860625	to	860807	.85	$3,893.76
860808	to	860828	.85	-$182.48
860717	to	860828	.75	$3,101.19
860829	to	860919	.75	$6,491.24
860807	to	860919	.75	$8,980.00
860922	to	861010	.75	-$1,210.00
860828	to	861010	1.05	$6,401.26
861013	to	861031	1.05	$3,100.00
860919	to	861031	1.2	$4,677.50
861103	to	861121	1.2	$890.00
861010	to	861121	.65	$7,553.75
861124	to	861215	.65	$438.74
861031	to	861215	.65	$1,968.74
861216	to	870107	.65	$3,237.50
861121	to	870107	.7	$3,705.01
870108	to	870128	.7	-$54.99

(continued)

```
---------------F O R W A R D   T E S T----------------
OPTIMIZED OVER 30 RECORDS AND TRADED OVER 15 RECORDS
```

OPTIMIZATION PERIOD			PARAMETERS	P & L
TRADING PERIOD			PARAMETERS	P & L

```
------------------------------------------------------
```

861215	to	870128	.9	$4,246.24
870129	to	870219	.9	$1,078.75
870107	to	870219	1.25	$4,450.00
870220	to	870312	1.25	$700.00
870128	to	870312	.65	$4,470.00
870313	to	870402	.65	$677.51
870219	to	870402	1.25	$3,209.99
870403	to	870424	1.25	$3,492.49
870312	to	870424	.75	$8,813.75
870427	to	870515	.75	-$2,082.51
870402	to	870515	.65	$10,491.24
870518	to	870608	.65	$798.76
870424	to	870608	.65	$2,906.25
870609	to	870629	.65	$1,975.00
870515	to	870629	.9	$5,154.99
870630	to	870721	.9	-$760.00
870608	to	870721	.85	$1,212.49
870722	to	870811	.85	$688.75
870629	to	870811	.85	$838.74
870812	to	870901	.85	$610.00
870721	to	870901	.9	$1,910.00
870902	to	870923	.9	$2,240.00
870811	to	870923	.9	$4,212.51
870924	to	871014	.9	-$291.25
870901	to	871014	.85	$3,006.26
871015	to	871104	.85	$10,731.25
870923	to	871104	.85	$10,630.00
871105	to	871125	.85	$1,470.00

```
Optimal Parameters Over the Entire Period...
 860102  to  871104          .65       $73,960.00
Versus Forward Test Results...
 860214  to  871125                     $58,130.00
                                        ==============
```

Notice how the parameter(s) in an anchored forward test get(s) more stable as time goes by.

The fifth and final rule for de-optimizing is *don't trade the peak parameter*. Recall that we look for robustness when we plot the parameter values along the X axis and the performance (usually the PRRs) along the Y axis. Rarely, however, does this chart resemble the neat curve of Figure 2-1. Rather, we get all sorts of spurious peaks and valleys, but the overall shape is that of a curve. Consider the following:

Parameter	PRR
.50	1.09
.55	1.10
.60	1.20
.65	1.35
.70	1.30
.75	1.79
.80	1.78
.85	1.90
.90	1.79
.95	1.87
1.00	1.75
1.05	1.30
1.10	1.50
1.15	1.50
1.20	1.50
1.25	1.00

Notice that the peak performance (in terms of PRR) is obtained at a parameter value of .85. Yet if you could imagine a smooth curve around this data you would see the curve peaking around the .85 to .95 area, as is demonstrated in Figure 2-2. There is a reason why we should not trade the peak of .85, but we would be better off to trade with a parameter value of .9. This is so because eventually parameters close to each other tend to have similar performance. Once you have located the optimal "neighborhood" of parameters, find one that has lower performance than the parameter immediately before and immediately after it. If the performances are going to tend toward each other, you are better off trading the parameter that will tend to go higher rather than the peak parameter (which will tend to go lower).

Eventually, after enough time and trades have elapsed, the performance/parameter curve will be a smooth one, due to a natural fact called entropy. Entropy is the process whereby things tend to decay into a

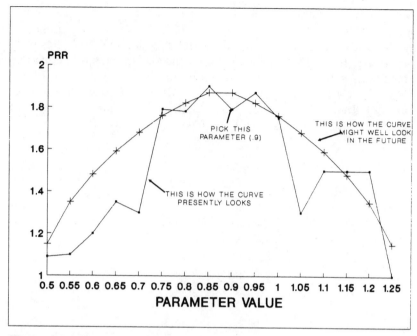

Figure 2-2   Choosing the correct parameter.

constant, uniform, isotropic state. This is the Second Law of Thermodynamics. The rather uniform density of the air at a given altitude comes as a result of entropy; the decomposition of biological things back to dust is entropy at work; the dispersion of light and other electromagnetic radiation is an example of entropy. Entropy goes in only one direction with respect to time. Pour a drop of dye into a swimming pool. At first you can see the dye in the water, but come back a few hours later and it will be uniformly dissolved throughout the pool. This is entropy. Of course, it is possible that all of the molecules of dye do not disperse among the molecules of water in the pool. This would be one of the exact sequences (among the multitude of exact sequences of arrangements of molecules in the pool) in which all of the molecules in the pool could arrange themselves, but most of the exact sequences that could occur would be more uniform in the dispersion of dye and pool water.

What follows is a little demonstration of entropy. To do it you need to pick one of the numbers in column one (the leftmost column). Whatever number you pick, count that amount of numbers forward. Say you pick the first number in the column, 8. Now count forward 8 numbers, and you land on 3, the first row, second column. Now count forward 3 spaces, and you land on 2, the fourth row, second column. Keep on doing this until you get to the last column. No matter where you start, the last number you will land on is 7, the sixth row, eighth column (right-most column).

This isn't rigged; these are all random digits. If you don't believe it, then pick a number in the first row. Say you pick 8 again. Now counting to the right 8 spaces, you come to the end of the row and therefore proceed down to the next row, where you land on 4. Keep going till you run through the entire course. Going in this direction, regardless of where you started you will invariably end up on 6 in the lower right-hand corner.

Still don't believe it? Then create a square of random digits and do it yourself. Whatever number you start on you will always end up on the same number for a given direction through the square (provided you have enough digits, which in this test are the equivalent to time in entropy). Like it or not, entropy is always present.

Entropy Square

8	3	5	9	3	6	4	7
4	6	2	5	2	5	3	1
2	5	5	5	2	7	2	8
4	2	9	3	5	1	6	3
1	5	4	3	7	2	9	1
7	5	9	4	5	9	4	7
9	7	4	8	4	6	4	9
8	7	5	1	6	4	8	6

Entropy will cause the performance/parameter value curve to become a smooth curve over time, losing its spurious peaks and valleys. Therefore, identify that region of parameter values that appear to be the peak, and pick the parameter with lowest performance value therein that has higher performance values for the parameters on either side. Ideally the parameters you choose will be almost the same for each market you are trading a particular system on. If that is the case, then you can be quite certain you have not curve-fit the system to the past data of any one particular market, and you can have confidence that the system should perform in the future.

To recap de-optimization: If you believe you have a good system, rather than working to fine tune the parameters of the system, as so many traders mistakenly do in order to show better historical results, you should work on the system so that it will perform in the future very much as it has performed in the past. You want a system you can "take into the foxhole" with you. This isn't to say that you shouldn't optimize a system, rather you should optimize it intelligently. That is the purpose of de-optimization, the rules of which are recapped here.

1. Optimize over as long a data set as possible.

2. Use as few parameters as possible.

3. Bias yourself to systems that show robustness across parameters.

4. Forward test—preferably using the anchored technique of forward testing to be consistent with rule 1.

5. Identify that region of parameter values that appears to be the peak, and pick the parameter with lowest performance value therein that has higher performance values for the parameters on either side. Ideally you will have the same parameter values for all markets you are trading a given system on.

Finally, if you have de-optimized a system and it still looks good, then don't mess with it—just trade it. Leave the rules alone. Put them up on a shelf. The system is done. The problem with system traders is that they keep reworking their systems. When you get a good system don't change it. If you want to tinker, start on a new system—one you might use in conjunction with the one you have finished. As for the one you have just finished, although it may seem like a crude system, simple and hardly optimized, leave it alone. Its simplicity and crudeness are the very reason it works. Go to work on another system if the system-tinkering bug bites you.

3
Reinvestment of Returns and Geometric Growth Concepts

TO REINVEST TRADING PROFITS OR NOT

Let's call the following system "System A." In it we have two trades—the first making 50%, the second losing 40%. Therefore, if we do not reinvest our returns we make 10%. If we do reinvest, the same sequence of trades loses 10%.

System A

Trade No.	No Reinvestment		With Reinvestment	
	P&L	Accum.	P&L	Accum.
		100		100
1	50	150	50	150
2	−40	110	−60	90

Now let's look at System B, a gain of 15% and a loss of 5%, which also nets out 10% over two trades on a non-reinvestment basis, just like System A. But look at the results of System B with reinvestment. Unlike System A, it makes money.

System B

Trade No.	No Reinvestment		With Reinvestment	
	P&L	Accum.	P&L	Accum.
		100		100
1	15	115	15	115
2	−5	110	−5.75	109.25

An important characteristic of trading with reinvestment that must be realized is that *reinvesting trading profits can turn a winning system into a losing system but not vice versa!* A winning system is turned into a losing system in trading with reinvestment if the returns are not consistent enough. Further, *changing the order or sequence of trades does not affect the final outcome.* This is not only true on a non-reinvestment basis, but also true on a reinvestment basis (contrary to most people's misconception).

System A

Trade No.	No Reinvestment P&L	Accum.	With Reinvestment P&L	Accum.
		100		100
1	−40	60	−40	60
2	50	110	30	90

System B

Trade No.	No Reinvestment P&L	Accum.	With Reinvestment P&L	Accum.
		100		100
1	−5	95	−5	95
2	15	110	14.25	109.25

This is not just an aberration caused by a two-trade example. Let's take system A and add two more trades and then examine the results under all four possible sequences of trades.

First Sequence
(System A)

Trade No.	No Reinvestment P&L	Accum.	With Reinvestment P&L	Accum.
		100		100
1	−40	60	−40	60
2	50	110	30	90
3	−40	70	−36	54
4	50	120	27	81

Second Sequence
(System A)

Trade No.	No Reinvestment		With Reinvestment	
	P&L	Accum.	P&L	Accum.
		100		100
1	50	150	50	150
2	− 40	110	− 60	90
3	50	160	45	135
4	− 40	120	− 54	81

Third Sequence
(System A)

Trade No.	No Reinvestment		With Reinvestment	
	P&L	Accum.	P&L	Accum.
		100		100
1	50	150	50	150
2	50	200	75	225
3	− 40	160	− 90	135
4	− 40	120	− 54	81

Fourth Sequence
(System A)

Trade No.	No Reinvestment		With Reinvestment	
	P&L	Accum.	P&L	Accum.
		100		100
1	− 40	60	− 40	60
2	− 40	20	− 24	36
3	50	70	18	54
4	50	120	27	81

As can obviously be seen, the sequence of trades has no bearing on the final outcome, whether viewed on a reinvestment or non-reinvestment basis. What *are* affected, however, are the drawdowns. Listed next are the drawdowns to each of the sequences of trades listed above.

First Sequence

No Reinvestment	Reinvestment
100 to 60 = 40 (40%)	100 to 54 = 46 (46%)

Second Sequence

No Reinvestment	Reinvestment
150 to 110 = 40 (27%)	150 to 81 = 69 (46%)

Third Sequence

No Reinvestment	Reinvestment
200 to 120 = 80 (40%)	225 to 81 = 144 (64%)

Fourth Sequence

No Reinvestment	Reinvestment
100 to 20 = 80 (80%)	100 to 36 = 64 (64%)

Reinvestment trading is never the best nor the worst drawdown of all possible sequences of trades, based on percent drawdown. It is never the best based on absolute drawdown. One side-benefit to trading on a reinvestment basis is that the drawdowns tend to be buffered. As a system goes into and through a drawdown period, each losing trade is followed by a trade with fewer and fewer contracts. That is why drawdowns as a percent of account equity are always less with reinvestment than with a non-reinvestment approach.

By inspection it would seem you are better off to trade on a non-reinvestment basis rather than to reinvest. This would seem so, since your probability of winning is greater. However, this is not a valid assumption, because in the real world we do not withdraw all of our profits and make up all of our losses by depositing new cash into an account. Further, the nature of investment or trading is predicated upon the effects of compounding. If we do away with compounding (as in the non-reinvestment plan) we can plan on doing little better in the future than we can today, no matter how successful our trading is between now and then. It is compounding that takes the linear function of account growth and makes it a geometric function.

Refer back to the statement that under a reinvestment plan a winning system can be turned into a losing system but not vice versa. Why, then, reinvest our profits into our trading? The sole reason is that by reinvestment, winning systems can be made to win far more than could ever be accomplished on a non-reinvestment basis.

The reader may still be inclined to prefer the non-reinvestment approach since an account that may not be profitable on a reinvestment basis may be profitable on a non-reinvestment basis. However, if a system is good enough, the profits generated on a reinvestment basis will be far greater than on a non-reinvestment basis, and that gap will widen as time goes by. If you have a system that can beat the market it doesn't make any sense to trade it any other way than to increase your amount wagered as your stake increases.

There is another phenomenon that lures traders away from reinvestment-based trading. That phenomenon is that a losing trade, or losing streak, is inevitable after a prolonged equity run-up. This is true by inspection. The only way a streak of winning trades can end is by a losing trade. The only way a streak of profitable months can end is with a losing month. The problem with reinvestment-based trading is that when the inevitable losses come along you will have the most contracts on. Hence, the losses will be bigger. Similarly, after a losing streak the reinvestment-basis trader will have fewer contracts on when the inevitable win comes along to break the streak.

This is not to say that there is any statistical reason to assume that winning streaks portend losing trades or vice versa. Rather what is meant is: If you trade long enough you will eventually encounter a loss. If you are trading on a reinvestment basis, that loss will be magnified, since, as a result of your winning streak, you will have more contracts on when the loss comes. Unfortunately, there is no way to avoid this—at least no way based on statistical fact in a stationary distribution environment, unless we are talking about a dependent trials process.

Therefore, assuming that the market system in question generates independent trades, there is no way to avoid this phenomenon. It is unavoidable when trading on a reinvestment basis, just as losses are unavoidable in trading under any basis. Losses are a part of the game. Since the goal of good money management is to exploit a profitable system to its fullest potential, the intelligent trader should realize that this phenomenon is part of the game and accept it as such to achieve the longer-term rewards that correct money-management techniques provide for.

MEASURING A GOOD SYSTEM FOR REINVESTMENT—THE GEOMETRIC MEAN

So far we have seen how a system can be sabotaged by not being consistent enough from trade to trade. Does this mean we should close up and put our money in the bank? Let's go back to System A, with its first two trades. For the sake of illustration we are going to add two winners of one point each.

System A

Trade No.	No Reinvestment		With Reinvestment	
	P&L	Accum.	P&L	Accum.
		100		100
1	50	150	50	150
2	− 40	110	− 60	90
3	1	111	0.9	90.9
4	1	112	0.909	91.809
Percent Wins		0.75		0.75
Avg. Trade		3		− 2.04775
Profit Factor		1.3		0.86
Std. Dev.		31.88		39.00
Avg. Trade/Std. Dev.		0.09		− 0.05

Now let's take System B and add two more losers of one point each.

System B

Trade No.	No Reinvestment		With Reinvestment	
	P&L	Accum.	P&L	Accum.
		100		100
1	15	115	15	115
2	− 5	110	− 5.75	109.25
3	− 1	109	− 1.0925	108.1575
4	− 1	108	− 1.08157	107.0759
Percent Wins		0.25		0.25
Avg. Trade		2		1.768981
Profit Factor		2.14		1.89
Std. Dev.		7.68		7.87
Avg. Trade/Std. Dev.		0.26		0.22

Now, if consistency is what we're really after, let's look at a bank account, the perfectly consistent vehicle (relative to trading), paying 1 percent per period. We'll call this series System C.

Notice that in reinvestment the standard deviation always goes up (and hence the Avg. Trade/Std. Dev. tends to come down). Furthermore, the Profit Factor measure is never higher in reinvestment than it is in non-reinvestment trading.

Our aim is to maximize our profits under reinvestment trading. With that as the goal, we can see that our best reinvestment sequence came

System C

Trade No.	No Reinvestment P&L	No Reinvestment Accum.	With Reinvestment P&L	With Reinvestment Accum.
		100		100
1	1	101	1	101
2	1	102	1.01	102.01
3	1	103	1.0201	103.0301
4	1	104	1.030301	104.0604
Percent Wins		1.00		1.00
Avg. Trade		1		1.015100
Profit Factor		infinite		infinite
Std. Dev.		0.00		0.01
Avg. Trade/Std. Dev.		infinite		89.89

from System B. How can we have known that, given only information regarding non-reinvestment trading? By percent of winning trades? By total dollars? Average trade? The answer to these questions is no, since that would have us trading System A (but this is the solution most futures traders opt for). What if we opted for most consistency (i.e., highest ratio of Avg. Trade/Std. Dev. or lowest standard deviation). How about highest profit factor or lowest drawdown? This is not the answer, either. If it were, we should put our money in the bank and forget about trading.

System B has the right mix of profitability and consistency. Systems A and C do not. That is why System B performs the best under reinvestment trading. How best to measure this "right mix"? It turns out there is a formula that will do just that: the *geometric mean*. This is simply the Nth root of the Terminal Wealth Relative (TWR), where N is the number of periods (trades). The TWR is simply what we've been computing when we figure what the final cumulative amount is under reinvestment. In other words, the TWRs for the three systems we just saw are:

SYSTEM	TWR
System A	91.809
System B	107.0759
System C	104.0604

Since there are four trades in each of these, we take the TWRs to the fourth root to obtain the geometric mean:

SYSTEM	GEO. MEAN
System A	0.978861
System B	1.017238
System C	1.009999

$$TWR = \prod_{i=1}^{N} HPR_i$$

Geometric Mean = TWR^(1/N)

where: N = Total number of trades.

HPR = Holding period returns (equal to 1 plus the rate of return).

For example, an HPR of 1.10 means a 10% return over a given period/ bet/trade. TWR shows the number of dollars of value at the end of a run of periods/bets/trades per dollar of initial investment, assuming gains and losses are allowed to compound. Here is another way of expressing these variables:

TWR = Final stake/Starting stake

Geometric Mean = Your growth factor per play, or

(Final stake/starting stake)^(1/number of plays).

or

Geometric Mean = exp((1/N) * log(TWR))

where: N = Total number of trades.

log(TWR) = The log base 10 of the TWR.
exp = The exponential function.

Think of the geometric mean as the "growth factor" of your stake, per play. The system or market with the highest geometric mean is the system or market with the highest utility to the trader trading on a reinvestment of returns basis. A geometric mean < 1 means that the system would have lost money if you were trading it on a reinvestment basis. Furthermore, it is vitally important that you use realistic slippage and commissions in calculating geometric means in order to have realistic results.

ESTIMATING THE GEOMETRIC MEAN

There exists a simple technique of finding the geometric mean, whereby you do not have to take the product of all HPRs to the Nth root. This is especially useful if you are doing your calculations by hand, or for certain computer languages that lack extensive math capability. The geometric mean squared can be very closely approximated as the arithmetic mean of the HPRs squared minus the population standard deviation of HPRs squared. So the way to approximate the geometric mean is to square the average HPR, then subtract the squared population standard deviation of those HPRs. Now take the square root of this answer and that will be a very close approximation of the actual geometric mean. As an example assume the following HPRs over four trades:

$$
\begin{array}{c}
1.00 \\
1.50 \\
1.00 \\
.60
\end{array}
$$

Arithmetic Mean	1.025
Population Standard Deviation	.3191786334
Estimated Geometric Mean	.9740379869
Actual Geometric Mean	.9740037464

Here is the formula for finding the estimated geometric mean (EGM):

$$\text{EGM} = ((\text{Arithmetic Mean}^2) - (\text{Pop. Std. Dev.}^2))^{(1/2)}$$

The formula given in Chapter 1 to find the standard deviation of a Normal Probability Function is not what you use here. If you already know how to find a standard deviation, skip this section and go on to the next section entitled "How Best to Reinvest."

The standard deviation is simply the square root of the variance:

$$\text{Variance} = (1/(N-1)) \sum_{i=1}^{N} ((X_i - \overline{X})^2)$$

where: $\overline{X}$ = The average of the data points.
$\quad\quad\ X_i$ = The i'th data point.
$\quad\quad\ N$ = The total number of data points.

This will give you what is called the *sample* variance. To find what is called the *population* variance you simply substitute the term $(N - 1)$ with (N). We will not go into why this is so, for the reasons pointed out in the section titled "What You Won't Find in This Book" in the Introduction.

Notice that if we take the square root of the sample variance we obtain the sample standard deviation. If we take the square root of the population variance we will obtain the population standard deviation. Now, let's run through an example using the four data points:

$$
\begin{array}{l}
1.00 \\
1.50 \\
1.00 \\
.60
\end{array}
$$

1. Find the average of the data points. In our example this is:

   $\overline{X} = (1.00 + 1.50 + 1.00 + .6)/4$

   $\phantom{\overline{X}} = 4.1/4$

   $\phantom{\overline{X}} = 1.025$

2. For each data point, take the difference between that data point and the answer just found in step 1 (the average). For our example this would be:

   $1.00 - 1.025 = -.025$

   $1.50 - 1.025 = .475$

   $1.00 - 1.025 = -.025$

   $.60 - 1.025 = -.425$

3. Square each answer just found in step 2. Note that this will make all answers positive numbers:

   $-.025 * -.025 = .000625$

   $.475 * .475 = .225625$

   $-.025 * -.025 = .000625$

   $-.425 * -.425 = .180625$

4. Sum up all of the answers found in step 3. For our example:

```
  .000625
  .225625
  .000625
+ .180625
  ───────
  .4075
```

5. Multiply the answer just found in step 4 by (1/N). If we were looking to find the sample variance we would multiply the answer just found in number 4 by (1/(N – 1)). Since we eventually want to find the population standard deviation of these four HPRs to find the estimated geometric mean, we will therefore multiply our answer to step 4 by the quantity (1/N).

Population Variance = (1/N) * (.4075)

$$= (1/4) * (.4075)$$

$$= .25 * .4075$$

$$= .101875$$

6. To go from variance to standard deviation, take the square root of the answer just found in step 5. For our example:

Population Standard Deviation = $.101875^{\wedge}(1/2)$

$$= .3191786334$$

Now, let's suppose we want to figure our estimated geometric mean for our example:

EGM = ((Arithmetic Mean $^{\wedge}2$) – (Pop. Std. Dev. $^{\wedge}2$))$^{\wedge}(1/2)$

$$= ((1.025^{\wedge}2) - (.3191786334^{\wedge}2))^{\wedge}(1/2)$$

$$= (1.050625 - .101875)^{\wedge}.5$$

$$= .94875^{\wedge}.5$$

$$= .9740379869$$

This compares to the actual geometric mean for our example data set of:

Geometric Mean = (1.00 * 1.50 * 1.00 * .60)$^{\wedge}(1/4)$

$$= .9^{\wedge}.25$$

$$= .9740037464$$

As you can see, the estimated geometric mean is very close to the actual geometric mean—so close, in fact, that we can use the two interchangeably throughout the text.

HOW BEST TO REINVEST

Thus far, we have discussed reinvestment of returns in trading whereby we reinvest 100% of our stake on all occasions. Although we know that in order to maximize a potentially profitable situation we must use reinvestment, a 100% reinvestment is rarely the wisest thing to do.

Take the case of a coin toss. Someone is willing to pay you $2 if you win the toss, but will charge you $1 if you lose. You can figure what you should make, on average, per toss by the mathematical expectation formula:

$$\text{Mathematical Expectation} = \sum_{i=1}^{N} (P_i * A_i)$$

where: P = Probability of winning or losing.

A = Amount won or lost.

N = Number of possible outcomes.

In the given example of the coin toss:

$$\text{Mathematical Expectation} = (2 * .5) + (1 * (-.5))$$

$$= 1 - .5$$

$$= .5$$

In other words, you would expect to make 50 cents per toss, on average. This is true of the first toss and all subsequent tosses, provided you do not step up the amount you are wagering. But in an independent trials process, that is exactly what you should do. As you win, you should commit more and more to each trade.

At this point it is important to realize the keystone rule to money-management systems, which states: *In an independent trials process, if the mathematical expectation is less than or equal to 0, no money-management technique, betting scheme, or progression can turn it into a positive-expectation game.*

This rule is applicable to trading one market system only. When you begin trading more than one market system, you step into a strange environment where it is possible to include a market system with a negative mathematical expectation as one of the market being traded, and actually have a net mathematical expectation higher than the net mathematical expectation of the group before the inclusion of the negative expectation system! Further, it is possible that the net mathematical expectation for the group with the inclusion of the negative mathematical expectation market system can be higher than the mathematical expectation of any of the individual market systems! (For more on this see Appendix A.)

For the time being, we will consider only one market system at a time, and therefore we must have a positive mathematical expectation in order for the money-management techniques to work.

Refer again to the two-to-one coin-toss example (which is a positive mathematical expectation game). Suppose you begin with an initial stake of $1. Now suppose you win the first toss and are paid $2. Since you had your entire stake ($1) riding on the last bet, you bet your entire stake ($3 now) on the next toss as well. However, this next toss is a loser and your entire $3 stake is gone. You have lost your original $1 plus the $2 you had won. If you had won the last toss, it would have paid you $6, since you had three full $1 bets on it. The point is that if you are betting 100% of your stake, then as soon as you encounter a losing wager (an inevitable event), you'll be wiped out.

If you were to replay the previous scenario and bet on a non-reinvestment basis (i.e., a constant bet size) you would make $2 on the first bet and lose $1 on the second. You would now be ahead $1 and have a total stake of $2. Somewhere between these two scenarios lies the optimal betting approach.

Now, consider four desirable properties of a money-management strategy. First, you want to make as much as mathematically possible, given a favorable game. Second, the tradeoff between the potential rate of growth of your stake and its security should be considered as well (this may not be possible given the first property, but it should at least be considered). Third, the likelihood of winning should be taken into consideration. Fourth and finally, the amounts you can win and the amounts you can lose should influence the bet size as well. If you know you have an edge over N bets, but you do not know which of those N bets will be winners, or for how much, and which will be losers, and for how much, you are best off (in the long run) treating each bet exactly the same in terms of what percentage of your total stake is at risk.

Let's go back to the coin toss. Suppose we have an initial stake of $2. We toss a coin 3 times; twice it comes up heads (whereby we win $1 per $1 bet) and once it comes up tails (whereby we lose $1 per every $1 bet). Also, assume this coin is flawed in that it always comes up heads 2 out of

3 times and comes up tails 1 out of 3 times. Let's further say that this flawed coin can never come up HHH or TTT on any 3-toss sequence. Since we know that this coin is flawed in these ways, but do not know where that loss will come in, how can we maximize this situation? The three possible exact sequences (the sample space), because of the flaws, are:

H H T
H T H
T H H

Here is our dilemma: We know we will win 66% of the time, but we do not know when we will lose, and we want to maximize what we make out of this situation.

Suppose now that rather than bet an equal fraction of our stake—which optimally is 1/3 of our stake on each bet (more on how to calculate this later)—we arbitrarily bet $2 on the first bet and $1 on each bet thereafter. Our $2 stake would grow to $4 at the end of both the H H T and the H T H sequences. However, for the T H H sequence we would have been tapped out on the first bet. Since there are 3 exact sequences, and 2 of them resulted in profits of $2 and 1 resulted in a complete loss, we can say that the sum of all sequences was $4 gained (2 + 2 + 0). The average sequence was therefore a gain of $1.33 (4/3).

You can try any other combination like this for yourself. Ultimately you will find that, since you do not know where the loss is due to crop up, you are best to bet the same fraction of your stake on each bet. Optimally this fraction is 1/3, or 33%, whereby you would make a profit of about $1.41 on each sequence, regardless of sequence(!), for a sum of all sequences of $4.23 gained (1.41 + 1.41 + 1.41). The average sequence was therefore a gain of $1.41 (4.23/3).

Many "staking" systems have been created by gamblers throughout history. One, the martingale, has you double your bet after each loss until ultimately, when a win does occur, you are ahead by one unit. However, the martingale strategy can have you making enormous bets during a losing streak. On the surface, this would appear to be the ultimate betting progression, as you will always come out ahead by one unit if you can follow the progression to termination. Of course, if you have a positive mathematical expectation there is no need to use a scheme such as this. Yet it seems this should work for an even-money game as well as for a game where you have a small negative expectancy.

Yet, as we saw in Chapter 1, the sum of a series of negative expectancy bets must be a negative expectation. Suppose you are betting à la martingale. You lose the first ten bets in succession. Going into the eleventh bet, you are now betting 1,024 units. The probabilities of winning are again the same as if you were betting one unit (assuming an independent trials process). Your mathematical expectation therefore, as a percentage, is the same as in the first bet, but in terms of units it is 1,024 times greater than the first bet. If you are betting with any kind of a negative expectation, it is now multiplied 1,024 times over.

"It doesn't matter," you, the martingale bettor, reply, "since I'll just double up for the twelfth bet if I lose the eleventh, and eventually I will come out ahead one unit." What eventually stymies the martingale bettor is a ceiling on the amount that may be bet, either by a house limit or inadequate capital to continue the progression on the bettor's part.

Theoretically, if you are gambling in a situation with no house limit it would seem you could work this progression successfully if you had unlimited capital. Yet who has unlimited capital? After roughly 46 losses in a row the player betting martingale who bet $1 on the first bet would now be betting an amount that exceeds the net worth of the world.[1]

Ultimately, the martingale bettor has a maximum bet size, imposed by either the house (as in casino gambling) or his capitalization (as in the markets). Eventually, the bettor will bet and lose this maximum bet size and thus go bust. Furthermore, this will happen regardless of mathematical expectation—that is why the martingale is completely foolish if you have a positive mathematical expectation, and just futile if you have an even-money game or a negative expectation. True, betting à la martingale you will most often walk away from the tables a winner. However, when you lose it will be for an amount that will more than compensate the casino for letting you walk away a winner the vast majority of the time.

It is not the maximum bet size that stymies the martingale as much as it is the number of bets required to reach the maximum bet size (this is

[1]In *The Mathematics of Gambling* Edward O. Thorp estimates the net worth of the world at roughly 30 trillion dollars. Any estimate made by Thorp, however rough, is certainly acceptable to this author. Thorp's book was published in 1984. Therefore, assuming a 6% annual growth rate, this figure approximates to a 1991 net worth of 30 trillion * (1.06^7) = roughly 45 trillion. Starting with a $1 bet, à la martingale, after 46 losses the bettor would then be required to wager $70,368,744,177,664 thus exceeding the current net worth of the world. The probability of having to do this is $.5^{46}$ = .00000000000001421086 (13 zeros) if we are discussing a fair 50/50 game. However, when betting red/black at roulette like this, you would still be required to put up the same amount on roll 47, but the probability of this happening becomes $(1 - .4736842105)^{46}$ = .0000000000001504301 (12 zeros). It is interesting to note that the slight negative expectation makes having to bet the net worth of the world 10 times more likely!

also one of the reasons why there are house minimums). To overcome this, gamblers have tried what is known as the small martingale—a somewhat watered-down version of the martingale.

The small martingale tries to provide survival for the bettor by increasing the number of bets required to reach the maximum bet size. Ultimately, the small martingale tries to win one unit per cycle. Since the system rules are easier to demonstrate than to describe, I will show this system through the use of examples. In the small martingale you keep track of a "progression list," and bet the amount that is the sum of the first and last values on the list. When a win is encountered, you cross off the first and last values on the list, thus obtaining new first and last values, giving you a new amount to wager on the next bet. The list starts at simply the number 1. When a loss is encountered, the next number is added on to the end of the list (i.e., 2, 3, 4, etc.). A cycle ends when one unit is won. If a list is ever composed of just the number 2, then convert it to a list of 1, 1. The following examples of four different cycles should make the progression clear:

Bet Number	List	Bet Size	Win/Loss
1	1	1	W

Bet Number	List	Bet Size	Win/Loss
1	1	1	L
2	1, 1	2	W

Bet Number	List	Bet Size	Win/Loss
1	1	1	L
2	1, 1	2	L
3	1, 1, 2	3	W
4	1	1	W

Bet Number	List	Bet Size	Win/Loss
1	1	1	L
2	1, 1	2	L
3	1, 1, 2	3	L
4	1, 1, 2, 3	4	W
5	1, 2	3	L
6	1, 2, 3	4	W
7	1, 1	2	L
8	1, 1, 2	. . . and continuing until the bettor is ahead by 1 unit.	

The small martingale is ultimately a loser too, for the same reasons that the martingale system is a loser. A sum of negative expectancy bets must have a negative expectancy.

Another system, the antimartingale, is just the opposite of the martingale (as its name implies). Here, you increase your bet size after each win. The idea is to hit a streak of winning bets and maximize the gains from that streak. Of course, just as the martingale ultimately makes one unit, the antimartingale will ultimately lose all of its units (even in a positive mathematical expectation game) once a loss is incurred, if 100% of the stake is placed on each bet.

Notice, however, that fixed fractional trading is actually a small antimartingale! Recall our flawed-coin example earlier in this chapter. In that example we saw how our "best" strategy was the small antimartingale. In the final analysis, fixed fractional trading, the small antimartingale, is the optimal betting system—provided you have a positive mathematical expectation.

Another famous system is the reserve strategy. Here you trade a base bet plus a fraction of your winnings. However, in the reserve strategy if the last bet was a winner then you bet the same amount on the next bet as you did the last. Suppose you encounter the sequence of Win $1, Win $1, Lose $1, then Win $1 for every $1 bet. If you are betting $1 plus 50% of winnings (in the reserve strategy), you would bet $1 on the first bet. Since it was a winner you would still bet $1 on the second bet—which was also a winner, boosting your total winnings to $2. Since the second bet was also a winner, you would not increase your third bet; rather, you would still bet $1. The third bet, being a loss of $1, lowers your total winnings to $1. Since you encountered a loss, however, you recapitalize your bet size to the base bet ($1) plus 50% of your winnings (.5 * $1) and hence bet $1.50 on the fourth bet. The fourth bet was a winner, paying 1 to 1, so you made $1.50 on the fourth bet, bringing your total winnings to $2.50. Since this last bet was a winner, you will not recapitalize (step up or down) your bet size into the fifth bet; instead, you stay with a bet size of $1.50 into the fifth bet.

On the surface, the reserve strategy seems like an ideal staking system. However, like all staking systems, its long-term performance falls short of the simple fixed fraction (small antimartingale) approach. Another popular idea of gamblers/traders has been the base bet plus square root strategy, whereby you essentially are always betting the same amount you started with plus the square root of any winnings. As you can see, the possibilities of staking systems are endless.

Many people seem to be partial, for whatever reason, to adding contracts after a losing trade, a streak of losing trades, or a drawdown.

Over and over again in computer simulations (by myself and others) this turns out to be a very poor method of money management. It is akin to the martingale and small martingale. Since we have determined that trading is largely an independent trials process, the past trades have no effect on the present trade. It doesn't matter whether the last 20 trades were all winners or all losers.

It is interesting to note that those computer tests that have been performed all bear out the same thing. In an independent trials process where you have an edge, you are better off to increase your bet size as your stake increases, and the bet size optimally is a fixed fraction of your entire stake. Time and again authors have performed studies that take a very long stream of independent outcomes with a net positive result, and have applied various staking systems to betting/trading on these outcomes. In a nutshell, the outcomes of every study of this type reach the same conclusion: that you are better off using a staking system that increases the size of the bet in direct proportion to the size of the total stake.

In another study, William T. Ziemba demonstrated in the June 1987 issue of *Gambling Times* magazine that proportional betting was superior to any other staking strategy.[2] Furthermore, Ziemba's article demonstrated how the optimal proportion (determined correctly by the Kelly formula in this study) far outperforms any other proportion. The study simulated 1,000 seasons of betting on 700 horse races, starting you out with an initial stake of $1,000. The test looked at such outcomes as how many seasons would have tapped you out, how many seasons were profitable, how many made more than $5,000, $10,000, $100,000, and so on, as well as what the minimum, maximum, mean, and median terminal amounts were. The results of this test, too, were quite clear— betting a fixed fraction of your bankroll is far and away the best staking system.

"Wait," you say. "Aren't staking systems foolish to begin with? Didn't we see in Chapter 1 that they do not overcome the house advantage, rather all they do is increase our total action?"

This is absolutely true for a situation with a negative mathematical expectation. For a positive mathematical expectation it is a different story altogether. In a positive expectancy situation the trader/gambler is posed with the question of how best to exploit the positive expectation.

[2]Ziemba, William T., "A Betting Simulation, The Mathematics of Gambling and Investment," *Gambling Times*, pp. 46–47, 80, June, 1987.

4

Optimal Fixed Fractional Trading

We have spent the last several chapters laying the groundwork for this chapter. It is the most important chapter in the entire book.

OPTIMAL FIXED FRACTION

We have seen that in order to consider betting/trading a given situation/ system you must first determine if a positive mathematical expectation exists. We have seen in the previous chapter that what is seemingly a "good bet" on a mathematical expectation basis (i.e., the mathematical expectation is positive) may in fact not be such a good bet when you consider reinvestment of returns.[1] Reinvesting returns never raises the mathematical expectation (as a percentage—although it can raise the mathematical expectation in terms of dollars, which it does geometrically, which is why we want to reinvest). If there is in fact a positive mathematical expectation, however small, the next step is to exploit this positive expectation to its fullest potential. This has been shown, for an independent trials process, to be by reinvesting a fixed fraction of your total stake[2], which leads to the following axiom: *For*

---

[1] If you are reinvesting too high a percentage of your winnings relative to the dispersion of outcomes of the system.

[2] For a dependent trials process the idea of betting a proportion of your total stake also yields the greatest exploitation of a positive mathematical expectation, just like an independent trials process. However, in a dependent trials process you optimally bet a variable fraction of your total stake, the exact fraction for each individual bet determined by the probabilities and payoffs involved for each individual bet.

any given independent trials situation where you have an edge (i.e., a positive mathematical expectation), there exists an optimal fixed fraction (f) between 0 and 1 as a divisor of your biggest loss to bet on each and every event.

Most people think that the optimal fixed fraction is the percentage of your total stake to bet. This is absolutely false. There is an interim step involved. Optimal f is not in itself the percentage of our total stake to bet, it is the divisor of our biggest loss, the result of which we divide our total stake by to know how many bets to make or contracts to have on.

You will also notice that *margin has nothing to do whatsoever with what is the mathematically optimal number of contracts to have on.*

Maximum TWRs

```
                                    *
                        *                       *

                   *                         *

              *                                   *
```

Minimum TWRs

f's→   0   0.2   0.4   0.6   0.8   1.00

As you can see, f is a curve cupped downward from 0 to 1. The highest point for f is that fraction of your stake to bet on each and every event (bet) to maximize your winnings.

Most people incorrectly believe that f is a straight-line function rising up and to the right. They believe this because they think it would mean that the more you are willing to risk the more you stand to make. People reason this way because they think that a positive mathematical expectation is just the mirror image of a negative expectancy. They mistakenly believe that if increasing your total action in a negative expectancy game results in losing faster, then increasing your total action in a positive expectancy game will result in winning faster. This is not true. At some point in a positive expectancy situation, to increase your total action further works against you. That point is a function of both the system's profitability and its consistency (i.e., its geometric mean), since you are reinvesting the returns.

ASYMMETRICAL LEVERAGE

Recall that the amount required to recoup a loss increases geometrically with the loss. We can show that the percentage gain to recoup a loss is:

Required Gain = (1/(1 − loss in percent)) − 1

A 20% loss requires a 25% gain afterwards to recoup. A 30% loss requires a 42% gain afterwards to recoup. This is asymmetrical leverage. In fixed fractional trading we have seen that the trader will tend to have on more contracts when she takes a loss than when she has a win. This is what amplifies the asymmetrical leverage. It is also what curves the f function, since the peak of the f function represents that point where the trader has the right amount of contracts on to go into the losses and come out of the losses (with asymmetrical leverage) and achieve the maximum growth on her money at the end of a sequence of trades (see Figure 4-1). The f value (X axis) that corresponds to the peak of this f curve will be known as the optimal f (f is always in lowercase).

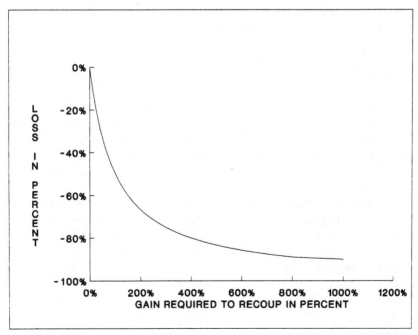

Figure 4-1   Asymmetrical leverage.

So f is a curved-line function, and this is due, in part, to the fact that asymmetrical leverage is amplified when reinvesting profits.

And how do we find this optimal f? Much work has been done in recent decades on this topic in the gambling community, the most famous and accurate of which is known as the Kelly Betting System. This is actually an application of a mathematical idea developed in early 1956 by John L. Kelly, Jr., and published in the July 1956 *Bell System Technical Journal*.[3] The Kelly criterion states that we should bet that fixed fraction of our stake (f) which maximizes the growth function $G(f)$:

$$G(f) = P * \ln(1 + B * f) + (1 - P) * \ln(1 - f)$$

where: f = The optimal fixed fraction.

P = The probability of a winning bet/trade.

B = The ratio of amount won on a winning bet to amount lost on a losing bet.

ln() = The natural logarithm function to the base $e = 2.71828. \ldots$

As it turns out, for an event with two possible outcomes, this optimal f can be found quite easily with the Kelly formulas.

KELLY

Beginning around the late 1940s, Bell System engineers were working on the problem of data transmission over long distance lines. The problem facing them was that the lines were subject to seemingly random, unavoidable "noise" that would interfere with the transmission. Some rather ingenious solutions were proposed by engineers at Bell Labs. Oddly enough, there are great similarities between this data communications problem and the problem of geometric growth as it pertains to gambling money management (as both problems are the product of an environment of favorable uncertainty). The Kelly formula is one of the outgrowths of these solutions.

The first equation here is:

$$f = 2 * P - 1$$

[3]Kelly, J. L., Jr., "A New Interpretation of Information Rate," *Bell System Technical Journal*, pp. 917–926, July, 1956.

where: f = The optimal fixed fraction.

P = The probability of a winning bet/trade.

This formula will yield the correct answer for optimal f provided the sizes of wins and losses are the same. As an example, consider the following stream of bets:

$$- 1, \ + 1, \ + 1, \ - 1, \ - 1, \ + 1, \ + 1, \ + 1, \ + 1, \ - 1$$

There are 10 bets, 6 winners, hence:

$$f = (.6 * 2) - 1$$
$$= 1.2 - 1$$
$$= .2$$

If the winners and losers were not all the same size, this formula would not yield the correct answer. Such a case would be our two-to-one coin-toss example, where all of the winners were for 2 units and all of the losers for 1 unit. For this situation the Kelly formula is:

$$f = ((B + 1) * P - 1)/B$$

where: f = The optimal fixed fraction.

P = The probability of a winning bet/trade.

B = The ratio of amount won on a winning bet to amount lost on a losing bet.

For the two-to-one coin toss:

$$f = ((2 + 1) * .5 - 1)/2$$
$$= (3 * .5 - 1)/2$$
$$= (1.5 - 1)/2$$
$$= .5/2$$
$$= .25$$

This formula will yield the correct answer for optimal f, provided all wins are always for the same amount and all losses are always for the same amount. If this condition is not met, the formula will not yield the correct answer.

Consider the following sequence of bets/trades:

$$+9, +18, +7, +1, +10, -5, -3, -17, -7$$

Since all wins and all losses are of different amounts, the previous formula does not apply. However, let's try it anyway and see what we get.

Since 5 of the 9 events are profitable, $P = .555$. Now let's take averages of the wins and losses to calculate B (here is where so many traders go wrong). The average win is 9 and the average loss is 8. Therefore we will say that $B = 1.125$. Plugging in the values we obtain:

$f = ((1.125 + 1) * .555 - 1)/1.125$

$\quad = (2.125 * .555 - 1)/1.125$

$\quad = (1.179375 - 1)/1.125$

$\quad = .179375/1.125$

$\quad = .159444444$

So we say $f = .16$. We will see later in this chapter that this is not the optimal f. The optimal f for this sequence of trades is .24. Applying Kelly when wins are not all for the same amount and/or losses are not all for the same amount is a mistake. It will not yield the optimal f.

Notice that the numerator in this formula equals the mathematical expectation for an event with two possible outcomes as defined in Chapter 1. Therefore, we can say that as long as all wins are for the same amount, and all losses are for the same amount (regardless of whether or not the amount that can be won equals the amount that can be lost), the optimal f is:

$f = $ Mathematical Expectation/B

where: $f = $ The optimal fixed fraction.

$\quad\quad\quad B = $ The ratio of amount won on a winning bet to amount lost on a losing bet.

FINDING THE OPTIMAL f
BY THE GEOMETRIC MEAN

In trading we can count on our wins being for various amounts and our losses being for various amounts. Therefore, the Kelly formula cannot give us the correct optimal f. How then can we find the optimal f to tell us how many contracts to have on and have it be mathematically correct?

As you will see later in this chapter, trading the correct quantities of contracts/shares is a far bigger problem than was previously thought. Quantity can mean the difference between winning and losing. All systems experience losing trades. All systems experience drawdown. These are givens, facts of life. Yet if you can always have the right amount of contracts on (i.e., the mathematically correct amount) then there is consolation in the losses. Trading the right amount of contracts as dictated by the optimal f will get you out of the drawdown in the least possible time.

Now here is the solution. To begin with, we must amend our formula for finding HPRs to incorporate f.

HPR = 1 + f * (− trade/biggest loss)

And again, TWR is simply the geometric product of the HPRs and geometric mean is simply the Nth root of the TWR.

$$TWR = \prod_{i=1}^{N} (1 + f * (- trade_i/biggest\ loss))$$

$$Geo.\ Mean = \left(\prod_{i=1}^{N} (1 + f * (- trade_i/biggest\ loss)) \right)^{\wedge}(1/N)$$

The geometric mean can also be calculated here by the procedure for finding the estimated geometric mean by using the HPRs as formulated above, or by taking the TWR, as formulated above, as an input to the equation:

Geo. Mean = exp((1/N) * log(TWR))

where: N = Total number of trades.

log(TWR) = The log base 10 of the TWR.
exp = The exponential function.

By looping through all values for f between .01 and 1, we can find that value for f which results in the highest TWR. This is the value for f that would provide us with the maximum return on our money using fixed fraction. We can also state that the optimal f is the f that yields the highest geometric mean. It matters not whether we look for highest TWR or geometric mean, as both are maximized at the same value for f.

Doing this with a computer is easy. Simply loop from f = .01 to f = 1.0
by .01. As soon as you get a TWR that is less than the previous TWR,
you know that the f corresponding to the previous TWR is the optimal f.
You can also calculate this by hand, but that is a lot more tedious,
especially as the number of trades increases. A quicker way to do it is to
use iteration to solve for the optimal f (you can use the iterative approach whether you are doing it by hand or by computer). Here, you
are initially bounded on f at f = 0 and f = 1.00. Pick a start value, say
f = .10, and find the corresponding TWR. Now step the f value up an
arbitrary amount. The example that follows steps it up by .10, but you
can use any amount you want to (so long as you do not have an f value
greater than 1.00, the upper bound). As long as your TWRs keep
increasing, you must step up the f value you are testing. Do this until
f = .30, where your TWR is less than at f = .20. Now, your f bounds are
.20 and .30. Keep on repeating the process until you zero in on the
optimal f. The following illustration demonstrates the iterative process
as well as the calculations:

At f = .10

TRADE	HPR	
9	1.052941	
18	1.105882	The HPRs are equal to
7	1.041176	$1 + (f*(-\text{trade/biggest loss}))$
1	1.005882	
10	1.058823	
-5	0.970588	
-3	0.982352	
-17	0.9	
-7	0.958823	
	TWR = 1.062409	The TWR is all of the HPRs multiplied together

At f = .20

TRADE	HPR
9	1.105882
18	1.211764
7	1.082352
1	1.011764
10	1.117647
-5	0.941176
-3	0.964705
-17	0.8
-7	0.917647
	TWR = 1.093231

At f = .30

TRADE	HPR
9	1.158823
18	1.317647
7	1.123529
1	1.017647
10	1.176470
− 5	0.911764
− 3	0.947058
− 17	0.7
− 7	0.876470
	TWR = 1.088113

At f = .25

TRADE	HPR
9	1.132352
18	1.264705
7	1.102941
1	1.014705
10	1.147058
− 5	0.926470
− 3	0.955882
− 17	0.75
− 7	0.897058
	TWR = 1.095387

At f = .23

TRADE	HPR
9	1.121764
18	1.243529
7	1.094705
1	1.013529
10	1.135294
− 5	0.932352
− 3	0.959411
− 17	0.77
− 7	0.905294
	TWR = 1.095634

At f = .24

TRADE	HPR
9	1.127058
18	1.254117
7	1.098823
1	1.014117
10	1.141176
− 5	0.929411
− 3	0.957647
− 17	0.76
− 7	0.901176
TWR =	1.095698

TO SUMMARIZE THUS FAR

In the previous chapter we demonstrated that a good system is the one with the highest geometric mean. Yet, to find the geometric mean you must know f. Understandably, the reader must be confused. Here now is a summary and clarification of the process:

1. Take the trade listing of a given market system.

2. Find the optimal f, either by testing various f values from 0 to 1 or through iteration. The optimal f is that which yields the highest TWR.

3. Once you have found f you can take the Nth root of that TWR corresponding to your f, where N is the total number of trades. This is your geometric mean for this market system. You can now use this geometric mean to make apples-to-apples comparisons with other market systems, as well as use the f to know how many contracts to trade for that particular market system.

Once the highest f is found, it can readily be turned into a dollar amount by dividing the biggest loss by the negative optimal f. For example, if our biggest loss is $100 and our optimal f is .25, then − $100/ − .25 = $400. In other words, we should bet 1 unit for every $400 we have in our stake.

In the sequence of bets that our coin-toss example would generate, we find that the optimal f value for the sequence + 2, − 1 is .25. Since our biggest loss is $1, 1/.25 = $4. In other words, we should bet $1 for every $4 we have in our stake in order to make the most money out of this game. To bet a higher number or a lower number will not result in a greater gain! After 10 bets, for every $4 we started out with in our stake, we will have $9.

This approach to finding the optimal f will yield the same result as:

$$f = ((B + 1) * P - 1)/B$$

You obtain the same result, of course, when losses are all for the same amount and wins are all for the same amount. In such a case, either technique is correct. When both wins and losses are for the same amount, you can use any of the three methods—the Kelly formula just shown, the f that corresponds to the highest TWR, or:

$$f = 2 * P - 1$$

Any of the three methods will give you the same answer when all wins and losses are for the same amount.

All three methods for finding the optimal f meet the four desirable properties of a money-management strategy outlined earlier, given the constraints of the two formulas (i.e., all wins being for the same amount and all losses being for the same amount, or all wins and losses being for the same amount). Regardless of constraints, the optimal f via the highest TWR will always meet the four desirable properties of a money-management strategy.

If you're having trouble with some of these concepts, try thinking in terms of betting in units, not dollars (e.g., one $5 chip or one futures contract or one 100-share unit of stock). The amount of dollars you allocate to each unit is calculated by figuring your largest loss divided by the negative optimal f.

The optimal f is a result of the balance between a system's profit-making ability (on a constant 1-unit basis) and its risk (on a constant 1-unit basis). Notice that margin doesn't matter, because the size of individual profits and losses are not the product of the amount of money put up as margin (they would be the same whatever the size of the margin). Rather, the profits and losses are the product of the exposure of one unit (one futures contract). The amount put up as margin is further made meaningless in a money-management sense, since the size of the loss is not limited to the margin.

HOW TO FIGURE THE GEOMETRIC
MEAN USING SPREADSHEET LOGIC

Here is an example of how to use a spreadsheet like Lotus 1-2-3™ to
calculate the geometric mean and TWR when you know the optimal f
or want to test a value for f.

(Assume f = .5, biggest loss = − 50)

	col A	col B	col C	col D	col E
row 1					1
row 2	15	0.3	0.15	1.15	1.15
row 3	− 5	− 0.1	− 0.05	0.95	1.0925

cell(s) explanation

A1 through D1 are blank.
E1   Set equal to 1 to begin with.
A2 down These are the individual trade P&Ls.
B2 down = A2/abs value of (biggest loss)
C2 down = B2/f
D2 down = C2 + 1
E2 down = E1 * D2

When you get to the end of the trades (the last row), your last value in
column E is your TWR. Now take the Nth root of this TWR (N is the
total number of trades); that is your geometric mean. In the above
example, your TWR (cell E3) raised to the power 1/2 (there are a total
of 2 trades here) = 1.045227. That is your geometric mean.

GEOMETRIC AVERAGE TRADE

At this point you may be interested in figuring your geometric average
trade. That is, what is the average garnered per contract per trade,
assuming profits are always reinvested and fractional contracts can be
purchased. In effect, this is the mathematical expectation when you are
trading on a fixed fractional basis. *This figure shows you what effect
there is from losers occurring when you have many contracts on and
winners occurring when you have fewer contracts on. In effect, this
approximates how a system would have fared per contract per trade*

doing fixed fraction. (Actually the geometric average trade is your mathematical expectation in dollars per contract per trade. The geometric mean minus 1 is your percent mathematical expectation per trade—e.g., a geometric mean of, say, 1.025 represents a mathematical expectation of 2.5% per trade, irrespective of size.) So many traders look simply at the average trade of a market system to see if it is high enough to justify trading the system. However, in making their decision, they should be looking at the geometric average trade (which is always lower than the average trade) as well as at the PRR.

Geo. Avg. Trade = G * (biggest loss/ − f)

where: G = Geometric mean − 1.

      f = Optimal fixed fraction.
      (And, of course, our biggest loss is always a negative number.)

For example, suppose a system has a geometric mean of 1.017238, the biggest loss is $8,000, and the optimal f is .31. Our geometric average trade would equal:

Geo. Avg. Trade = (1.017238 − 1) * (− 8,000/ − .31)

                = .017238 * 25,806.45

                = $444.85

A SIMPLER METHOD FOR FINDING THE OPTIMAL f

There are numerous ways to arrive at the optimal value for f. The technique for finding the optimal f that has been presented thus far in this chapter is perhaps the most mathematically logical. That is to say, it is obvious upon inspection that this technique will yield the optimal f. It makes more intuitive sense when you can see the HPRs laid out than does the next and somewhat easier method. So here is another way for calculating the optimal f, one that some readers may find simpler and more to their liking. It will give the same answer for optimal f as the technique previously described.

Under this method we still need to loop through different test values for f to see which value for f results in the highest TWR. However, we calculate our TWR without having to calculate the HPRs. Let's assume the following stream of profits and losses from a given system:

+ $100
− $500
+ $1,500
− $600

Again, we must isolate the largest losing trade. This is − $600.

Now we want to obtain the TWR for a given test value for f. Our first step is to calculate what we'll call the *starting value*. To begin with, take the largest loss and divide it by the test value for f. Let's start out by testing a value of .01 for f. So we will divide the largest loss, − $600, by .01. This yields an answer of − $60,000. Now we make it a positive value. Therefore, our starting value for this example sequence of a .01 test value for f is $60,000.

For each trade we must now calculate a *working value*. To do this, for each trade we must take the previous working value and divide it by the starting value. (For the first trade, the answer will be 1, since the previous working value is the same as the starting value.) Next, we multiply the answer by the current trade amount. Finally, we add this answer and the previous working value to obtain the current working value.

P&L	WORKING VALUE	
	60000	← This is the starting value
+ 100	60100	
− 500	59599.166667	
+ 1500	61089.14583	
− 600	60478.25437	

Our TWR is obtained simply by taking the last entry in the working value column and dividing it by our starting value. In this instance:

TWR = 60478.25437/60000

$$= 1.007970906$$

Now we repeat the process, only we must increment our test value for f. This time through, rather than dividing the absolute value of the largest loss of − $600 by .01 we will divide it by .02. Therefore, we will begin this next pass through with a starting value of 600/.02 = 30000.

	WORKING	
P&L	VALUE	
	30000	
+ 100	30100	((30000/30000) * 100) + 30000
− 500	29598.33	((30100/30000) * − 500) + 30100
+ 1500	31078.2465	((29598.33/30000) * 1500) + 29598.33
− 600	30456.68157	((31078.2465/30000) * − 600) + 31078.2465

Here the TWR = 30456.68157/30000 = 1.015222719

We keep on repeating the procedure until we obtain the value for f that results in the highest TWR. The answers we obtain for TWRs, as well as for the optimal f, will be the same with this technique as with the previous technique using the HPRs.

THE VIRTUES OF THE OPTIMAL f

It is a mathematical fact that when two people face the same sequence of favorable betting/trading opportunities, if one uses the optimal f and the other uses any different money-management system, then the ratio of the optimal f bettor's stake to the other person's stake will increase as time goes on, with higher and higher probability. In the long run, the optimal f bettor will have infinitely greater wealth than any other money-management system bettor with a probability approaching one.

Furthermore, if a bettor has the goal of reaching a prespecified fortune, and is facing a series of favorable betting/trading opportunities, the expected time needed to reach the fortune will be less with optimal f than with any other betting system.

Obviously, the optimal f strategy satisfies desirable property number 1 for money management, as it makes the most amount of money that is mathematically possible using a fixed fractional betting strategy on a game where you have the edge. Since optimal f incorporates the probability of winning as well as the amounts won and lost, it also satisfies desirable properties numbers 3 and 4. Not much has been discussed about desirable property number 2, the security aspect, but this will be treated in the next chapter, "Risk of Ruin."

Let's go back and reconsider the following sequence of bets/trades:

$$+9, \ +18, \ +7, \ +1, \ +10, \ -5, \ -3, \ -17, \ -7$$

Recall that we determined earlier in this chapter that the Kelly formula did not apply to this sequence, since wins were not all for the same

amount and losses were not all for the same amount. We also decided to
average the wins and average the losses and take these averages as our
values into the Kelly formula (as many traders mistakenly do). Doing
this we arrived at an f value of .16. It was stated that this is an incorrect
application of Kelly, that it would not yield the optimal f. The Kelly
formula must be specific to a single bet. We cannot average our wins
and losses from trading and obtain the true optimal f using the Kelly
formula.

Our highest TWR on this sequence of bets/trades is obtained at .24,
or betting $1 for every $71 in our stake. That is the optimal geometric
growth we can squeeze out of this sequence of bets/trades trading fixed
fraction. Let's look at the TWRs at different points along 100 loops
through this sequence of bets.

At one loop through, 9 bets/trades, the TWR for f = .16 is 1.085; for
f = .24 it is 1.096. This means that for one pass through this sequence of
bets an f = .16 made 99% of what an f = .24 would have made. To
continue:

Passes Through	Total Bets/Trades	TWR for f = .24	TWR for f = .16	Percentage Difference
1	9	1.096	1.085	1%
10	90	2.494	2.261	9.4%
40	360	38.694	26.132	32.5%
100	900	9313.312	3490.761	62.5%

As can be seen, using an f value that we mistakenly figured from
Kelly only made 37.5% as much as our optimal f of .24 after 900 bets/
trades (100 cycles through the series of 9 outcomes). In other words, our
optimal f of .24 (which is only .08 more than .16) made almost 267%
the profit that f = .16 did after 900 bets!

Let's go another 11 cycles through this sequence of trades, so we have
a total of 999 trades. Now our TWR for f = .16 is 8563.302 (not even
what it was for f = .24 at 900 trades) and our TWR for f = .24 is
25,451.045. At 999 trades f = .16 is only 33.6% of f = .24, or f = .24 is
297% of f = .16! Here is the proof that using the Kelly formula does not
yield the true optimal f for trading.

*As can be seen from the above, using the optimal f does not appear to
offer much advantage over the short run, but over the long run it
becomes more and more important to use the optimal f. The point is you
must give the program time when trading at the optimal f and not
expect miracles in the short run. The more time (i.e., bets/trades) that
elapses, the greater the difference between using the optimal f and any
other money-management strategy.*

UNANSWERED QUESTIONS

This brings us to an interesting point, that being the question, "How big a time window, or sample of trades, do we need in order to accurately find the optimal f?" Remember that when we obtain the optimal f we are obtaining that value for f which was optimal in the past over the time segment we obtained it on. We have no guarantee that the same optimal value will hold for future trades, but we have nothing to go on, other than past data. So how much past data should we use to obtain the optimal f? Surely one trade is not enough, for that would give us only two possible answers, 0 or 1. Either invest all of it or none of it depending upon whether that one trade was a winner or loser.

At present the best answer to this question is one based on theoretical reason rather than physical proof. Imagine we are writing a computer program to tell us how many times we get 12 when two dice are rolled. Further, suppose we know nothing about the odds involved. All that we can do is simulate outcomes. We would want a variable to keep track of how many times 12 came up. We would also want a second variable, to use as a divisor, for how many rolls have elapsed in total. Then we could derive a ratio, which would be the expected probability of 12 coming up on any given roll. The longer we ran the program, the closer our expected probability would be to what the actual probability is (the actual probability of throwing a 12 in one throw of a pair of fair dice is .0277777, or 1/36).

Simply stated, this is again the famous Law of Averages. The ratio of total profits or losses divided by total action approaches the expected outcome divided by the total action as the total action approaches infinity. Applying this same logic to trading, we can assume that the more trade history we have for a given market/system the more the optimal f derived therefrom will equal the optimal f in the future.

Consider the Kelly formula again. This formula is used when we know the following:

1. The probability of winning

2. How much we will make when we win

3. How much we will lose when we lose

That is, the probability distribution of the outcomes is known before the event.

This luxury does not exist in trading. We must therefore use the past history of trades that a given system has generated as a proxy for the probability distribution applicable to the next trade. The more trades we use as past data, the greater the resolution of this distribution.

Here we have decided that, by and large, the stream of profits from a trading system is independent of the outcomes of previous trades. In Chapter 1, footnote 2, however, we described a stationary distribution and contrasted it to a non-stationary distribution. Stationary distributions are quite easy to handle. With a stationary distribution, either we have a positive mathematical expectation (which can be capitalized on) or we do not (in which case the best course of action is to avoid a game with a negative expectation on an independent trials stationary distribution). Non-stationary distributions, on the other hand, can get pretty mean. Most events in real life seem to belong to the non-stationary variety. Perhaps that is where we get such "laws" of life as Murphy's. Perhaps that is why events in the lives of so many people seem to go through periods of prolonged good times and bad, the lengths and depths of which seem to be rather unpredictable beforehand.

The stream of profits and losses generated from a trading system, although independent, do conform to a probability distribution that is non-stationary (i.e., of the mean variety). When we observe the profit and loss stream of a trading system through time, the system seems to have periods where it does better than other periods (i.e., the probability distribution of the trade profits and losses is dynamic, it moves around). Often, however, when we look at the results of a system and decide that the results look good enough to us that we are willing to trade it, what we are really looking at are the results of an amalgam of the distributions of profits and losses that the system experienced through time.

Likewise, when we calculate our optimal f on a system we are actually calculating it on an amalgam of the probability distributions of the trade profits and losses through time. At some points in time, a value for f other than what we regard as the optimal would in fact have been the optimal. Therefore, we can expect that in the future, as the probability distribution of the trade profits and losses changes and moves around, so too will the value for the optimal f *at that moment*. Yet over time, as the distribution moves around, we hope that the optimal f will converge to what we have calculated it to be.

The next question that naturally arises is, "How often should you recalculate the optimal f?" By the same reasoning as was just illustrated with the Law of Averages, the optimal f should be found after each new trade. In actual practice, though, once you have a sufficient trade history (at least 30 trades), each new trade (unless it makes an unusually large profit or loss) will most likely not change the optimal f in any significant way. Certainly a new largest loss will affect the optimal f. Recall the stock index futures after October 1987. The optimal f values were quite different at the end of that month than they were at the beginning.

An interesting avenue of research now opens. What if you were to take the trade history for a given market/system and drop the biggest winning and biggest losing trades out before finding the optimal f in order to obtain an optimal "robust" f?

Optimized results will often give values for f that are too optimistic, putting the trader too far out to the right of the peak of the f curve (i.e., too many contracts on). Rarely will the optimal values in the past be the optimals in the future. Finding f via forward testing can eliminate this and give a far more realistic appraisal of what is the best value to use for f in the future than simple optimized results can provide. So, if you are using an optimized system and you have the computer resources, the best way to find f is by way of forward testing. This eliminates the possibility of arriving at a value for f that is too optimistic. By optimizing over a certain time period, taking those optimal parameters, and using them on the next segment of data, you can obtain out-of-sample results. You then repeat the process until you have gone through all of your data. Then use all of these out-of-sample trades to find your optimal f.

If you do not or cannot forward-test, then either trade a system that has no optimizeable parameters or pad the f considerably to try to take into account the fact that the future won't be as good as the past (using the past's optimal parameters).

This gets a little sticky, since the value for f itself is arrived at by optimization. Furthermore, the f curve is not very robust. If the optimal f in the future is not the same as the optimal f in the past, there is not a great deal of room for error. Ideally, you would trade a system that had no optimizeable parameters and a lengthy trade history. Of course the historical results of such a system could not be expected to rival those of an optimizeable system. However, the optimal f value obtained could be relied upon to hold up better in the future than would the optimal f for an optimizeable system. And as you will see shortly, there is a tremendous penalty to be paid for not being near the optimal f in the future. As you can see, *the role of the computer in futures trading has been misdirected; the concentration should be on account management more than on parameter optimization.*

WHY YOU MUST KNOW YOUR OPTIMAL f

Figures 4-2 through 4-6 demonstrate the importance of using optimal f in fixed fractional trading. The graphs are constructed by plotting the f values from 0 to 1.0 along the X axis and the respective TWRs along the Y axis. Values are plotted at intervals of .05.

Each graph has a corresponding spreadsheet. Each column heading in the spreadsheet has a different f value. Under each f value is the corresponding start value, figured as the biggest loss divided by the negative f value. For every unit of start value you have in your stake you bet one unit. Along the far left is the sequence of 40 bets. This sequence is the only difference between the various spreadsheets and graphs.

As you go down through the sequence of trades you will notice that each cell equals the previous cell divided by that cell's starting value. This result is then multiplied by the outcome of the current bet, and the product added to the original value of the previous cell, to obtain the value of the current cell. When you reach the end of the column you can figure your TWR as the last value of the column divided by the start value of the column (i.e., the biggest loss divided by negative f). This is the alternative and somewhat easier way to figure your TWRs. Both methods shown thus far make the calculations non-quantum. In other words, you do not need an integer amount to multiply the current bet result by; you can use a decimal amount of the starting value as well. An example may help clarify.

In the $+1.2$, -1 sequence (Figure 4-2), for an f value of .05, we have a starting value of 20:

$$-1/-.05 = 20$$

In other words, we will bet 1 unit for every 20 units in our stake. With the first bet, a gain of 1.2, we now have 21.2 units in our stake. (Since we had 20 units in our stake prior to this bet and we bet 1 unit for every 20 in our stake, we only bet 1 unit on this bet.) Now the next bet is a loss of 1 unit. The question now is, "How many units were we betting on this one?"

We could argue that we were only betting 1 unit, since 21.20 (our stake prior to the bet) divided by 20 (the starting value) = 1.06. Since most bets must be in integer form—i.e., no fractional bets (chips are not divisible and neither are futures contracts)—we could only bet 1 unit in real life in this situation. However, in these simulations the fractional bet is allowed. The reasoning here behind allowing the fractional bet is to keep the outcome consistent regardless of the starting stake. Notice that each simulation starts with only enough stake to make 1 full bet. What if each simulation started with more than that? Say each simulation started with enough to make 1.99 bets. If we were only allowing integer bets, our outcomes (TWRs) would be altogether different.

Further, the larger the amount we begin trading with is, relative to the starting value (biggest loss/ − optimal f), the closer the integer bet will be to the fractional bet. Again, clarity is provided by way of an example. What if we began trading with 400 units in the previous example? After the first bet our stake would have been:

Stake = 400 + ((400/20) * 1.2)

      = 400 + (20 * 1.2)

      = 400 + 24

      = 424

For the next bet, we would wager 21.2 units (424/20), or the integer amount of 21 units. Note that the percentage difference between the fractional and the integer bet here is only 0.952381% versus a 6.0% difference, had the amount we began trading with been only 1 starting value, 20 units. The following axiom can now be drawn: *The greater the ratio of the amount you have as a stake to begin trading relative to the starting value (biggest loss/ – optimal f), the more the percentage difference will tend to zero between integer and fractional betting.*

By allowing fractional bets, making the process non-quantum, we obtain a more realistic assessment of the relationship of f values to TWRs. *The fractional bets represent the average (of all possible values of the size of initial bankrolls) of the integer bets.* So the argument that we cannot make fractional bets in real life does not apply, since the fractional bet represents the average integer bet. If we made graphs of the TWRs at each f value for the + 2, – 1 coin toss, and used integer bets, we would have to make a different graph for each different initial bankroll. If we did this and then averaged the graphs to create a composite graph of the TWRs at each f value, we would have a graph of the fractional bet situation exactly as shown.

This is not a contention that the fractional bet situation is the same as the real-life integer-bet situation. Rather the contention is that for the purposes of studying these functions we are better off considering the fractional bet, since it represents the universe of integer bets. The fractional bet situation *is* what we can expect in real life in an asymptotic sense (i.e., in the long run).

This discussion leads to another interesting point that is true in a fixed fractional betting situation where fractional bets are allowed (think of fractional bets as the average outcome of all integer bets at different initial bankroll values, since that is what fractional betting represents here). This point is that *the TWR is the same regardless of the starting value.* In the examples just cited, if we have an initial stake of 1 starting value, 20 units, our TWR (ending stake divided by initial stake) is 1.15. If we have an initial stake of 400 units, 20 starting values, our TWR is still 1.15.

20 TRIALS

EVENT	f VALUES -->								
	0.05	0.1	0.15	0.2	0.25	0.3	0.35	0.4	0.45
START VALUES -->	20.00	10.00	6.67	5.00	4.00	3.33	2.86	2.50	2.22
1.2	21.20	11.20	7.87	6.20	5.20	4.53	4.06	3.70	3.42
-1	20.14	10.08	6.69	4.96	3.90	3.17	2.64	2.22	1.88
1.2	21.35	11.29	7.89	6.15	5.07	4.32	3.74	3.29	2.90
-1	20.28	10.16	6.71	4.92	3.80	3.02	2.43	1.97	1.59
1.2	21.50	11.38	7.91	6.10	4.94	4.11	3.46	2.92	2.46
-1	20.42	10.24	6.73	4.88	3.71	2.88	2.25	1.75	1.35
1.2	21.65	11.47	7.94	6.05	4.82	3.91	3.19	2.59	2.08
-1	20.57	10.32	6.75	4.84	3.61	2.74	2.07	1.55	1.14
1.2	21.80	11.56	7.96	6.00	4.70	3.72	2.94	2.30	1.76
-1	20.71	10.41	6.77	4.80	3.52	2.61	1.91	1.38	0.97
1.2	21.95	11.66	7.99	5.96	4.58	3.54	2.72	2.04	1.49
-1	20.85	10.49	6.79	4.76	3.44	2.48	1.77	1.23	0.82
1.2	22.11	11.75	8.01	5.91	4.47	3.37	2.51	1.81	1.26
-1	21.00	10.57	6.81	4.73	3.35	2.36	1.63	1.09	0.69
1.2	22.26	11.84	8.03	5.86	4.36	3.21	2.32	1.61	1.07
-1	21.15	10.66	6.83	4.69	3.27	2.25	1.51	0.97	0.59
1.2	22.42	11.94	8.06	5.81	4.25	3.06	2.14	1.43	0.91
-1	21.30	10.74	6.85	4.65	3.18	2.14	1.39	0.86	0.50
1.2	22.57	12.03	8.08	5.77	4.14	2.91	1.97	1.27	0.77
-1	21.44	10.83	6.87	4.61	3.11	2.04	1.28	0.76	0.42
1.2	22.73	12.13	8.11	5.72	4.04	2.77	1.82	1.13	0.65
-1	21.60	10.92	6.89	4.58	3.03	1.94	1.18	0.68	0.36
1.2	22.89	12.23	8.13	5.68	3.94	2.64	1.68	1.00	0.55
-1	21.75	11.00	6.91	4.54	2.95	1.85	1.09	0.60	0.30
1.2	23.05	12.32	8.15	5.63	3.84	2.51	1.55	0.89	0.47
-1	21.90	11.09	6.93	4.50	2.88	1.76	1.01	0.53	0.26
1.2	23.21	12.42	8.18	5.59	3.74	2.39	1.43	0.79	0.40
-1	22.05	11.18	6.95	4.47	2.81	1.67	0.93	0.47	0.22
1.2	23.37	12.52	8.20	5.54	3.65	2.28	1.32	0.70	0.33
-1	22.21	11.27	6.97	4.43	2.74	1.59	0.86	0.42	0.18
1.2	23.54	12.62	8.23	5.50	3.56	2.17	1.22	0.62	0.28
-1	22.36	11.36	6.99	4.40	2.67	1.52	0.79	0.37	0.16
1.2	23.70	12.72	8.25	5.45	3.47	2.06	1.13	0.55	0.24
-1	22.52	11.45	7.01	4.36	2.60	1.44	0.73	0.33	0.13
1.2	23.87	12.82	8.28	5.41	3.38	1.96	1.04	0.49	0.20
-1	22.68	11.54	7.04	4.33	2.54	1.38	0.68	0.29	0.11
1.2	24.04	12.93	8.30	5.37	3.30	1.87	0.96	0.44	0.17
-1	22.83	11.63	7.06	4.29	2.47	1.31	0.62	0.26	0.09
1.2	24.20	13.03	8.33	5.32	3.21	1.78	0.89	0.39	0.15
-1	22.99	11.73	7.08	4.26	2.41	1.25	0.58	0.23	0.08
TWR --------->	1.15	1.17	1.06	0.85	0.60	0.37	0.20	0.09	0.04

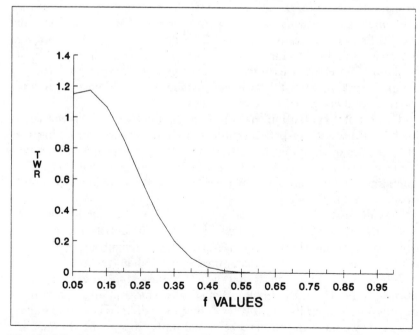

Figure 4-2   Values of f for 20 sequences at + 1.2, − 1.

0.5	0.55	0.6	0.65	0.7	0.75	0.8	0.85	0.9	0.95	1
2.00	1.82	1.67	1.54	1.43	1.33	1.25	1.18	1.11	1.05	1.00
3.20	3.02	2.87	2.74	2.63	2.53	2.45	2.38	2.31	2.25	2.20
1.60	1.36	1.15	0.96	0.79	0.63	0.49	0.36	0.23	0.11	0.00
2.56	2.25	1.97	1.71	1.45	1.20	0.96	0.72	0.48	0.24	0.00
1.28	1.01	0.79	0.60	0.44	0.30	0.19	0.11	0.05	0.01	0.00
2.05	1.68	1.36	1.06	0.80	0.57	0.38	0.22	0.10	0.03	0.00
1.02	0.76	0.54	0.37	0.24	0.14	0.08	0.03	0.01	.00	0.00
1.64	1.26	0.93	0.66	0.44	0.27	0.15	0.07	0.02	.00	0.00
0.82	0.57	0.37	0.23	0.13	0.07	0.03	0.01	.00	.00	0.00
1.31	0.94	0.64	0.41	0.24	0.13	0.06	0.02	.00	.00	0.00
0.66	0.42	0.26	0.14	0.07	0.03	0.01	.00	.00	.00	0.00
1.05	0.70	0.44	0.26	0.13	0.06	0.02	0.01	.00	.00	0.00
0.52	0.32	0.18	0.09	0.04	0.02	.00	.00	.00	.00	0.00
0.84	0.52	0.30	0.16	0.07	0.03	0.01	.00	.00	.00	0.00
0.42	0.24	0.12	0.06	0.02	0.01	.00	.00	.00	.00	0.00
0.67	0.39	0.21	0.10	0.04	0.01	.00	.00	.00	.00	0.00
0.34	0.18	0.08	0.03	0.01	.00	.00	.00	.00	.00	0.00
0.54	0.29	0.14	0.06	0.02	0.01	.00	.00	.00	.00	0.00
0.27	0.13	0.06	0.02	0.01	.00	.00	.00	.00	.00	0.00
0.43	0.22	0.10	0.04	0.01	.00	.00	.00	.00	.00	0.00
0.21	0.10	0.04	0.01	.00	.00	.00	.00	.00	.00	0.00
0.34	0.16	0.07	0.02	0.01	.00	.00	.00	.00	.00	0.00
0.17	0.07	0.03	0.01	.00	.00	.00	.00	.00	.00	0.00
0.27	0.12	0.05	0.02	.00	.00	.00	.00	.00	.00	0.00
0.14	0.05	0.02	0.01	.00	.00	.00	.00	.00	.00	0.00
0.22	0.09	0.03	0.01	.00	.00	.00	.00	.00	.00	0.00
0.11	0.04	0.01	.00	.00	.00	.00	.00	.00	.00	0.00
0.18	0.07	0.02	0.01	.00	.00	.00	.00	.00	.00	0.00
0.09	0.03	0.01	.00	.00	.00	.00	.00	.00	.00	0.00
0.14	0.05	0.02	.00	.00	.00	.00	.00	.00	.00	0.00
0.07	0.02	0.01	.00	.00	.00	.00	.00	.00	.00	0.00
0.11	0.04	0.01	.00	.00	.00	.00	.00	.00	.00	0.00
0.06	0.02	.00	.00	.00	.00	.00	.00	.00	.00	0.00
0.09	0.03	0.01	.00	.00	.00	.00	.00	.00	.00	0.00
0.05	0.01	.00	.00	.00	.00	.00	.00	.00	.00	0.00
0.07	0.02	.00	.00	.00	.00	.00	.00	.00	.00	0.00
0.04	0.01	.00	.00	.00	.00	.00	.00	.00	.00	0.00
0.06	0.02	.00	.00	.00	.00	.00	.00	.00	.00	0.00
0.03	0.01	.00	.00	.00	.00	.00	.00	.00	.00	0.00
0.05	0.01	.00	.00	.00	.00	.00	.00	.00	.00	0.00
0.02	0.01	.00	.00	.00	.00	.00	.00	.00	.00	0.00
0.01	.00	.00	.00	.00	.00	.00	.00	.00	.00	0.00

Figure 4–3 shows the f curve for 20 sequences of the + 1.5, − 1.

Refer now to the + 2, − 1 graph (Figure 4-4). Notice that here the optimal f is .25 where the TWR is 10.55 after 40 bets (20 sequences of + 2, − 1). Now look what happens if you bet only 15% away from the optimal .25 f. At an f of .1 or .4 your TWR is 4.66. This is not even half of what it is at .25, yet you are only 15% away from the optimal and only 40 bets have elapsed! What does this mean in terms of dollars? At f = .1, you would be making 1 bet for every $10 in your stake. At f = .4 you would be making 1 bet for every $2.50 in your stake. Both make the same amount, with a TWR of 4.66. At f = .25, you are making 1 bet for every $4 in your stake. Notice that if you make 1 bet for every $4 in your stake you will make more than twice as much as you would if you were making 1 bet for every $2.50 in your stake! Clearly, it does not pay to overbet. At 1 bet for every $10 in your stake you make the same amount as if you had bet 4 times that amount, 1 bet for every $2.50 in your stake! Notice that in a 50/50 game where you win twice the amount that you lose, at an f of .5 you are only breaking even! That means you are only breaking even if you made 1 bet for every $2 in your stake. At an f greater than .5 you are losing in this game, and it is simply a matter of time until you are completely tapped out!

Now let's increase the winning payout from 2 units to 5 units, as is

20 TRIALS f VALUES --> EVENT	0.05	0.1	0.15	0.2	0.25	0.3	0.35	0.4	0.45
START VALUES -->	20.00	10.00	6.67	5.00	4.00	3.33	2.86	2.50	2.22
1.5	21.50	11.50	8.17	6.50	5.50	4.83	4.36	4.00	3.72
-1	20.43	10.35	6.94	5.20	4.13	3.38	2.83	2.40	2.05
1.5	21.96	11.90	8.50	6.76	5.67	4.91	4.32	3.84	3.43
-1	20.86	10.71	7.23	5.41	4.25	3.43	2.81	2.30	1.89
1.5	22.42	12.32	8.85	7.03	5.85	4.98	4.28	3.69	3.16
-1	21.30	11.09	7.53	5.62	4.39	3.49	2.78	2.21	1.74
1.5	22.90	12.75	9.22	7.31	6.03	5.05	4.24	3.54	2.91
-1	21.75	11.48	7.84	5.85	4.52	3.54	2.76	2.12	1.60
1.5	23.39	13.20	9.60	7.60	6.22	5.13	4.21	3.40	2.68
-1	22.22	11.88	8.16	6.08	4.67	3.59	2.73	2.04	1.47
1.5	23.88	13.66	10.00	7.91	6.41	5.21	4.17	3.26	2.47
-1	22.69	12.29	8.50	6.33	4.81	3.64	2.71	1.96	1.36
1.5	24.39	14.14	10.41	8.22	6.62	5.28	4.13	3.13	2.28
-1	23.17	12.72	8.85	6.58	4.96	3.70	2.69	1.88	1.25
1.5	24.91	14.63	10.84	8.55	6.82	5.36	4.10	3.01	2.10
-1	23.66	13.17	9.21	6.84	5.12	3.75	2.66	1.80	1.15
1.5	25.44	15.14	11.28	8.90	7.04	5.44	4.06	2.89	1.93
-1	24.17	13.63	9.59	7.12	5.28	3.81	2.64	1.73	1.06
1.5	25.98	15.67	11.75	9.25	7.26	5.53	4.03	2.77	1.78
-1	24.68	14.11	9.99	7.40	5.44	3.87	2.62	1.66	0.98
1.5	26.53	16.22	12.23	9.62	7.48	5.61	3.99	2.66	1.64
-1	25.20	14.60	10.40	7.70	5.61	3.93	2.59	1.60	0.90
1.5	27.10	16.79	12.74	10.01	7.72	5.69	3.96	2.55	1.51
-1	25.74	15.11	10.83	8.01	5.79	3.99	2.57	1.53	0.83
1.5	27.67	17.38	13.26	10.41	7.96	5.78	3.92	2.45	1.39
-1	26.29	15.64	11.28	8.33	5.97	4.05	2.55	1.47	0.77
1.5	28.26	17.99	13.81	10.82	8.21	5.87	3.89	2.35	1.28
-1	26.85	16.19	11.74	8.66	6.15	4.11	2.53	1.41	0.70
1.5	28.86	18.61	14.38	11.26	8.46	5.95	3.85	2.26	1.18
-1	27.42	16.75	12.22	9.00	6.35	4.17	2.50	1.36	0.65
1.5	29.47	19.27	14.98	11.71	8.73	6.04	3.82	2.17	1.09
-1	28.00	17.34	12.73	9.36	6.54	4.23	2.48	1.30	0.60
1.5	30.10	19.94	15.59	12.17	9.00	6.13	3.79	2.08	1.00
-1	28.59	17.95	13.25	9.74	6.75	4.29	2.46	1.25	0.55
1.5	30.74	20.64	16.24	12.66	9.28	6.23	3.75	2.00	0.92
-1	29.20	18.57	13.80	10.13	6.96	4.36	2.44	1.20	0.51
1.5	31.39	21.36	16.91	13.17	9.57	6.32	3.72	1.92	0.85
-1	29.82	19.23	14.37	10.53	7.18	4.42	2.42	1.15	0.47
1.5	32.06	22.11	17.60	13.69	9.87	6.41	3.69	1.84	0.78
-1	30.46	19.90	14.96	10.96	7.40	4.49	2.40	1.11	0.43
TWR --------->	1.52	1.99	2.24	2.19	1.85	1.35	0.84	0.44	0.19

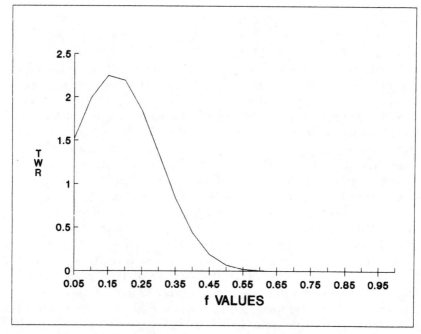

Figure 4-3   Values of f for 20 sequences at + 1.5, − 1.

0.5	0.55	0.6	0.65	0.7	0.75	0.8	0.85	0.9	0.95	1
2.00	1.82	1.67	1.54	1.43	1.33	1.25	1.18	1.11	1.05	1.00
3.50	3.32	3.17	3.04	2.93	2.83	2.75	2.68	2.61	2.55	2.50
1.75	1.49	1.27	1.06	0.88	0.71	0.55	0.40	0.26	0.13	0.00
3.06	2.73	2.41	2.10	1.80	1.51	1.21	0.91	0.61	0.31	0.00
1.53	1.23	0.96	0.74	0.54	0.38	0.24	0.14	0.06	0.02	0.00
2.68	2.24	1.83	1.45	1.11	0.80	0.53	0.31	0.14	0.04	0.00
1.34	1.01	0.73	0.51	0.33	0.20	0.11	0.05	0.01	.00	0.00
2.34	1.84	1.39	1.00	0.68	0.42	0.23	0.11	0.03	.00	0.00
1.17	0.83	0.56	0.35	0.20	0.11	0.05	0.02	.00	.00	0.00
2.05	1.51	1.06	0.69	0.42	0.23	0.10	0.04	0.01	.00	0.00
1.03	0.68	0.42	0.24	0.13	0.06	0.02	0.01	.00	.00	0.00
1.80	1.24	0.80	0.48	0.26	0.12	0.05	0.01	.00	.00	0.00
0.90	0.56	0.32	0.17	0.08	0.03	0.01	.00	.00	.00	0.00
1.57	1.02	0.61	0.33	0.16	0.06	0.02	.00	.00	.00	0.00
0.79	0.46	0.24	0.12	0.05	0.02	.00	.00	.00	.00	0.00
1.37	0.84	0.46	0.23	0.10	0.03	0.01	.00	.00	.00	0.00
0.69	0.38	0.19	0.08	0.03	0.01	.00	.00	.00	.00	0.00
1.20	0.69	0.35	0.16	0.06	0.02	.00	.00	.00	.00	0.00
0.60	0.31	0.14	0.06	0.02	.00	.00	.00	.00	.00	0.00
1.05	0.56	0.27	0.11	0.04	0.01	.00	.00	.00	.00	0.00
0.53	0.25	0.11	0.04	0.01	.00	.00	.00	.00	.00	0.00
0.92	0.46	0.20	0.08	0.02	0.01	.00	.00	.00	.00	0.00
0.46	0.21	0.08	0.03	0.01	.00	.00	.00	.00	.00	0.00
0.81	0.38	0.15	0.05	0.01	.00	.00	.00	.00	.00	0.00
0.40	0.17	0.06	0.02	.00	.00	.00	.00	.00	.00	0.00
0.70	0.31	0.12	0.04	0.01	.00	.00	.00	.00	.00	0.00
0.35	0.14	0.05	0.01	.00	.00	.00	.00	.00	.00	0.00
0.62	0.26	0.09	0.02	0.01	.00	.00	.00	.00	.00	0.00
0.31	0.12	0.04	0.01	.00	.00	.00	.00	.00	.00	0.00
0.54	0.21	0.07	0.02	.00	.00	.00	.00	.00	.00	0.00
0.27	0.09	0.03	0.01	.00	.00	.00	.00	.00	.00	0.00
0.47	0.17	0.05	0.01	.00	.00	.00	.00	.00	.00	0.00
0.24	0.08	0.02	.00	.00	.00	.00	.00	.00	.00	0.00
0.41	0.14	0.04	0.01	.00	.00	.00	.00	.00	.00	0.00
0.21	0.06	0.02	.00	.00	.00	.00	.00	.00	.00	0.00
0.36	0.12	0.03	0.01	.00	.00	.00	.00	.00	.00	0.00
0.18	0.05	0.01	.00	.00	.00	.00	.00	.00	.00	0.00
0.32	0.10	0.02	.00	.00	.00	.00	.00	.00	.00	0.00
0.16	0.04	0.01	.00	.00	.00	.00	.00	.00	.00	0.00
0.28	0.08	0.02	.00	.00	.00	.00	.00	.00	.00	0.00
0.14	0.04	0.01	.00	.00	.00	.00	.00	.00	.00	0.00
0.07	0.02	.00	.00	.00	.00	.00	.00	.00	.00	0.00

demonstrated in the data in Figure 4-5. Here your optimal f is .4, or bet $1 for every $2.50 in your stake. After 20 sequences of + 5, − 1, 40 bets, your $2.50 stake has grown to $127,482, thanks to optimal f. Now look what happens in this extremely favorable situation if you miss the optimal f by 20%. At f values of .6 and .2 you don't make one-tenth as much as you do at .4 in this case! This particular situation, a 50/50 bet paying 5 to 1, has a mathematical expectation of $(5 * .5) + (1 * (− .5)) = 2$. Yet if you bet using an f value greater than .8, you lose money in this situation. Clearly the question of what the correct quantity to bet or trade is has been terribly underrated.

The graphs bear out a few more interesting points. The first is that *at no other fixed fraction will you make more money than optimal f.* In other words it does not pay to bet one dollar for every two in your stake in the above example of + 5, − 1. In such a case, you would make less money than if you bet one dollar for every $2.50 in your stake. *It does not pay to risk more than the optimal f—in fact you pay a price to do so!* Notice in Figure 4-6 that you make less at f = .55 than at f = .5. The second interesting point to notice is how important the biggest loss is in the calculations. Traders may be incorrectly inclined to use maximum drawdown rather than biggest loss.

20 TRIALS

EVENT	f VALUES -->								
	0.05	0.1	0.15	0.2	0.25	0.3	0.35	0.4	0.45
START VALUES -->	20.00	10.00	6.67	5.00	4.00	3.33	2.86	2.50	2.22
2	22.00	12.00	8.67	7.00	6.00	5.33	4.86	4.50	4.22
-1	20.90	10.80	7.37	5.60	4.50	3.73	3.16	2.70	2.32
2	22.99	12.96	9.58	7.84	6.75	5.97	5.37	4.86	4.41
-1	21.84	11.66	8.14	6.27	5.06	4.18	3.49	2.92	2.43
2	24.02	14.00	10.58	8.78	7.59	6.69	5.93	5.25	4.61
-1	22.82	12.60	8.99	7.02	5.70	4.68	3.85	3.15	2.54
2	25.11	15.12	11.69	9.83	8.54	7.49	6.55	5.67	4.82
-1	23.85	13.60	9.94	7.87	6.41	5.25	4.26	3.40	2.65
2	26.24	16.33	12.92	11.01	9.61	8.39	7.24	6.12	5.04
-1	24.92	14.69	10.98	8.81	7.21	5.87	4.71	3.67	2.77
2	27.42	17.63	14.28	12.34	10.81	9.40	8.00	6.61	5.26
-1	26.05	15.87	12.14	9.87	8.11	6.58	5.20	3.97	2.89
2	28.65	19.04	15.78	13.82	12.16	10.53	8.84	7.14	5.50
-1	27.22	17.14	13.41	11.05	9.12	7.37	5.75	4.28	3.02
2	29.94	20.57	17.43	15.47	13.68	11.79	9.77	7.71	5.75
-1	28.44	18.51	14.82	12.38	10.26	8.25	6.35	4.63	3.16
2	31.29	22.21	19.26	17.33	15.39	13.21	10.80	8.33	6.00
-1	29.72	19.99	16.37	13.87	11.55	9.24	7.02	5.00	3.30
2	32.69	23.99	21.29	19.41	17.32	14.79	11.93	9.00	6.27
-1	31.06	21.59	18.09	15.53	12.99	10.35	7.75	5.40	3.45
2	34.17	25.91	23.52	21.74	19.48	16.56	13.18	9.72	6.56
-1	32.46	23.32	19.99	17.39	14.61	11.60	8.57	5.83	3.61
2	35.70	27.98	25.99	24.35	21.92	18.55	14.57	10.49	6.85
-1	33.92	25.18	22.09	19.48	16.44	12.99	9.47	6.30	3.77
2	37.31	30.22	28.72	27.27	24.66	20.78	16.10	11.33	7.16
-1	35.44	27.20	24.41	21.82	18.49	14.54	10.46	6.80	3.94
2	38.99	32.64	31.74	30.54	27.74	23.27	17.79	12.24	7.48
-1	37.04	29.37	26.98	24.44	20.81	16.29	11.56	7.34	4.12
2	40.74	35.25	35.07	34.21	31.21	26.06	19.65	13.22	7.82
-1	38.71	31.72	29.81	27.37	23.41	18.25	12.78	7.93	4.30
2	42.58	38.07	38.75	38.31	35.11	29.19	21.72	14.27	8.17
-1	40.45	34.26	32.94	30.65	26.33	20.43	14.12	8.56	4.49
2	44.49	41.11	42.82	42.91	39.50	32.70	24.00	15.42	8.54
-1	42.27	37.00	36.40	34.33	29.62	22.89	15.60	9.25	4.70
2	46.49	44.40	47.32	48.06	44.44	36.62	26.52	16.65	8.92
-1	44.17	39.96	40.22	38.45	33.33	25.63	17.24	9.99	4.91
2	48.59	47.95	52.28	53.83	49.99	41.01	29.30	17.98	9.32
-1	46.16	43.16	44.44	43.06	37.49	28.71	19.05	10.79	5.13
2	50.77	51.79	57.77	60.29	56.24	45.93	32.38	19.42	9.74
-1	48.23	46.61	49.11	48.23	42.18	32.15	21.05	11.65	5.36
TWR --------->	2.41	4.66	7.37	9.65	10.55	9.65	7.37	4.66	2.41

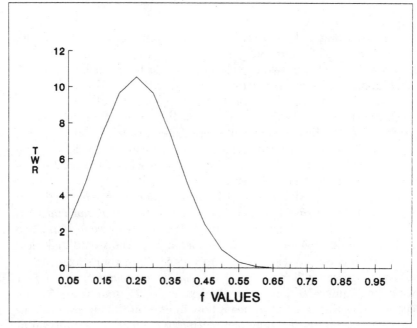

Figure 4-4   Values of f for 20 sequences at + 2, − 1.

0.5	0.55	0.6	0.65	0.7	0.75	0.8	0.85	0.9	0.95	1
2.00	1.82	1.67	1.54	1.43	1.33	1.25	1.18	1.11	1.05	1.00
4.00	3.82	3.67	3.54	3.43	3.33	3.25	3.18	3.11	3.05	3.00
2.00	1.72	1.47	1.24	1.03	0.83	0.65	0.48	0.31	0.15	0.00
4.00	3.61	3.23	2.85	2.47	2.08	1.69	1.29	0.87	0.44	0.00
2.00	1.62	1.29	1.00	0.74	0.52	0.34	0.19	0.09	0.02	0.00
4.00	3.41	2.84	2.29	1.78	1.30	0.88	0.52	0.24	0.06	0.00
2.00	1.53	1.14	0.80	0.53	0.33	0.18	0.08	0.02	.00	0.00
4.00	3.22	2.50	1.85	1.28	0.81	0.46	0.21	0.07	0.01	0.00
2.00	1.45	1.00	0.65	0.38	0.20	0.09	0.03	0.01	.00	0.00
4.00	3.04	2.20	1.49	0.92	0.51	0.24	0.09	0.02	.00	0.00
2.00	1.37	0.88	0.52	0.28	0.13	0.05	0.01	.00	.00	0.00
4.00	2.88	1.94	1.20	0.66	0.32	0.12	0.03	0.01	.00	0.00
2.00	1.29	0.77	0.42	0.20	0.08	0.02	0.01	.00	.00	0.00
4.00	2.72	1.70	0.96	0.48	0.20	0.06	0.01	.00	.00	0.00
2.00	1.22	0.68	0.34	0.14	0.05	0.01	.00	.00	.00	0.00
4.00	2.57	1.50	0.78	0.34	0.12	0.03	0.01	.00	.00	0.00
2.00	1.16	0.60	0.27	0.10	0.03	0.01	.00	.00	.00	0.00
4.00	2.43	1.32	0.62	0.25	0.08	0.02	.00	.00	.00	0.00
2.00	1.09	0.53	0.22	0.07	0.02	.00	.00	.00	.00	0.00
4.00	2.29	1.16	0.50	0.18	0.05	0.01	.00	.00	.00	0.00
2.00	1.03	0.46	0.18	0.05	0.01	.00	.00	.00	.00	0.00
4.00	2.17	1.02	0.40	0.13	0.03	.00	.00	.00	.00	0.00
2.00	0.98	0.41	0.14	0.04	0.01	.00	.00	.00	.00	0.00
4.00	2.05	0.90	0.33	0.09	0.02	.00	.00	.00	.00	0.00
2.00	0.92	0.36	0.11	0.03	.00	.00	.00	.00	.00	0.00
4.00	1.94	0.79	0.26	0.07	0.01	.00	.00	.00	.00	0.00
2.00	0.87	0.32	0.09	0.02	.00	.00	.00	.00	.00	0.00
4.00	1.83	0.70	0.21	0.05	0.01	.00	.00	.00	.00	0.00
2.00	0.82	0.28	0.07	0.01	.00	.00	.00	.00	.00	0.00
4.00	1.73	0.61	0.17	0.03	.00	.00	.00	.00	.00	0.00
2.00	0.78	0.24	0.06	0.01	.00	.00	.00	.00	.00	0.00
4.00	1.63	0.54	0.14	0.02	.00	.00	.00	.00	.00	0.00
2.00	0.74	0.22	0.05	0.01	.00	.00	.00	.00	.00	0.00
4.00	1.54	0.47	0.11	0.02	.00	.00	.00	.00	.00	0.00
2.00	0.69	0.19	0.04	0.01	.00	.00	.00	.00	.00	0.00
4.00	1.46	0.42	0.09	0.01	.00	.00	.00	.00	.00	0.00
2.00	0.66	0.17	0.03	.00	.00	.00	.00	.00	.00	0.00
4.00	1.38	0.37	0.07	0.01	.00	.00	.00	.00	.00	0.00
2.00	0.62	0.15	0.02	.00	.00	.00	.00	.00	.00	0.00
4.00	1.30	0.32	0.06	0.01	.00	.00	.00	.00	.00	0.00
2.00	0.59	0.13	0.02	.00	.00	.00	.00	.00	.00	0.00
1.00	0.32	0.08	0.01	.00	.00	.00	.00	.00	.00	0.00

DRAWDOWN IS MEANINGLESS, BIGGEST LOSING TRADE ISN'T

First, if you have f = 1.00, then as soon as the biggest loss is encountered, you would be tapped out. This is as it should be. You want f to be bounded at 0 (nothing at stake) and 1 (the lowest amount at stake where you would lose 100%).

Second, in an independent trials process the sequence of trades that results in the drawdown is, in effect, arbitrary (as a result of the independence). Suppose we toss a coin 6 times, and we get heads 3 times and tails 3 times. Suppose that we win $1 every time heads comes up and lose $1 every time tails comes up. Considering all possible sequences here our drawdown could be $1, $2, or $3, the extreme case where all losses bunch together. If we went through this exercise once, and came up with a $2 drawdown, it wouldn't mean anything. Since drawdown is an *extreme* case situation, and we are speaking of exact sequences of trades that are independent, we have to assume that the extreme case can be all losses bunching together in a row (the extreme worst case in the sample space). Just because we experienced one exact sequence of 6 coin flips wherein the drawdown was $2 doesn't mean we can use that as any kind of a meaningful benchmark, since the next exact sequence is

20 TRIALS f VALUES --> EVENT	0.05	0.1	0.15	0.2	0.25	0.3	0.35	0.4	0.45
START VALUES -->	20.00	10.00	6.67	5.00	4.00	3.33	2.86	2.50	2.22
5	25.00	15.00	11.67	10.00	9.00	8.33	7.86	7.50	7.22
-1	23.75	13.50	9.92	8.00	6.75	5.83	5.11	4.50	3.97
5	29.69	20.25	17.35	16.00	15.19	14.58	14.04	13.50	12.91
-1	28.20	18.23	14.75	12.80	11.39	10.21	9.13	8.10	7.10
5	35.25	27.34	25.81	25.60	25.63	25.52	25.10	24.30	23.08
-1	33.49	24.60	21.94	20.48	19.22	17.86	16.32	14.58	12.69
5	41.86	36.91	38.40	40.96	43.25	44.66	44.87	43.74	41.25
-1	39.77	33.22	32.64	32.77	32.44	31.26	29.17	26.24	22.69
5	49.71	49.82	57.12	65.54	72.98	78.16	80.21	78.73	73.73
-1	47.23	44.84	48.55	52.43	54.74	54.71	52.14	47.24	40.55
5	59.03	67.26	84.96	104.86	123.16	136.78	143.38	141.72	131.80
-1	56.08	60.53	72.22	83.89	92.37	95.74	93.20	85.03	72.49
5	70.10	90.80	126.38	167.77	207.83	239.36	256.30	255.09	235.58
-1	66.60	81.72	107.43	134.22	155.87	167.55	166.59	153.06	129.57
5	83.25	122.58	187.99	268.44	350.71	418.88	458.13	459.17	421.11
-1	79.09	110.32	159.80	214.75	263.03	293.21	297.78	275.50	231.61
5	98.86	165.49	279.64	429.50	591.82	733.03	818.90	826.50	752.73
-1	93.91	148.94	237.70	343.60	443.87	513.12	532.29	495.90	414.00
5	117.39	223.41	415.97	687.19	998.70	1282.81	1463.79	1487.69	1345.50
-1	111.52	201.07	353.57	549.76	749.03	897.96	951.46	892.62	740.03
5	139.40	301.60	618.75	1099.51	1685.31	2244.91	2616.53	2677.85	2405.09
-1	132.43	271.44	525.94	879.61	1263.98	1571.44	1700.74	1606.71	1322.80
5	165.54	407.16	920.39	1759.22	2843.96	3928.60	4677.04	4820.13	4299.10
-1	157.27	366.44	782.33	1407.37	2132.97	2750.02	3040.08	2892.08	2364.50
5	196.58	549.66	1369.09	2814.75	4799.19	6875.04	8360.21	8676.24	7684.64
-1	186.75	494.70	1163.72	2251.80	3599.39	4812.53	5434.14	5205.74	4226.55
5	233.44	742.05	2036.51	4503.60	8098.63	12031.32	14943.88	15617.22	13736.29
-1	221.77	667.84	1731.04	3602.88	6073.97	8421.93	9713.52	9370.33	7554.96
5	277.21	1001.76	3029.31	7205.76	13666.44	21054.82	26712.18	28111.00	24553.62
-1	263.35	901.58	2574.92	5764.61	10249.83	14738.37	17362.92	16866.60	13504.49
5	329.19	1352.38	4506.11	11529.22	23062.12	36845.93	47748.02	50599.80	43889.60
-1	312.73	1217.14	3830.19	9223.37	17296.59	25792.15	31036.22	30359.88	24139.28
5	390.91	1825.71	6702.83	18446.74	38917.33	64480.37	85349.59	91079.65	78452.66
-1	371.37	1643.14	5697.41	14757.40	29188.00	45136.26	55477.24	54647.79	43148.96
5	464.21	2464.71	9970.46	29514.79	65672.99	112840.65	152562.40	163943.37	140234.12
-1	441.00	2218.24	8474.89	23611.83	49254.74	78988.46	99165.56	98366.02	77128.77
5	551.25	3327.35	14831.06	47223.66	110823.17	197471.14	272705.29	295098.06	250668.50
-1	523.68	2994.62	12606.40	37778.93	83117.38	138229.80	177258.44	177058.84	137867.67
5	654.60	4491.93	22061.21	75557.86	187014.10	345574.49	487460.70	531176.51	448069.94
-1	621.87	4042.74	18752.03	60446.29	140260.58	241902.14	316849.46	318705.91	246438.47
TWR ---------->	31.09	404.27	2812.80	12089.26	35065.14	72570.64	110897.31	127482.36	110897.31

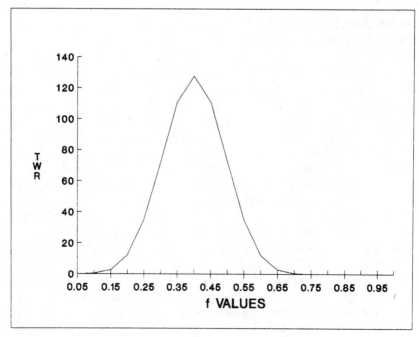

Figure 4-5   Values of f for 20 sequences at +5, -1.

0.5	0.55	0.6	0.65	0.7	0.75	0.8	0.85	0.9	0.95	1
2.00	1.82	1.67	1.54	1.43	1.33	1.25	1.18	1.11	1.05	1.00
7.00	6.82	6.67	6.54	6.43	6.33	6.25	6.18	6.11	6.05	6.00
3.50	3.07	2.67	2.29	1.93	1.58	1.25	0.93	0.61	0.30	0.00
12.25	11.51	10.67	9.73	8.68	7.52	6.25	4.86	3.36	1.74	0.00
6.13	5.18	4.27	3.40	2.60	1.88	1.25	0.73	0.34	0.09	0.00
21.44	19.42	17.07	14.47	11.72	8.93	6.25	3.83	1.85	0.50	0.00
10.72	8.74	6.83	5.06	3.51	2.23	1.25	0.57	0.18	0.03	0.00
37.52	32.76	27.31	21.52	15.82	10.61	6.25	3.02	1.02	0.14	0.00
18.76	14.74	10.92	7.53	4.75	2.65	1.25	0.45	0.10	0.01	0.00
65.65	55.29	43.69	32.01	21.35	12.59	6.25	2.38	0.56	0.04	0.00
32.83	24.88	17.48	11.20	6.41	3.15	1.25	0.36	0.06	.00	0.00
114.89	93.30	69.91	47.62	28.83	14.96	6.25	1.87	0.31	0.01	0.00
57.45	41.99	27.96	16.67	8.65	3.74	1.25	0.28	0.03	.00	0.00
201.06	157.45	111.85	70.83	38.92	17.76	6.25	1.47	0.17	.00	0.00
100.53	70.85	44.74	24.79	11.67	4.44	1.25	0.22	0.02	.00	0.00
351.86	265.69	178.96	105.36	52.54	21.09	6.25	1.16	0.09	.00	0.00
175.93	119.56	71.58	36.88	15.76	5.27	1.25	0.17	0.01	.00	0.00
615.75	448.35	286.33	156.72	70.92	25.04	6.25	0.91	0.05	.00	0.00
307.87	201.76	114.53	54.85	21.28	6.26	1.25	0.14	0.01	.00	0.00
1077.56	756.59	458.13	233.12	95.75	29.74	6.25	0.72	0.03	.00	0.00
538.78	340.47	183.25	81.59	28.72	7.43	1.25	0.11	.00	.00	0.00
1885.73	1276.75	733.01	346.77	129.26	35.32	6.25	0.57	0.02	.00	0.00
942.86	574.54	293.20	121.37	38.78	8.83	1.25	0.08	.00	.00	0.00
3300.02	2154.52	1172.81	515.82	174.50	41.94	6.25	0.45	0.01	.00	0.00
1650.01	969.53	469.12	180.54	52.35	10.48	1.25	0.07	.00	.00	0.00
5775.04	3635.75	1876.50	767.29	235.57	49.80	6.25	0.35	.00	.00	0.00
2887.52	1636.09	750.60	268.55	70.67	12.45	1.25	0.05	.00	.00	0.00
10106.31	6135.33	3002.40	1141.34	318.02	59.14	6.25	0.28	.00	.00	0.00
5053.16	2760.90	1200.96	399.47	95.41	14.78	1.25	0.04	.00	.00	0.00
17686.04	10353.36	4803.84	1697.75	429.33	70.23	6.25	0.22	.00	.00	0.00
8843.02	4659.01	1921.54	594.21	128.80	17.56	1.25	0.03	.00	.00	0.00
30950.58	17471.30	7686.14	2525.40	579.59	83.39	6.25	0.17	.00	.00	0.00
15475.29	7862.09	3074.46	883.89	173.88	20.85	1.25	0.03	.00	.00	0.00
54163.51	29482.82	12297.83	3756.53	782.45	99.03	6.25	0.14	.00	.00	0.00
27081.76	13267.27	4919.13	1314.79	234.73	24.76	1.25	0.02	.00	.00	0.00
94786.15	49752.27	19676.53	5587.04	1056.30	117.60	6.25	0.11	.00	.00	0.00
47393.07	22388.52	7870.61	1955.74	316.89	29.40	1.25	0.02	.00	.00	0.00
165875.76	83956.95	31482.44	8311.92	1426.01	139.65	6.25	0.08	.00	.00	0.00
82937.88	37780.63	12592.98	2909.17	427.80	34.91	1.25	0.01	.00	.00	0.00
290282.57	141677.35	50371.91	12363.97	1925.11	165.83	6.25	0.07	.00	.00	0.00
145141.29	63754.81	20148.76	4327.39	577.53	41.46	1.25	0.01	.00	.00	0.00
72570.64	35065.14	12089.26	2812.80	404.27	31.09	1.00	0.01	.00	.00	0.00

equally likely to be any other possible sequence as it is to be the sequence we are basing this drawdown figure on.

Return to the coin toss, whereby if we win we win $1 and if we lose we lose $1. Suppose 20 tosses have gone by and you have experienced a drawdown of $5 at one point. What does this mean? Does this mean that we can expect "about" a $5 drawdown on the next 20 tosses? Since coin tossing is an independent trials process (as trading is for the most part), the answer to all of these questions is no. The only estimating we can perform here is one based on the losing streaks involved. With a 20-coin toss we can figure probabilities of getting 20 tosses against us, 19 tosses, and so on. But what we are talking about with drawdown is absolute worst case—an extreme. What we are looking for is an answer to the question, "How far out on the tails of the distribution, to the adverse side, is the limit?" The answer is that there is no limit—all future coin tosses, the next 20 tosses and all sequences of 20 tosses, could go against us. It's highly unlikely, but it could happen. To assume that there is a maximum drawdown that we can expect is simply an illusion. The idea is propagated for a trader's peace of mind. Statistically it has no significance. If we are trading on a fixed fractional basis (where the drawdown is also a function of when it happens—i.e., how big the

20 TRIALS	f VALUES -->								
EVENT	0.05	0.1	0.15	0.2	0.25	0.3	0.35	0.4	0.45
START VALUES -->	20.00	10.00	6.67	5.00	4.00	3.33	2.86	2.50	2.22
-1	19.00	9.00	5.67	4.00	3.00	2.33	1.86	1.50	1.22
-1	18.05	8.10	4.82	3.20	2.25	1.63	1.21	0.90	0.67
-1	17.15	7.29	4.09	2.56	1.69	1.14	0.78	0.54	0.37
-1	16.29	6.56	3.48	2.05	1.27	0.80	0.51	0.32	0.20
-1	15.48	5.90	2.96	1.64	0.95	0.56	0.33	0.19	0.11
-1	14.70	5.31	2.51	1.31	0.71	0.39	0.22	0.12	0.06
-1	13.97	4.78	2.14	1.05	0.53	0.27	0.14	0.07	0.03
-1	13.27	4.30	1.82	0.84	0.40	0.19	0.09	0.04	0.02
-1	12.60	3.87	1.54	0.67	0.30	0.13	0.06	0.03	0.01
-1	11.97	3.49	1.31	0.54	0.23	0.09	0.04	0.02	0.01
1	12.57	3.84	1.51	0.64	0.28	0.12	0.05	0.02	0.01
1	13.20	4.22	1.74	0.77	0.35	0.16	0.07	0.03	0.01
1	13.86	4.64	2.00	0.93	0.44	0.21	0.09	0.04	0.02
1	14.56	5.11	2.30	1.11	0.55	0.27	0.13	0.06	0.02
1	15.28	5.62	2.64	1.34	0.69	0.35	0.17	0.08	0.04
1	16.05	6.18	3.04	1.60	0.86	0.45	0.23	0.11	0.05
1	16.85	6.79	3.49	1.92	1.07	0.59	0.31	0.16	0.08
1	17.69	7.47	4.01	2.31	1.34	0.77	0.42	0.22	0.11
1	18.58	8.22	4.62	2.77	1.68	1.00	0.57	0.31	0.16
1	19.51	9.04	5.31	3.32	2.10	1.30	0.77	0.44	0.23
1	20.48	9.95	6.11	3.99	2.62	1.69	1.04	0.61	0.34
1	21.50	10.94	7.02	4.79	3.28	2.19	1.41	0.86	0.49
1	22.58	12.04	8.08	5.74	4.10	2.85	1.90	1.20	0.71
1	23.71	13.24	9.29	6.89	5.12	3.71	2.57	1.68	1.02
1	24.89	14.57	10.68	8.27	6.40	4.82	3.47	2.35	1.48
1	26.14	16.02	12.28	9.93	8.00	6.27	4.68	3.29	2.15
1	27.45	17.62	14.12	11.91	10.00	8.15	6.32	4.61	3.12
1	28.82	19.39	16.24	14.29	12.50	10.59	8.53	6.45	4.52
1	30.26	21.32	18.68	17.15	15.63	13.77	11.52	9.03	6.55
1	31.77	23.46	21.48	20.58	19.54	17.89	15.55	12.65	9.50
1	33.36	25.80	24.70	24.70	24.42	23.26	20.99	17.71	13.78
1	35.03	28.38	28.41	29.64	30.53	30.24	28.34	24.79	19.98
1	36.78	31.22	32.67	35.57	38.16	39.31	38.26	34.71	28.97
1	38.62	34.34	37.57	42.68	47.70	51.11	51.65	48.59	42.00
1	40.55	37.78	43.21	51.22	59.62	66.44	69.73	68.02	60.90
1	42.58	41.56	49.69	61.46	74.53	86.37	94.13	95.23	88.30
1	44.71	45.71	57.14	73.75	93.16	112.29	127.08	133.32	128.04
1	46.94	50.28	65.71	88.50	116.45	145.97	171.56	186.65	185.66
1	49.29	55.31	75.57	106.20	145.57	189.77	231.60	261.32	269.21
1	51.75	60.84	86.90	127.44	181.96	246.69	312.66	365.84	390.35
TWR --------->	2.59	6.08	13.04	25.49	45.49	74.01	109.43	146.34	175.66

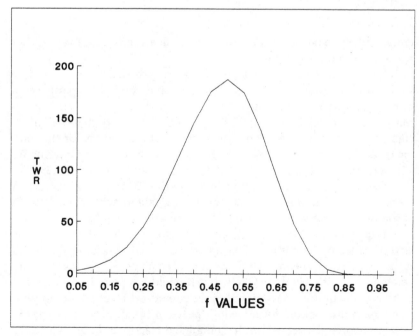

Figure 4-6   Values of f for 10 sequences at − 1, 30 at + 1.

0.5	0.55	0.6	0.65	0.7	0.75	0.8	0.85	0.9	0.95	1
2.00	1.82	1.67	1.54	1.43	1.33	1.25	1.18	1.11	1.05	1.00
1.00	0.82	0.67	0.54	0.43	0.33	0.25	0.18	0.11	0.05	0.00
0.50	0.37	0.27	0.19	0.13	0.08	0.05	0.03	0.01	.00	0.00
0.25	0.17	0.11	0.07	0.04	0.02	0.01	.00	.00	.00	0.00
0.13	0.07	0.04	0.02	0.01	0.01	.00	.00	.00	.00	0.00
0.06	0.03	0.02	0.01	.00	.00	.00	.00	.00	.00	0.00
0.03	0.02	0.01	.00	.00	.00	.00	.00	.00	.00	0.00
0.02	0.01	.00	.00	.00	.00	.00	.00	.00	.00	0.00
0.01	.00	.00	.00	.00	.00	.00	.00	.00	.00	0.00
.00	.00	.00	.00	.00	.00	.00	.00	.00	.00	0.00
.00	.00	.00	.00	.00	.00	.00	.00	.00	.00	0.00
.00	.00	.00	.00	.00	.00	.00	.00	.00	.00	0.00
.00	.00	.00	.00	.00	.00	.00	.00	.00	.00	0.00
0.01	.00	.00	.00	.00	.00	.00	.00	.00	.00	0.00
0.01	.00	.00	.00	.00	.00	.00	.00	.00	.00	0.00
0.01	0.01	.00	.00	.00	.00	.00	.00	.00	.00	0.00
0.02	0.01	.00	.00	.00	.00	.00	.00	.00	.00	0.00
0.03	0.01	.00	.00	.00	.00	.00	.00	.00	.00	0.00
0.05	0.02	0.01	.00	.00	.00	.00	.00	.00	.00	0.00
0.08	0.03	0.01	.00	.00	.00	.00	.00	.00	.00	0.00
0.11	0.05	0.02	0.01	.00	.00	.00	.00	.00	.00	0.00
0.17	0.08	0.03	0.01	.00	.00	.00	.00	.00	.00	0.00
0.25	0.12	0.05	0.02	.00	.00	.00	.00	.00	.00	0.00
0.38	0.18	0.08	0.03	0.01	.00	.00	.00	.00	.00	0.00
0.57	0.29	0.13	0.05	0.01	.00	.00	.00	.00	.00	0.00
0.86	0.44	0.20	0.08	0.02	0.01	.00	.00	.00	.00	0.00
1.28	0.69	0.32	0.13	0.04	0.01	.00	.00	.00	.00	0.00
1.92	1.07	0.52	0.21	0.07	0.02	.00	.00	.00	.00	0.00
2.89	1.65	0.83	0.35	0.12	0.03	0.01	.00	.00	.00	0.00
4.33	2.56	1.32	0.58	0.20	0.05	0.01	.00	.00	.00	0.00
6.49	3.97	2.11	0.95	0.34	0.09	0.02	.00	.00	.00	0.00
9.74	6.15	3.38	1.57	0.58	0.16	0.03	.00	.00	.00	0.00
14.61	9.53	5.41	2.58	0.99	0.28	0.05	0.01	.00	.00	0.00
21.92	14.77	8.65	4.26	1.68	0.49	0.10	0.01	.00	.00	0.00
32.88	22.89	13.85	7.04	2.86	0.87	0.17	0.02	.00	.00	0.00
49.32	35.49	22.15	11.61	4.87	1.51	0.31	0.03	.00	.00	0.00
73.98	55.00	35.45	19.16	8.28	2.65	0.56	0.06	.00	.00	0.00
110.97	85.25	56.71	31.61	14.07	4.64	1.00	0.11	.00	.00	0.00
166.45	132.14	90.74	52.16	23.92	8.12	1.80	0.21	0.01	.00	0.00
249.68	204.82	145.19	86.06	40.66	14.21	3.24	0.38	0.01	.00	0.00
374.51	317.48	232.30	142.00	69.12	24.86	5.83	0.70	0.03	.00	0.00
187.26	174.61	139.38	92.30	48.38	18.64	4.66	0.60	0.02	.00	0.00

account was when the drawdown started) then drawdown is absolutely meaningless.

Third, the drawdown under fixed fraction is not the drawdown we would encounter on a constant contract basis (i.e., non-reinvestment). This was demonstrated in the previous chapter. Fourth and finally, in this exercise we are only trying to discern how much to commit to the next trade, not the next sequence of trades. Drawdown is a sequence of trades—should the maximum drawdown occur on one trade, then that one trade would also be the biggest losing trade.

If you want to measure the downside of a system then you should look at the biggest losing trade, since drawdown is arbitrary and, in effect, meaningless. This becomes even more so when you are considering fixed fractional (i.e., reinvestment of returns) trading. Many traders try to "limit their drawdown" either consciously (as when they are designing trading systems) or subconsciously. This is understandable, as drawdown is the trader's nemesis. Yet we see that, as a result of its arbitrary nature, drawdown is uncontrollable. What is controllable, at least to an extent, is the largest loss. As you have seen, optimal f is a function of the largest loss. It is possible to control your largest loss by many techniques, such as only daytrading, using options, etc. The point here is that you can control your largest loss as well as your frequency of large losses (at least to some extent), but by and large you cannot control your draw-down.

It is important to note at this point that the drawdown you can expect with fixed fractional trading, as a percentage retracement of your account equity, historically would have been at least as much as f percent. In other words, if f is .55, then your drawdown would have been at least 55 percent of your equity (leaving you with 45% at one point). This is so because if you are trading at the optimal f, as soon as your biggest loss is hit, you would experience the drawdown equivalent to f. Again, assuming f for a system is .55, and assuming that translates into trading one contract for every $10,000, your biggest loss would be $5,500. As should by now be obvious, when the biggest loss was encountered (again we're speaking historically, i.e., about what would have happened), you would have lost $5,500 for each contract you had on, and you would have had one contract on for every $10,000 in the account. Therefore, at that point your drawdown would have been 55% of equity. However, it is possible that the drawdown would continue, that the next trade or series of trades would draw your account down even more. Therefore, the better a system, the higher the f. The higher the f, generally the higher the drawdown, since the drawdown (as a percentage) can never be any less than the f. There is a paradox involved here, in that if a system is good enough to generate an optimal f that is a high percentile, then the drawdown for such a good system will also be quite high. While optimal f allows you to experience the greatest geometric growth, it also gives you enough rope to hang yourself. This paradox is remedied, to some extent, in Chapter 6.

CONSEQUENCES FOR STRAYING TOO FAR FROM THE OPTIMAL f

The fact that the difference between being at the optimal value for f and being at any other value increases geometrically over time is particularly important to gamblers. Time in this sense is synonymous with action. For years, a simple system for blackjack has been to simply keep track of how many fives have fallen from the deck. The fewer the fives contained in the remaining deck the greater is the player's advantage over the casino. Depending on the rules of the casino, this advantage could range to almost as high as 3.6% for a deck with no remaining fives. Roughly, then, the optimal f for this strategy would range from 0 to about .075 to .08 for each hand, depending on how many fives had fallen (i.e., you would use a different f value for each different number of remaining fives in a deck. This is a dependent trials process, and therefore your optimal betting strategy would be to trade variable fraction based on the optimal f for each scenario of the ratio of fives left in the deck). If you go into the casino and play through only one deck, you will not be penalized for deviating from the optimal f (as you would if you were to play 1,000 hands). It is incorrect to think that if you have an edge on a particular hand, you should simply increase the size of your wager. How much you increase it by is paramount.

To illustrate, if you have a stake of $500 and start playing at a table where $5 is the minimum bet, your minimum bet is therefore 1% of your stake. If you encounter, during the course of the deck, a situation where all fives are depleted from the deck, you then have an edge of anywhere from 3 to 3.6%, depending on the house rules. Say your optimal f now is .08, or one bet per every $62.50 in your stake ($5, the maximum possible loss on the next hand, divided by .08).

Suppose you had been breaking even to this point in the game and still had $500 in your stake. You would then bet $40 on the next hand ($500/$62.50 * $5). If you were to bet $45, you could expect a decrease in performance. There is no benefit to betting the extra $5 unit. This decrease in performance grows geometrically over time. If you calculate your optimal f on each hand, and slightly over- or underbet, you can expect a decrease in performance geometrically proportional to the length of the game (the action). If you were to bet, say, $100, on the situation described above, you would be at an f factor way out to the right of the optimal f. You wouldn't stand a chance over time—no matter how good a card counter you were! If you are too far to the right of the optimal f, even if you know exactly what cards remain in the deck, you are in a losing situation!

Next are four more charts, which, if you still do not see, drive home the importance of being near the optimal f. These are equity curve charts. An equity curve is simply the total equity of an account (plotted on the Y axis) over a period of time or series of trades (the X axis). On these four charts, we assume an account starts out with 10 units. Then the following sequence of 21 trades/bets is encountered:

$$1, 2, 1, -1, 3, 2, -1, -2, -3, 1, -2, 3, 1, 1, 2, 3, 3, -1, 2, -1, 3$$

If you have done the calculations yourself you will find that the optimal f is .6, or bet 1 unit for every 5 in your stake (since the biggest losing trade is for 3 units).

The first equity curve (Figure 4-7) shows this sequence on a constant one-contract basis. Nice consistency. No roller-coaster drawdowns. No geometric growth, either.

Next comes an equity curve with f at .3, or bet 1 unit for every 10 units in your stake (Figure 4-8). Makes a little more than constant contract.

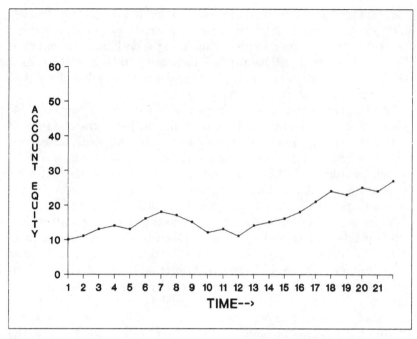

Figure 4-7   Equity curve for 21 trades on a constant contract basis.

On the third equity curve graph you see the sequence at the optimal f value of .6, or 1 bet for every 5 in your stake (Figure 4-9). Notice how much more it has made than at f = .3.

The final equity curve shows the sequence of bets at f = .9, or 1 bet for every 3⅓ units in your stake (Figure 4-10). Notice how quickly the equity took off until it hit the drawdown periods (7 through 12). When f is too high, the market systems get beaten down so low during a drawdown that it takes far longer to come out of them, if ever, than at the optimal values.

Even at the optimal values the drawdowns can be quite severe for any market/system. It is not unusual for a market system trading one contract under optimal f to see 80 to 95% of its equity erased in the bad drawdowns. But notice how at the optimal values the equity curve is able to recover in short order and go on to higher ground. These four charts have all traded the same sequence of trades, yet look at how using the optimal f affects performance, particularly after drawdowns.

Obviously, the greater an account's capitalization, the more accurately its traders can stick to optimal f, as the dollars per single contract required are a smaller percentage of the total equity. For example, suppose optimal f for a given market system dictates we trade one

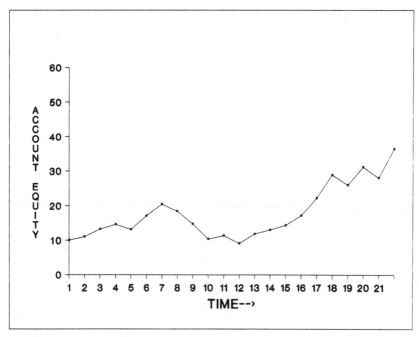

Figure 4-8   Equity curve for 21 trades with f = .30, or 1 contract for every
10 units in the stake.

contract for every $5,000 in an account. If an account starts out with
$10,000 equity, then it can gain (or lose) 50% before a quantity adjust-
ment is necessary. Contrast this to a $500,000 account, where there
would be a contract adjustment for every 1% change in equity. Clearly
the larger account can take advantage of the benefits provided by
optimal f better than a smaller account can. Theoretically, optimal f
assumes you can trade in infinitely divisible quantities, which is not the
case in real life, where the smallest quantity you can trade in is a single
contract. In the asymptotic sense this does not matter. In the real-life
integer-bet scenario, a good case could be presented for trading a
market system that requires as small a percentage of the account equity
as possible, especially for smaller accounts. But there is a tradeoff here
as well. Since we are striving to trade in markets that would require us
to trade in greater multiples, we will be paying greater commissions,
execution costs, and slippage. Bear in mind that the amount required
per contract in real life is the greater of the initial margin requirement
or the dollar amount per contract dictated by the optimal f.

As the charts bear out, you pay a substantial penalty for deviating
from the optimal fixed dollar fraction. *Being at the right value for f is*

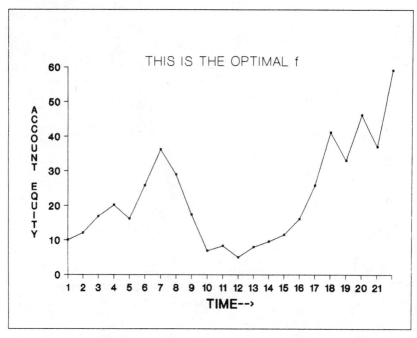

Figure 4-9   Equity curve for 21 trades with f = .60, or 1 contract for every
5 units in the stake.

more important than how good your trading system is (provided of
course that the system is profitable on a single-contract basis)! Therefore, the finer you can cut it (i.e., the more frequently you adjust the
size of the positions you are trading, so as to align yourself with what the
optimal f dictates), the better off you are. Most accounts, therefore,
would be better off trading the smaller markets. Corn may not seem like
a very exciting market to you compared to the S&Ps. Yet for most people
the corn market can get awfully exciting if they have a few hundred
contracts on.

   Throughout the text, we refigure the amount of contracts you should
have on for the next trade based on the dictates of the optimal f for a
given market system. However, the finer you can cut it the better. If you
refigure how many contracts you should have on every day as opposed to
simply every trade, you will be that much better off. If you refigure how
many contracts you should have on every hour as opposed to every day,
you will be even better off. However, there is the old tradeoff of commissions, slippage, and fees, not to mention the cost of mistakes, which will
be more likely the more frequently you realign yourself with the dictates
of the optimal f. Bear in mind that realigning yourself on every trade is

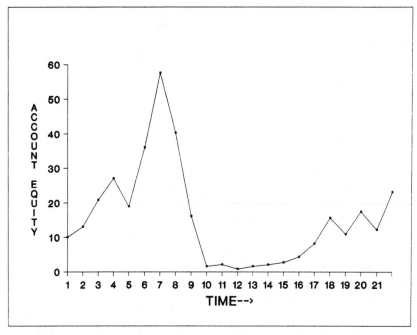

Figure 4-10   Equity curve for 21 trades with f = .90, or 1 contract for every 3.33 units in the stake.

not the only way to do it, and the finer (more frequently) you can cut it—the more often you realign yourself with the dictates of the optimal f—the more the benefits of the optimal f will work for you. Ideally, you will realign yourself with optimal f on as close to a continuous basis as possible with respect to the tradeoffs of commissions, fees, slippage, and the costs of human error.

It is doubtful whether anyone in the history of the markets has been able to religiously stick to trading on a constant contract basis. If someone quadrupled their money, would they still stick to trading in the same exact size? Conversely, would someone trading ten contracts on every trade who was suddenly cut down to trading less than ten contracts inject enough capital into the account to margin ten contracts again on the next trade? It's quite unlikely. Any time a trader trading on a constant contract basis deviates from always trading the same constant contract size, the problem of what quantities to trade in arises. This is so whether the trader recognizes this problem or not. As you have seen demonstrated in this chapter, this is a problem for the trader. Constant contract trading is not the solution, because you can never experience geometric growth trading constant contract. So, like it or not, the question of what quantity to take on the next trade is inevitable for everyone. To simply select an arbitrary quantity is a costly mistake. Optimal f is factual; it is mathematically correct.

Are there traders out there who aren't planning on reinvesting their profits? Unless we're looking at optimal f via the highest TWR we wouldn't know a good market system if it bit us on the leg. This is the problem with Gann, Elliott Wave, the "high priest hunch," or any other approach to trading that is not totally mechanical. Unless you have a totally mechanical approach with a performance history you have no way of knowing where your optimal f is. You are completely lost. This is why so many technicians, good market analysts, good systems traders, cannot beat the markets. This is why so many traders who are on a prolonged winning streak give it back to the markets. They don't know where their optimal f is and they eventually stray to the right of the peak.

If a system is good enough, it is often possible to have a value for f that implies applying a dollar amount per contract that is less than the initial margin. Remember that f gives us the peak of the curve; to go off to the right of the peak (take on more contracts) provides no benefit. But the trader need not use that value for f that puts him at the peak; he may want to go to the left of the peak (i.e., apply more dollars in equity to each contract he puts on). You could, for instance, divide your account into two equal parts and resolve to keep one part cash and one part as dollars to apply to trading positions and use f on that half. This in effect would amount to a half f or fractional f strategy.

By now it should be obvious that we have a working range for usable values of f, that range being from zero to the optimal value. The higher you go within this range, the greater the return (up to but not beyond the optimal f) and the greater the risk (the greater the expected draw-downs in size—not, however, in frequency). The lower you go in this range, the less the risk (again in terms of extent but not frequency of drawdowns), and the less the potential returns. However, as you move down this range toward zero, the greater the probability is that an account will be profitable (remember that a constant-contract-based account has the greatest probability of being profitable). Ziemba's *Gambling Times* articles on Kelly demonstrated that *at smaller profit targets the half Kelly was more apt to reach these levels before halving than was a full Kelly bet. In other words the fractional Kelly (fractional f) bet is safer—it has less variance in the final outcome after X bets. This ability to choose a fraction of the optimal f (choosing a value between 0 and the optimal f) allows you to have any desired risk/return tradeoff that you like.*

Referring back to our four equity curve charts where the optimal f = .60, notice how nice and smooth the half f chart of f = .30 is. Half f makes for a much smoother equity curve than does full f. Of course the tradeoff is less return—again, a difference that grows as time passes.

Here a word of caution is in order. Just as there is a price to be paid (in reduced return and greater drawdowns) for being too far to the right of the peak of the f curve (i.e., too many contracts on), there is also a price to be paid for being to the left of the peak of the f curve (i.e., too few contracts on). This price is not as steep as being too far to the right, so if you must err, err to the left.

*As you move to the left of the peak of the f curve (i.e., allocate more dollars per contract) you reduce your drawdowns **arithmetically**. However, you also reduce your returns **geometrically**.* Reducing your returns geometrically is the price you pay for being to the left of the optimal f on the f curve. However, using the fractional f still makes good sense in many cases. When viewed from the perspective of time required to reach a specific goal (as opposed to absolute gain), the fractional f strategy makes a great deal of sense. Very often, a fractional f strategy will not take much longer to reach a specific goal than will the full f (the height of the goal and what specific fraction of f you choose will determine how much longer). If minimizing the time required to reach a specific goal times the potential drawdown as a percentage of equity retracement is your priority, then the fractional f strategy is most likely for you.

Aside from, or in addition to, diluting the optimal f by using a percentage or fraction of the optimal f, you could diversify into other markets and systems (as was just done by putting 50% of the account into cash, as if cash were another market or system). This subject is addressed in Chapter 6.

FINDING OPTIMAL f VIA
PARABOLIC INTERPOLATION

Originally, I had hoped to find a method of finding the optimal f by way of a single equation like the Kelly formula. As computer speed has become cheaper, you can find the optimal f by way of a simple loop through the trade history of a given market system, starting f at .01 and incrementing by .01 until the generated TWR is less than the TWR of the previous loop, at which point the optimal f is the f used during the previous loop. This takes but a few seconds on an ordinary PC, even if hundreds of trades are involved. It will give you the correct answer, and in very little time.

Not that many years ago more of a premium was placed on speed vis-à-vis the logic of the program. As an example, using BASIC:

```
RANGE = 0
FOR X = 1 TO 5
RANGE = RANGE + (H(X) − L(X))
NEXT
RANGE = RANGE/5
AVG = 0
FOR X = 1 TO 3
AVG = AVG + C(X)
NEXT
AVG = AVG/3
```

In the above segment of BASIC code we are calculating a 5-day average of the daily ranges and a 3-day average of the closes. There are 2 loops. The first one is executed 5 times; the second, 3. Altogether 8 loops are performed. This code segment could also have been programmed as:

```
RANGE = 0
AVG = 0
FOR X = 1 TO 5
RANGE = RANGE + (H(X) − L(X))
IF X < 4 THEN AVG = AVG + C(X)
NEXT
RANGE = RANGE/5
AVG = AVG/3
```

Here we have performed the exact same thing in one loop. So now there are only 5 passes through a loop versus 8 passes in the former code. Now there are only 8 statements of code versus 10 statements in the former code. Both segments of code give the same answer. The latter method executes more rapidly, but speed is no longer the concern that it used to be. Computers today have become quite fast. Now, when we speak of a slower code we're usually talking about waiting a few nanoseconds.

Once again, our technology allows us the time to appreciate the more aesthetic aspects of life. The second code segment is preferable to the first because it is more elegant. (That is why I have never been fond of finding the optimal f by setting it equal to .01 and looping through the trade history until the TWR starts to decline. It is clumsy. It is akin to finding f by brute force because you do not have the mathematical tools to do it elegantly.) In finding the optimal f we are looking for that value for f which generates the highest TWR in the domain 0 to 1.0 for f. Since f is the only variable we have to maximize the TWR for, we say that we are *maximizing in one dimension.*

We can use another technique to iterate to the optimal f with a little more style than the brute methods already described. Recall that in the iterative technique we bracket an intermediate point (A, B), test a point within the bracket (X) and obtain a new, smaller bracketing interval (either A, X or X, B). This process continues until the answer is converged upon. This is still brutish, but not so brutish as the simple 0 to 1 by .01 loop method.

The best (i.e., fastest and most elegant) way to find a maximum in one dimension, when you are certain that only one maximum exists, that each successive point to the left of the maximum lessens, and that each successive point to the right of the maximum lessens (as is the case with the shape of the f curve) is to use *parabolic interpolation.* When there is only one local extreme (be it a maximum or a minimum) in the range you are searching, parabolic interpolation will work. If there is more than one local extreme, parabolic interpolation will not work (see Figure 4-11).

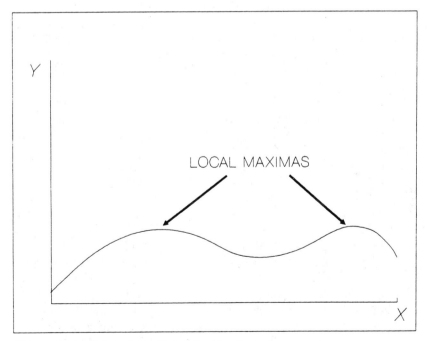

Figure 4-11   A function with two local extremes.

With this technique we simply input three coordinate points. The axes of these points are the TWRs (Y axis) and the f values (X axis). We can find the abscissa (the X axis, or f value corresponding to the peak of a parabola) by the following formula, given the three coordinates:

$$\text{ABSCISSA} = X2 - .5 * \frac{(((X2-X1)^2) * (Y2-Y3) - ((X2-X3)^2) * (Y2-Y1))}{((X2-X1) * (Y2-Y3) - (X2-X3) * (Y2-Y1))}$$

The result returned by this equation is the value for f (or X if you will) that corresponds to the abscissa of a parabola where the three coordinates (X1, Y1), (X2, Y2), (X3, Y3) lie on the parabola.

The object now is to superimpose a parabola over the f curve, change one of the input coordinates to draw an amended parabola, and keep on doing this until the abscissa of the most recent parabola converges with the previous parabola's abscissa. Convergence is determined when the absolute value of the difference between two abscissas is less than a prescribed amount called the tolerance, or TOL for short. This amount should be chosen with respect to how accurate you want your f to be. Generally, I use a value of .005 for TOL. This gives the same accuracy in searching for the optimal f as the brute force techniques described earlier.

We can start with two of the three coordinate points as (0, 0), (1.0, 0). The third coordinate point must be a point that lies on the actual f curve itself. Let us choose the X value here to be 1 – TOL, or .995. To make sure that the coordinate lies on the f curve, we determine our Y value by finding what the TWR is at f = .995. Assume we are looking for the optimal f for the four-trade example – 1, – 3, 3, 5. For these four trades the TWR at f = .995 is .01772207367. Now we have the three coordinates: (0, 0), (.995, .01772207367), (1.0, 0). We plug them into the above described equation to find the abscissa of a parabola that contains these three points, and our result is .5.

Now we compute the TWR corresponding to this abscissa; this equals 1.145834247. Since the X value here now (.5) is to the left of the value for X2 previously (.995), we move our three points over to the left, and compute a new abscissa to the parabola that contains the three points (0, 0), (.5, 1.145834247), (.995, .01772207367).

This abscissa is at .550806. The TWR corresponding to this f value is 1.090797389. Since this value for X is to the right of the previous value for X2, we drop the leftmost coordinate (0, 0), and look for an abscissa of the parabola that contains the three coordinates (.5, 1.145834247), (.550806, 1.090797389), (.995, .01772207367). Note that the last difference in abscissas was .550806 minus .5, or .050806. When we encounter a difference in abscissas that is less than or equal to TOL, we will have converged to the optimal f. In our example this would occur at the end of the seventh pass through. Is this not a superior way to find the optimal f?

Shown here are the full seven passes and the values used in each pass so that you may better understand this technique. In Appendix B is the computer code that utilizes this technique.

PARABOLIC INTERPOLATION

Pass#	X1	Y1	X2	Y2	X3	Y3	abscissa
1	0	0	0.995	0.017722	1	0	0.5
2	0	0	0.5	1.145834	0.995	0.017722	0.550806
3	0.5	1.145834	0.550806	1.090797	0.995	0.017722	0.475298
4	0.5	1.145834	0.475298	1.167507	0.550806	1.090797	0.345946
5	0.5	1.145834	0.345946	1.227846	0.475298	1.167507	0.327823
6	0.5	1.145834	0.327823	1.229368	0.345946	1.227846	0.321288
7	0.5	1.145834	0.321288	1.229508	0.327823	1.229368	0.32048

Convergence is extremely rapid. Using a value of .005 for TOL, convergence is obtained at an average of less than 7 iterations. Rarely does convergence take more than 11 iterations to find the optimal f.

Refer now to Figure 4-12. This graphically shows the parabolic interpolation process for the coin-toss example with a 2:1 payoff, where the optimal f is .25. On the graph, notice the familiar f curve, which peaks out at .25. The first step here is to draw a parabola through three points: A, B, and C. The coordinates for A are (0,0). For C the coordinates are (1,0). For point B we now pick a point whose coordinates lie on the f curve itself. Once parabola ABC is drawn, we obtain its abscissa (the f value corresponding to the peak of the parabola ABC). We find what the TWR is for this f value. This gives us coordinates for point D. We repeat the process, this time drawing a parabola through points A, B, and D. Once the abscissa to parabola ABD is found, we can find the TWR that corresponds to an f value of the abscissa of parabola ABD. These coordinates (f value, TWR) give us point E.

Notice how quickly we are converging to the peak of the f curve at f = .25. If we were to continue with the exercise in Figure 4-12, we would next draw a parabola through points E, B, and D, and continue until we converged upon the peak of the f curve.

One potential problem with this technique from a computer standpoint is that the denominator in the equation that solves for the abscissa might equal zero while running. One possible solution is the following fast and dirty patch in BASIC:

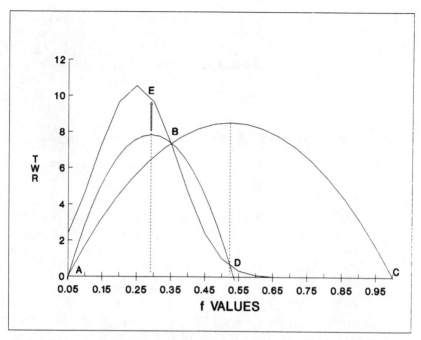

Figure 4-12   Parabolic interpolation performed on TWRs of 20 sequences of +2, −1.

DM = ((X2 − X1) * (Y2 − Y3) − (X2 − X3) * (Y2 − Y1))
IF DM = 0 THEN DM = .00001
ABSCISSA = X2 − .5 * ((((X2 − X1)^2) * (Y2 − Y3) − ((X2 − X3)^2) * (Y2 − Y1))/DM)

This patch will not detract from the integrity of the results.

Note that this method can be used to find a local maximum for a given function, provided only one maximum exists within the range. The same technique could be used to find a local minimum for a function that opened upward (for example, the function Y equals X squared is such a function). Again, the technique will work provided there is only one local minimum (as is the case with our example). The only change from looking for a local maximum is in the equation for finding the abscissa:

$$\text{ABSCISSA} = X2 + .5 * \frac{(((X2 - X1)^2) * (Y2 - Y3) - ((X2 - X3)^2) * (Y2 - Y1))}{((X2 - X1) * (Y2 - Y3) - (X2 - X3) * (Y2 - Y1))}$$

Note that here, for a local minimum, the first operator is a plus (+) sign, not a minus (−) sign as when we were looking for a local maximum.

OPTIMAL f AND OPTIONS

Optimal f presents the options trader with a very powerful new tool. As will be made clear, the value for f that will be the optimal in the future can be found with greater accuracy than by using the previously described techniques. This is so because we are not using any past data to find the optimal f. Rather, we can do it entirely with statistical techniques.

Previously, we have taken a sequence of system trades—preferably a minimum of 30 trades—and derived our optimal f from those trades, assuming that the trades in the future would mimic the ones in the past in terms of profit and loss distribution. Now, using options, an even more formidable technique can be adopted to find the optimal f. (This technique can also be used on instruments other than options.) It is necessary at this point to state that this technique is almost impossible to perform by hand since the calculations are so numerous. A computer is a necessity.

Let us begin our discussion by assuming that we are speaking about the simple outright purchase of a call option. Rather than taking a full history of option trades that a given market system produced and deriving our optimal f therefrom, we are going to take a look at all the possible outcomes of what this particular option might do throughout the term that we hold it. We are going to weight each outcome by the probability of its occurrence. This probability-weighted outcome will be derived as an HPR relative to the purchase price of the option. Finally, we will look at the full spectrum of outcomes (i.e., the geometric mean) for each value for f until we obtain the optimal value.

Options are unique in that they very strongly conform to mathematical models for their price (the arbitrage process provides for this). Using these models, we can determine, with a high degree of accuracy, what the option price will be when we change one or more of the variables in the pricing model. Before returning to the procedure for finding the optimal f, we must discuss these pricing models.

Theoretical option pricing models are numerous, and for numerous reasons. There are mathematical differences in the options prices that must be addressed—between stocks and futures, between American or European settlement, and between delivery of the stock(s)/commodities or cash. There are foreign currency differences and aggregate stock index dividends to consider, and so on. This is why there are so many good theoretical option pricing models around—such as the Black-Scholes model for stock options, the Fisher Black commodity option model, the Garman Kohlhagen foreign currencies option model, the Cox-Ross-Rubinstein (binomial) model, and so forth. However, this is not a book on theoretical option pricing models (and it takes at least a book to cover them all). So, for our purposes, we will assume the reader has access to a good pricing model for the options on that item of intended evaluation. The specific mathematics of calculating the theoretical prices will not be covered here. There are many good books on options available that will also get you started on the theoretical pricing models. For further reference, consult Appendix E.

In almost all of the good options pricing models the input variables that have the most effect on the theoretical options price are (a) time remaining till expiration, (b) the strike price, (c) the underlying price, and (d) the volatility. Different models have different input, but basically these four have the greatest bearing on the theoretical value returned from the various models.

Of the four basic inputs, two—the time remaining till expiration and the underlying price—are certain to change. One, volatility, may change, yet not as surely and rarely as much as these two. One, the strike price, is certain *not* to change.

Therefore, we must look at the theoretical price returned by our model for all of these different values of different underlying prices, and different times left till expiration.

$$HPR = (1 + (f * ((Z(T,U)/S) - 1)))^{\wedge}P(T,U)$$

where: f = The tested value for f.

S = The current price of the option.

$Z(T,U)$ = The theoretical option price if the underlying instrument were at price U with time remaining till expiration of T.

$P(T,U)$ = The probability of the underlying instrument being at price U by time remaining till expiration of T.

This formula will give us the HPR (which is probability-weighted to the probability of the outcome) of one possible outcome for this option—namely, that the underlying instrument will be at price U by time T.

In the preceding equation the variable T represents the decimal part of the year remaining until option expiration. Therefore, at expiration, $T = 0$. If there are 365 days left to expiration, $T = 1$. Finding T is relatively simple with the help of a few calendar algorithms found in Appendix D. To find T:

1. Convert the expiration day from YYMMDD format to Julian.

2. Convert the day you are looking at from YYMMDD format to Julian.

3. Subtract the answer in number 2 from the answer in number 1. The result is how many calendar days are left till expiration.

4. Divide the answer in number 3 by 365. This gives the decimal portion of the year remaining to expiration.

The variable $Z(T,U)$ in the preceding equation is found via whatever option model you are using. The only other variable you need to calculate in the equation is the variable $P(T,U)$, the probability of the underlying instrument being at price U after T calendar days have elapsed on the trade.

Figure 4-13 shows graphically the relationship between the Normal Probability Distribution and the percentage of area under the curve at given points on the curve. Note that the percentage area is symmetrical, i.e., it represents that area under the curve to the left of the point if the point is left of center, or the area under the curve and to the right of the point if the point in question is right of the center of the curve. In doing so, the percentage area represents the probabilities of being at different points on the curve.

In order to calculate $P(T,U)$, we need to perform the following equation(s):

if U < or = to Q:
$$P(T,U) = N ((\ln(U/Q))/(V * (T^{(1/2)})))$$

if U > Q:
$$P(T,U) = 1 - N ((\ln(U/Q))/(V * (T^{(1/2)})))$$

where: U = The price in question.

Q = Current price of the underlying instrument.

V = The annual volatility of the underlying instrument.[4]

T = Decimal fraction of the year elapsed since the option was put on. For the first day of the trade this would be 1/365, for the second, 2/365, etc. After one week in the trade this value would be 7/365 or .01917808219.

---

[4]The annual volatility in options is usually expressed as the annualized sample standard deviation of prices. For our purposes in these computations, however, we are best to use the implied volatility. For a further discussion of volatility, implied and actual, see *Options as a Strategic Investment* by Lawrence MacMillan, New York Institute of Finance.

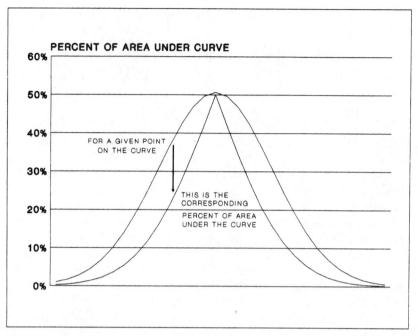

Figure 4-13   Normal probability function and the percentage of area under the curve at a given point on the curve.

N = The Cumulative Normal Distribution Function. (This function is available in Appendix C.)

ln = The natural logarithm function (available in most statistics books as well as most hand-held calculators). Most computer languages have a function to return the natural logarithm of a number.

Having performed the forementioned equations, we can derive a probability-weighted HPR for a particular outcome in the option. Yet a broad range of outcomes are possible. Fortunately, these outcomes are not continuous. Take the time remaining till expiration. This is not a continuous function. Rather, a discrete number of days are left till expiration. The same is true for the price of the underlying instrument. If a stock is at a price of, say, 35, and we want to know how many possible price outcomes there are between the possible prices of 30 and 40, and if the stock is traded in eighths, then we know that there are 81 possible price outcomes between 30 and 40.

What we must now do is calculate all the probability-weighted HPRs on the option for the expiration date or some other mandated exit date (see appendix D for how to determine what day of the week a given date is). Let's say we know we will be out of the option no later than a week from today. In such a case, we do not need to calculate HPR's for the expiration day, since that is immaterial to the question of how many of these options to buy, given all of the available information (time to expiration, time expected in the trade, price of the underlying instrument, price of the option, and volatility). If we do not have a time frame for when we will be out of the trade, then we must use the expiration day as the date to use to calculate probability-weighted HPRs on.

Once we know what date to calculate for (and we will assume here that we will calculate for the expiration day) we must now calculate the probability-weighted HPRs for all possible prices for that market day. Again this is not as overwhelming as you might think. Recall from Chapter 1 that in a Normal Probability Distribution,[5] 99.73% of all outcomes will fall within 3 standard deviations of the mean. The mean here is the current price of the underlying instrument. Therefore, we really only need to calculate the probability-weighted HPRs for a particular market day, for each discrete price between -3 and $+3$ standard deviations. This should get us quite accurately close to the correct answer. Of course, if we wanted to we could go out to 4, 5, 6 or more standard deviations, but that would not be much more accurate. Likewise, we could contract the price window in if we wanted to by only looking at 2 or 1 standard deviations. There is no gain in accuracy by doing this, though. The point is that 3 standard deviations is not set in stone, but should provide for sufficient accuracy.

To determine how much 1 standard deviation is above a given underlying price, Q, use this formula:

$$\text{Std. Dev.} = Q * \exp(V * (T^{(1/2)}))$$

where: Q = Current price of the underlying instrument.

V = The annual volatility of the underlying instrument.

---

[5]Repeatedly throughout the text mention has been made of the fact that prices do not conform to the Normal Probability Distribution. Yet it is the Normal Probability Distribution that is used throughout so much of the mathematics on options, primarily for lack of a better distribution. Again, any calculation will only be accurate to the extent that the prices conform to the distribution. Someday, perhaps, someone will alleviate this problem. I believe there are people within the industry that have determined better (more accurate) distribution functions for prices, but they keep an extremely low profile about it. This is quite understandable in that if you have a more realistic distribution function, then you also have a more realistic pricing model, which would give you an enormous edge over the other participants in these markets.

T = Decimal fraction of the year elapsed since the option was put on. For the first day of the trade this would be 1/365, for the second, 2/365, and so on. After one week in the trade, this value would be 7/365 or .01917808219.

exp = The exponential function, available in most statistics books, hand-held calculators, and computer languages.

Notice that the standard deviation is a function of the time elapsed in the trade (i.e., you must know how much time has elapsed in order to know where the 3-standard-deviation points are).

Building upon this equation, to determine that point that is 3 standard deviations above the current underlying price:

$$+ 3 \text{ Std. Dev.} = Q + 3 * ((Q * \exp(V * (T^{(1/2)}))) - Q)$$

Likewise, 3 standard deviations below Q is found by:

$$- 3 \text{ Std. Dev.} = Q - 3 * ((Q * \exp(V * (T^{(1/2)}))) - Q)$$

Remember, you must first determine how many days old the trade is and divide by 365 before you can determine what price constitutes X standard deviations above or below a given price Q.

Here, then, is a summary of the procedure for finding the optimal f for a given option.

1. Determine if there is a definite date by which you will be out of the option. If not, then use the expiration date.

2. Counting the first day as day 1, determine how many days you will have been in the trade by the date in number 1. Now divide this number of days by 365 to convert it to a decimal fraction of a year.

3. For the day in number 1, calculate those points that are + and − 3 standard deviations from the current underlying price.

4. Convert the ranges of values of prices in number 3 to discrete values. In other words, using increments of one tick, determine all of the possible prices between and including those values in number 3 that bound the range.

5. For each of these outcomes now calculate Z(T,U) and P(T,U) for the probability-weighted HPR equation. In other words, for each of

these outcomes now calculate the resultant theoretical option price as well as the probability of the underlying instrument being at that price by the dates in question.

6. After you have completed step 5, you have all of the input required to calculate the probability-weighted HPRs for all of the outcomes.

$$HPR = (1 + (f * ((Z(T,U)/S) - 1)))^{\wedge}P(T,U)$$

where: f = The tested value for f (0 to 1.0).

S = The current price of the option.

Z(T,U) = The theoretical option price if the underlying instrument were at price U with time remaining till expiration of T.

P(T,U) = The probability of the underlying instrument being at price U by time remaining till expiration of T.

7. Now you can begin the process of finding the optimal f. Again, you can do this by iteration, by looping through all of the possible f values between 0 and 1, or by parabolic interpolation. By plugging in the test values for f into the HPRs (and you have an HPR for each of the possible price increments between + and − 3 standard deviations on the expiration date or mandated exit date) you can find your geometric mean. By multiplying all of the HPRs for a given f value together you will obtain your geometric mean. This differs from the more "empirical" methods described in this chapter wherein multiplying all of your HPRs for a given f value would give you the TWR. Under this "theoretical" method, multiplying all of your HPRs together gives you the geometric mean itself. In fact, under this method, the TWR is never calculated since the TWR is a function of the number of trades elapsed. Since we are only looking at 1 individual trade, and the myriad of possible outcomes of this trade, the TWR is irrelevant. Hence, the f value which yields the highest geometric mean is the optimal f. From this geometric mean we can now discern what the geometric mathematical expectation is (geometric mean − 1).

Once you know the optimal f for a given option, you can readily turn it into how many contracts to buy based on the following equation:

Account Equity/(Current Option Price in Dollars/Optimal f)

The answer derived from this equation must be "floored to the integer." In other words, for example, if the answer is to buy 4.53 contracts, you would buy 4 contracts.

Now a new avenue opens up. Say we want to find what the optimal f is for a given option for each day between now and expiration. In other words, what if we ran this procedure over and over, starting with tomorrow as the mandated exit date and finding the optimal f, then starting the whole process over again with the next day as the mandated exit date? We keep moving the mandated exit date forward until the mandated exit date is the expiration date. We record the optimal f's and geometric means for each mandated exit date. When we are through with this entire procedure, we can find that mandated exit date which results in the highest geometric mean. Now we know the date by which we must be out of the option position in order to have the highest mathematical expectation (i.e., the highest geometric mean). By using the f value that corresponds to the highest geometric mean, we also know how many contracts to buy.

This is quite a startling revelation. We now have a mathematical technique whereby if we just blindly go out and buy an option, as long as we are out of it by the mandated exit date that has the highest geometric mean (provided that it is greater than 1.0, of course) and buy the number of contracts indicated by the optimal f corresponding to that highest geometric mean, we are in a positive mathematical expectation. Contemporary thought has been that positive mathematical expectations only exist if we are shorting options, because then we have the advantage of time premium decay. However, as we have seen, positive mathematical expectations can be found for long options as well. Furthermore, these are geometric positive mathematical expectations. By that I mean that the geometric mean (minus 1.0) is the mathematical expectation when reinvesting returns. The true arithmetic positive mathematical expectation would be actually higher than the geometric! As you can see, these techniques give a new insight into a mathematically correct strategy for options that has been heretofore unnoticed.

Sometimes you will get an optimal f value less than zero. This tells you that the bet is bad, a loser, and that you should not play it. Often this happens when you are looking to hold an option to expiration.

This technique can be applied to other and more advanced option strategies. We have only looked at the outright purchase of a put or a call. The applications of this approach to other, more sophisticated options strategies, as well as applications to other instruments, will be left to the reader's own resourcefulness. There is neither space nor time to cover all of the potential applications in this chapter or in this book. These concepts are presented to break new ground and generate interest in the many applications that can be derived from them.

5

Risk of Ruin

This is perhaps the most tangential and unnecessary chapter in the book. There isn't much connection between this chapter and the next chapter, nor is there much connection between this chapter and the previous chapters. This chapter is placed where it is within this book because in order to understand risk of ruin you must first have a good understanding of the differences between fixed fraction and constant contract trading. There are marked differences in the risk of ruin depending on whether you are trading on a fixed fraction or a constant contract basis.

No book on the topic of money management in trading could be considered complete unless it devoted the necessary coverage to risk of ruin calculations. However, as I hope to bear out, nothing in the realm of money management could be more useless to the trader. Yet when people speak of money management they almost invariably mention risk of ruin. These risk of ruin measures are meaningless because there is nothing you can do about them. They do not dictate any action on your part. Unlike concepts such as dependency, robustness of parameters, optimal f, and so on, risk of ruin tells you nothing about how to handle your money or your trading. It's an interesting figure—and nice to know, since it is almost always small (i.e., there is little risk of ruin)—but it is virtually useless in terms of helping you to trade or manage your account more effectively. Yet when the banter of traders turns to money management doubtlessly you will hear the term "risk of ruin" emerge as if there were some money-management secret buried within its calculations.

The calculations presented here are for completeness, but the reader is forewarned not to make too much of these risk of ruin concepts. We start with a definition for ruin. *Ruin is a state your equity is so depleted that you are no longer able to trade a system.* The risk of ruin is a probability statement between 0 (ruin is impossible) and 1 (ruin is certain).

Once again, understanding is aided by simplicity. Let's start with a scenario for determining risk of ruin where all losses are for the same amount and all wins for the same amount, say, $1. Suppose we have a history of 3 trades, of which 2 were winners. Further, we will assume we are betting 1 unit on each trade, and our entire stake is 1 unit. Therefore, on the first trade there is a 33% chance we will be ruined, since only 2 out of the 3 possible outcomes are winners.

Looking now into the future series of trades, if we won our first trade we would then need to lose the next two trades in order to be ruined. The probability of this occurring is .33 * .33, so our risk of ruin probability statement now appears as:

$$.33 + (.33 * .33)$$

which represents the possibility of ruin on the first trade plus the possibility of ruin on the second trade (assuming ruin is not encountered on the first trade).

If we profited on the first two trades, we would now need to lose 3 units before profiting by another one in order to be ruined. Amending our probability statement to encompass this occurrence we have:

$$.33 + (.33 * .33) + (.33 * .33 * .33)$$

As you can see, the logic carries out to infinity, our ultimate risk of ruin probability statement being defined as:

$$.33 + (.33 * .33) + (.33 * .33 * .33) + \cdots + (.33 \text{ to the power of infinity})$$

For such a scenario, where you win $1 or lose $1, with a 66% chance of winning, your ultimate risk of ruin is .5.

Notice, however, that we only incorporated three trades into our calculations. This is certainly not enough in the real world. What if instead of three trades we used three coin tosses? Obviously three coin tosses can never be a good sample for coin tossing. The more trades you can incorporate, the more extensive the history you are using to calculate your risk of ruin, the more accurate your calculation should be.

THE EQUATIONS

We now see that the risk of ruin is the sum of the probabilities of being ruined on the first event, on the second event, on third event, and so on. Further, we have seen that each successive event has a lower probability, since each successive event is the probability of ruin of the previous event multiplied by the probability of ruin of the current event, as if the current event were the first event in the sequence. Mathematically, we can demonstrate this process for calculating the risk of ruin (which we will call R0) as:

$$R0 = \sum_{M=1}^{\infty} \prod_{X=1}^{M} 1 - P_x$$

where: P = The probability of a win.

The obvious question that arises here is, "If you are summing something an infinite number of times, won't the final sum be infinitely large?" In other words, you keep on summing in this process, so won't R0 be some infinitely large number?

The answer is no. R0 is really a formula that tends to converge on the risk of ruin. Each value that gets added to the sum, R0, is smaller and smaller. By way of an analogy, say you start with the number 1. Now add 1/10th of 1 to it to obtain 1.1. Now add 1/100th of one to that sum to obtain 1.11. Now add 1/1000th of 1 to further obtain 1.111. If we continue with this process we will never reach 1.2. The same logic applies to the formula for R0.

If you want a computer demonstration, the following snippet of code in BASIC will allow you to input any percentage of winning trades, then see how the risk of ruin (R0) converges to a certain value:

```
10 INPUT "PERCENTAGE OF WINS (0 TO 1) ";P
20 Z = 1–P
30 X = Z:A = 1
40 PRINT A,X,Z^A
50 A = A + 1
60 X = X + (Z^A)
70 GOTO 40
```

Now we can show a formula that will find our risk of ruin (R1) when all wins and all losses are for the same amount, without having to carry out the computations to infinity:

$$R1 = \frac{1-A}{1+A}$$

where: $A = P - (1 - P)$

P = The probability of a win.

For our 3-trade example, where the probability of a win was 2 in 3:

$$R1 = \frac{1 - .333}{1 + .333} = \frac{.666}{1.333} = .5$$

The probability of ruin in this case is therefore .5.

It should be noted at this point that these risk of ruin calculations assume an independent trials process. Furthermore, the probability of ruin is presented as the probability of ruin if you trade forever.

What about an even money game? What would the risk of ruin be if we had a 50% chance of winning $1 and a 50% chance of losing $1?

$$A = .5 - (1 - .5)$$

$$= .5 - .5$$

$$= 0$$

Therefore, the risk of ruin (R1) equals:

$$R1 = \frac{1-0}{1+0} = \frac{1}{1} = 1$$

Since R1 = 1 we can state that *ruin is certain in an even money game!*

The risk of ruin equation (R1) can now be amended so that we do not assume we are trading our entire stake on the first trade.

$$R2 = ((1 - A)/(1 + A))^{\wedge}J$$

where: $J = \dfrac{\text{Total stake}}{\text{Percent of total stake allocated per trade}}$

So, if we win 2 out of 3 times, and we are trading with a $100 stake, allocating $20 per trade, J = 5. In this case the probability of ruin (R2) would equal .03125, or .5^5.

Notice that for our even-money game, where ruin is certain, no matter what power you raise 1 to it will always equal 1. This means that in an even-money game ruin is certain *regardless of how small a fraction of your total stake you bet on each event!* The moral once again is clear, albeit from a different proof: *You must have a positive mathematical expectation in order to have a chance at winning.*

The risk of ruin equations presented thus far (R1 and R2) only apply to trading on a constant contract basis, where the amount won when you win is always the same and always equal to the amount lost when you lose. This of course is rarely the case. A more powerful formula for finding risk of ruin is necessary.

When wins and losses are not all for the same amount, we can use a derivation of the formula originally presented by Peter Griffin,[1] which we will call R3:

$$R3 = ((1 - P)/P)^U$$

where: $P = .5 * (1 + (Z/A))$

$Z = (abs(AW/Q) * PW) - (abs(AL/Q) * (1 - PW))$

$A = ((PW * (AW/Q)^2) + ((1 - PW) * (AL/Q)^2))^{(1/2)}$

AW = Amount you win (i.e., average win).

PW = Probability of winning.

AL = Amount you lose (i.e., average loss).

Q = The size of the stake in dollars.

$U = G/A$

G = Percent of account depletion until ruin (e.g., if 1, then 100% of the account must be depleted before you call it a ruin).

abs = The absolute value function.

This formula will approximate the risk of ruin when wins and losses are not all equal. To obtain the true risk of ruin requires the use of compli-

[1] *The Theory of Blackjack*, P. Griffin, Gamblers Press, Las Vegas, Nevada. 1981.

cated difference equations. However, this derivation of Dr. Griffin's equation is a fair approximation.

In this as in all of the other risk of ruin calculations in this chapter, to accommodate slippage and commissions you simply deduct them from each trade before figuring your variables. Your average win trade (AW) and average loss trade (AL) will thus reflect the commissions and slippage as well as the variables PW, A, Z, P, and of course our answer R3.

Now let's run through our previous 3-trade example in this risk of ruin calculation. We know that PW = .666, that AW = 20 and that AL = − 20. Furthermore, we know that Q = $100, and G = 1. Therefore:

$$A = ((PW * (AW/Q)^\wedge 2) + ((1 - PW) * (AL/Q)^\wedge 2))^\wedge (1/2)$$

$$= ((.666 * (20/100)^\wedge 2) + ((1 - .666) * (-20/100)^\wedge 2))^\wedge (1/2)$$

$$= ((.666 * .2^\wedge 2) + (.333 * - .2^\wedge 2))^\wedge (1/2)$$

$$= ((.666 * .04) + (.333 * .04))^\wedge (1/2)$$

$$= (.0264 + .01332)^\wedge (1/2)$$

$$= .03972^\wedge (1/2)$$

$$= .1992987707$$

$$Z = (abs(AW/Q) * PW) - (abs(AL/Q) * (1 - PW))$$

$$= (abs(20/100) * .666) - (abs(-20/100) * (1 - .666))$$

$$= (abs(.2) * .666) - (abs(-.2) * .333)$$

$$= (.2 * .666) - (.2 * .333)$$

$$= .1332 - .0666$$

$$= .0666$$

$$U = G/A$$

$$= 1/.1992987707$$

$$= 5.017592414$$

$P = .5 * (1 + (Z/A))$

$\quad = .5 * (1 + (.0666/.1992987707))$

$\quad = .5 * (1 + .3341716548)$

$\quad = .5 * 1.3341716548$

$\quad = .6670858275$

$R3 = ((1 - P)/P)^\wedge U$

$\quad = ((1 - .6670858275)/.6670858275)^\wedge 5.017592414$

$\quad = (.3329141725/.6670858275)^\wedge 5.017592414$

$\quad = .4990574807^\wedge 5.017592414$

$\quad = .03058035969$

Under this formula, risk of ruin is again slightly over 3%. This formula allows us to closely approximate the risk of ruin when wins and losses are not for the same amount, hence it is the preferred formula. The formula assumes that the outcomes are generated by an independent trials process (that there exists no dependency between the outcomes used as input to the formula). Also, this approximate risk of ruin is the approximate probability of ruin for an account trading on a constant contract basis.

In establishing the value for the variable G, you must figure what percentage of your total stake the initial margin for one contract is. For example, a trader with a $50,000 account trading two markets where the initial margin for one is $3,000 and the initial margin for the other is $5,000 is in effect ruined should the account's equity decline below $8,000, since then the system can no longer be traded.

This formula (R3) assumes you will trade forever. Since no one will trade forever, three possible alternatives are left. The first of these is ruin. If you do not experience ruin, if you are profitable, at some level of profits you will either quit trading or at least withdraw some of your winnings. This changes the risk of ruin. To account for this, the risk of ruin formula becomes:

$R4 = 1 - (((((1 - P)/P)^\wedge U) - 1)/((((1 - P)/P)^\wedge C) - 1))$

where: $C = ((L - ((1 - G) * Q))/Q)/A$

> L = The amount a trader's stake must grow to in order for the trader to quit trading.

> All other variables are as previously defined.

Let's go back to our 3-trade example, where we started out with a $100 stake, won $20 two thirds of the time, and lost $20 one third of the time. When we set G equal to 1 we found we had a risk of ruin of .03058035969. Now, suppose we say we are going to quit trading if our stake of $100 grows to $200. In this case L will equal $200. Therefore:

$$C = ((200 - ((1 - 1) * 100))/100)/.1992987707$$

$$= ((200 - (0 * 100))/100)/.1992987707$$

$$= ((200 - 0)/100)/.1992987707$$

$$= (200/100)/.1992987707$$

$$= 2/.1992987707$$

$$= 10.03518483$$

We know from our earlier example that P = .6670858275, and therefore:

$$(1 - P)/P = (1 - .6670858275)/.6670858275$$

$$= .3329141725/.6670858275$$

$$= .4990574807$$

Substituting .4990574807 for $(1 - P)/P$ in the equation for R4:

$$R4 = 1 - (((((1 - P)/P)^U) - 1)/((((1 - P)/P)^C) - 1))$$

$$= 1 - \frac{((.4990574807^5.017592414) - 1)}{((.4990574807^10.03518483) - 1)}$$

$$= 1 - \frac{.03058035969 - 1}{.0009351583976 - 1}$$

$$= 1 - \frac{- .9694196403}{- .9990648416}$$

$$= 1 - .9703270498$$

$$= .0296729502$$

The risk of ruin under this formula (R4) will always be less than that given by the previous formula (R3). Therefore, if the previous formula

(R3) gives an acceptable (low enough) risk of ruin, then certainly this later (more accurate) formula (R4) will also.

WITHDRAWING FUNDS

Suppose the trader doesn't want to quit trading altogether, but rather to let profits build up to the value L and then withdraw enough funds to drop the stake back to Q. The latest risk of ruin formula will give us the risk of ruin if the trader only wants to withdraw funds once (i.e., quit trading). However, when the trader wants to withdraw funds more than one time, the formula for the risk of being ruined at least once when N withdrawals are made (R5) is:

$R5 = 1 - (1 - R)^N$

where: N = The number of withdrawals to be made.

R = The risk of ruin as calculated for R4.

All other variables are as previously defined.

Now let's go back to our 3-trade example, where we started out with a $100 stake, won $20 two thirds of the time and lost $20 one third of the time. When we set G equal to 1 and L to $200 (the point at which we were going to quit trading), we found we had a risk of ruin R4 = .0296729502. Suppose that rather than quit we are going to withdraw $100, bringing our stake back down to our starting level of $100, and try to do this 10 times over. In this case:

$R5 = 1 - (1 - R)^N$

$= 1 - (1 - .0296729502)^{10}$

$= 1 - (.9703270498)^{10}$

$= 1 - .7399142368$

$= .2600857632$

As can be seen, *removing funds sharply increases the risk of ruin*. Yet this is hardly a problem in that a trader who has removed an amount equal to his starting stake Q can be ruined yet start anew with those funds withdrawn, provided the trader has them still. These risk of ruin equations assume you are trading on a constant contract basis. How then can they be amended to accommodate fixed fractional trading?

RISK OF RUIN IN FIXED FRACTIONAL TRADING

By the nature of fixed fractional trading, ruin is theoretically impossible. In theory, in fixed fractional trading an account's equity approaches zero with each successive loss but never converges to zero.

For example, suppose you have a stake of $10. Say you are betting half of that on each bet. Furthermore, say you just happen to get in before a large losing streak, a losing streak that continues to infinity (as we saw in Chapter 1, this can happen). After the first loss your stake is cut down to $5. After the second loss, $2.50, then $1.25, then $.625, and so on. Yet your stake is never completely tapped out.

However, there is a lowest denomination allowable (a base unit), which in U.S. dollars is one cent. In a casino it is the minimum bet amount. In futures trading the lowest denomination allowable is one contract (it can even be a minicontract). So we can say that theoretically the risk of ruin in fixed fractional trading is zero. Yet in reality, ruin, defined as the inability to continue trading a system, is that point at which you could not trade one base unit (one contract).

As we saw in the last chapter, when you get too far out to the right of the f curve (too high a value for f) your TWR gets below 1. Now a TWR (or geometric mean) of less than 1 means you are losing money trading the system at such a value for f. Remember that the geometric mean minus 1 is a proxy for the mathematical expectation under fixed fractional trading. If the geometric mean is less than 1, then you are in a situation of negative expectancy. Recall from Chapter 1 that when gambling in a negative expectancy situation you are not only certain to lose, you are certain to lose your entire stake (ruin) with a probability approaching 1 as the action approaches infinity. Therefore, we can state with near certainty that in fixed fractional trading, if the f value is so high as to cause the TWR or geometric mean to be less than 1, the risk of ruin is 1. This also explains the extreme case, that if f = 1.0 then the risk of ruin also = 1.0.

I have devised a formula for calculating the risk of ruin in fixed fractional trading, assuming that you are going to trade indefinitely. This equation we call R6. First, however, let's take the equation for R4, and we will build R6 from there.

If we substitute the amount we allocate per contract in fixed fractional trading for the variable Q in our risk of ruin calculations, we can figure what our risk of ruin would be if we were trading on a constant contract basis with a stake equal to the amount we would allocate per trade:

$$Q = abs(\text{biggest loss}/\text{optimal f})$$

Going back to the 3-trade example we have been using throughout this chapter, we can determine our optimal f, which is .33. Now we find abs($-20/.33$) equals $60.61. Therefore, we would trade one contract per every $60.61 in equity. If we substitute $60.61 for the value Q in our pertinent risk of ruin calculation, R4, and set the variable L equal to 2 times this value, or $121.22, we can determine what the risk of ruin is in progressing from one contract ($60.61) to that level where we would begin trading two contracts ($121.22).

$$A = ((PW * (AW/Q)\verb|^|2) + ((1 - PW) * (AL/Q)\verb|^|2))\verb|^|(1/2)$$

$$= ((.666 * (20/60.61)\verb|^|2) + ((1 - .666) * (-20/100)\verb|^|2))\verb|^|(1/2)$$

$$= ((.666 * .3299785514\verb|^|2) + (.333 * -.3299785514\verb|^|2))\verb|^|(1/2)$$

$$= ((.666 * .1088858444) + (.333 * .1088858444))\verb|^|(1/2)$$

$$= (.07251797237 + .03625898619)\verb|^|(1/2)$$

$$= .1087769586\verb|^|(1/2)$$

$$= .3298135209$$

$$Z = (abs(AW/Q) * PW) - (abs(AL/Q) * (1 - PW))$$

$$= (abs(20/60.61) * .666) - (abs(-20/60.61) * (1 - .666))$$

$$= (abs(.3299785514) * .666) - (abs(-.3299785514) * .333)$$

$$= (.3299785514 * .666) - (.3299785514 * .333)$$

$$= .2197657152 - .1098828576$$

$$= .1098828576$$

$$U = G/A$$

$$= 1/.3298135209$$

$$= 3.032016387$$

$$P = .5 * (1 + (Z/A))$$

$$= .5 * (1 + (.1098828576/.3298135209))$$

$$= .5 * (1 + .3331666249)$$

$$= .5 * 1.333166625$$

$$= .6665833125$$

$$C = ((L - ((1 - G) * Q))/Q)/A$$

$$= ((121.22 - ((1 - 1) * 60.61))/60.61)/.3298135209$$

$$= ((121.22 - (0 * 60.61))/60.61)/.3298135209$$

$$= (121.22/60.61)/.3298135209$$

$$= 2/.3298135209$$

$$= 6.064032774$$

$$R4 = 1 - (((((1 - P)/P)^{\wedge}U) - 1)/((((1 - P)/P)^{\wedge}C) - 1))$$

$$(1 - P)/P = (1 - .6665833125)/.6665833125$$

$$= .3334166875/.6665833125$$

$$= .5001875703$$

$$= 1 - \frac{((.5001875703^{\wedge}3.032016387) - 1)}{((.5001875703^{\wedge}6.064032774) - 1)}$$

$$= 1 - \frac{.1223956571 - 1}{.01498069687 - 1}$$

$$= 1 - \frac{-.8776043429}{-.9850193031}$$

$$= 1 - .890951416$$

$$R4 = .109048584$$

So there is approximately an 11% chance that, under such a scenario, an account would see 100% of the equity wiped out ($G = 1.00$) before it doubled and started trading 2 contracts.

Now we want to look at what the probability of dropping back to trading 1 contract would be before getting up to trading 3 contracts. We can find this by using R4, setting $L = Q * 3$ and $G = .5$ (i.e., if we're trading 2 contracts, we need a 50% equity retracement to drop back to trading 1 contract). Then we need to double the amount for Q. There is an easier way to state this whole thing. Let Q equal its initial amount of abs(biggest loss/optimal f). Set $L = Q + (Q/2)$, thus representing a 50% gain, the amount needed to progress from trading 2 contracts to 3. Let

$G = 1/2$, the percentage loss to go from trading 2 contracts back down to trading 1 contract. Now, run R4 with these new values:

$U = G/A$

    $= .5/.3298135209$

    $= 1.516008193$

$C = ((L - ((1 - G) * Q))/Q)/A$

    $= ((90.915 - ((1 - .5) * 60.61))/60.61)/.3298135209$

    $= ((90.915 - (.5 * 60.61))/60.61)/.3298135209$

    $= (90.915/30.305)/.3298135209$

    $= 3/.3298135209$

    $= 9.096049161$

$R4 = 1 - (((((1 - P)/P)\wedge U) - 1)/((((1 - P)/P)\wedge C) - 1))$

        $(1 - P)/P = (1 - .6665833125)/.6665833125$

                  $= .3334166875/.6665833125$

                  $= .5001875703$

$$= 1 - \frac{((.5001875703\wedge 1.516008193) - 1)}{((.5001875703\wedge 9.096049161) - 1)}$$

$$= 1 - \frac{.3498509071 - 1}{.001833572237 - 1}$$

$$= 1 - \frac{-.6501490929}{-.9981664278}$$

$$= 1 - .651343378$$

$R4 = .348656622$

So we can say that once we are at the level of trading 2 contracts, the probability of dropping back down to trading 1 contract before going up to trading 3 contracts is .348656622. Therefore, once we are trading 2 contracts, the probability of ruin is the probability of dropping back down to 1 contract (.348656622) times the probability of being ruined when trading 1 contract (.109048584), or .348656622 * .109048584 = .03802051093. In other words, once we are up to trading 2 contracts, our risk of ruin is slightly under 4%.

So our total risk of ruin up to this point is the sum of the risk of ruin while trading 1 contract until we are trading 2 contracts (.109048584) plus the risk of ruin while trading 2 contracts before advancing to 3 contracts (.03802051093) or .109048584 + .03802051093 = .1470690949. Note that we are summing these individual risks of ruin per the definition of R0!

Here, then, is the formula for calculating the approximate risk of ruin in fixed fractional trading, R6:

$$R6 = \sum_{M=1}^{\infty} \prod_{X=1}^{M} 1 - \left(\frac{(((1-P)/P)^{\wedge}(Y/A)) - 1}{(((1-P)/P)^{\wedge}(((((Q/X) + Q) - ((1-Y) * Q))/Q)/A)) - 1} \right)$$

where: $Y = 1/X$, if $X = 1$ then $Y = G$

Q = abs (biggest loss/optimal f)

$P = .5 * (1 + (Z/A))$

$Z = (\text{abs}(AW/Q) * PW) - (\text{abs}(AL/Q) * (1 - PW))$

$A = ((PW * (AW/Q)^{\wedge}2) + ((1 - PW) * (AL/Q)^{\wedge}2))^{\wedge}(1/2)$

AW = Amount you win (i.e., average win).

PW = Probability of winning.

AL = Amount you lose (i.e., average loss).

G = Percent of account depletion until ruin (e.g., if 1 then 100% of the account must be depleted before you call it a ruin).

abs = The absolute value function.

A few notes on the above equation for R6 are in order. First of all, there is no need to carry the calculations to infinity. Once you have decided on the precision you want for R6 (e.g., 4 decimal places, or .0001), then, once a geometric product of the equation (i.e., the amount you are adding onto the sum for R6) is less than the precision (e.g., a geometric product < .0001), there is no need to carry the calculations any further.

You will also note that the risk of ruin when you are fixed fractional trading is not nearly as high as you might think. The reason for this is that when you are trading under fixed fraction and your account is depleted to the point where you are trading one contract, at that point you are actually trading on a constant contract basis. This is partially why R6 does not usually equal 1 when f equals 1. Before you are ruined, you inevitably go back to trading on a constant contract basis of one contract! R6 reflects this fact.

The fact that R6 tends to also be quite small is rather reassuring. We know that the risk of ruin when trading on a constant contract basis is quite small. Now we have seen that the risk of ruin when trading on a fixed fraction basis is also quite small, even though the potential gain is geometrically greater.

It is worth repeating that all of these risk of ruin calculations (R0 through R6) are simply approximations, since the equations use *average win* and *average loss* as inputs. This does not take the distribution of the individual trades into account. It is akin to finding your optimal f for a given sequence of trades by using the Kelly formula. As an example, consider the following two sequences of trades/bets:

Sequence 1	Sequence 2
+ 1	+ 7
+ 13	+ 7
− 11	− 6
− 1	− 6

The average win and the average loss are the same for both sequences. If we were to calculate R3 for both of these sequences, we would get the same answer, provided we define ruin as the probability of touching 0 (i.e., we set G = 1). Clearly, sequence 1 is riskier in that the variance is greater than for sequence 2, and hence, the risk of ruin for sequence 1 should really be greater than for sequence 2, especially if the starting stake was 11. Here is another instance where futures traders have tried to force a technique to fit the nature of futures trading. By this I mean that *these equations are designed to apply to gambling. As such, the inputs are the amount you can win and the amount you can lose. Futures traders take this to be the same as your average win and your average loss. It isn't. Using averages makes the equations incorrect to the extent of the dispersion of the wins about the average win and the dispersion of the losses about the average loss. Furthermore, all of these risk of ruin equations not only assume an independent trials process, they further assume a stationary distribution of outcomes/bets/trades.*

This last fact, that these risk of ruin calculations assume a stationary distribution, is quite important. The fact that we are dealing with non-stationary distributions makes the risk of ruin greater than these equations may imply, for in assuming a stationary distribution, these equations do not account for the fact that the distribution can shift to an unfavorable state and stay there for a prolonged period of time. So, the trader is more likely to be ruined than these equations may indicate.

Yet futures traders will still figure these calculations down to the last decimal place as though they were gospel. Therefore, as we continue with our discussion of these risk of ruin calculations, be on notice that they are really rather rough approximations. *Even R6 is but a rough approximation of the risk of ruin.* The equations were meant for a gambling situation, which is not synonymous with a trading situation because the distribution of outcomes is a factor in a trading situation, as is the non-stationary distribution of outcomes from trading systems, and these points are not addressed in these equations.

RISK OF RUIN VERSUS f

Next, we have a graph of our coin-toss example that pays $2 for a win and costs $1 on a loss. Superimposed over the f curve is the risk of ruin curve for trading fixed fraction indefinitely with $G = 1$ and $Q =$ abs $(-1/\text{the f value})$, the absolute value of the biggest loss divided by the given f value.

The ratio of the TWR (or geometric mean) to the risk of ruin is at its greatest at $f = 0$. At that point the ratio is infinitely high. Now, as you increase f from 0 towards 1 the ratio continually declines (see Figure 5-1). *Using the optimal f doesn't minimize the risk of ruin, not trading does!* Therefore, if you want the smallest possible risk of ruin (or the highest ratio of TWR or geometric mean to the risk of ruin), then don't trade. So long as the risk of ruin is acceptable to you (and we have seen with R6 that the risk of ruin, even for fixed fractional trading, is usually quite small), then the risk of ruin poses no potential problem with trading at the optimal f level. Not that the risk of ruin calculation matters much anyhow, but if the calculation is excessively high you may well want to not trade that market system at the optimal f level or at all.

As for the risk of ruin calculations themselves, not only are they rather rough approximations, since they do not take the distributions of the trades or the dynamic nature of these distributions into account, they are usually unimportant in a decision-making sense (unless of course the probability of ruin is too high for the trader to bear). Traders pay an undue amount of attention to these equations. The important point to note about them, though, is that you are far better off being left of center on the f curve!

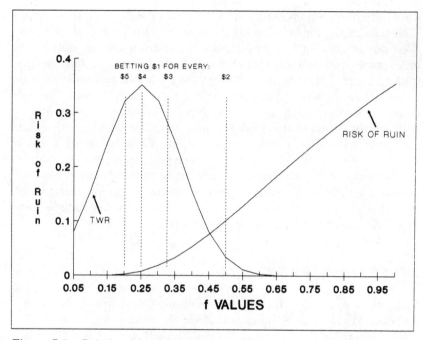

Figure 5-1   Relationship of risk of ruin and TWR for 2:1 coin-toss example.

Risk of ruin calculations are, at best, reassuring to the trader and interesting from an academic standpoint. Beyond that they are of little value in trading. They have been presented here for completeness and to introduce you to the concepts and equations involved.

6

The Total Portfolio Approach

MODERN PORTFOLIO THEORY

Recall from Chapter 4 the paradox of the optimal f and a market system's drawdown. The better a market system is, the higher the value for f. Yet the drawdown (historically), if you are trading the optimal f, can never be lower than f. Generally speaking, then, the better the market system, the greater the drawdown will be as a percent of account equity (if you are trading optimal f). That is, if you want to have the greatest geometric growth in an account then you can count on severe drawdowns along the way.

Diversification among other market systems is the most effective way to buffer this drawdown while still staying close to the peak of the f curve (i.e., without having to trim back to half f, and so on). When one market system goes into a drawdown, another one that is being traded in the account will come on strong, thus canceling the drawdown of the other. This also provides for a catalytic effect on the entire account. The market system that just experienced the drawdown (and now is getting back to performing well) will have no less funds to start with than it did when the drawdown began (thanks to the other market system canceling out the drawdown).

With optimal f you must diversify. As should be apparent to you from the last paragraph, diversification won't hinder the upside of a system (quite the reverse—the upside is far greater, since after a drawdown you aren't starting back with fewer contracts) yet it will buffer the downside. Of course, what has been described is the case of an optimally diversified portfolio—one where a drawdown in one market system is completely offset by a drawup in another market system.

Given a group of market systems and their respective optimal f's, a quantifiable, optimal portfolio mix does exist. Although we cannot be certain that what was the optimal portfolio mix in the past will be optimal in the future, it is more likely to be optimal or near optimal than is the case for the optimal system parameters of the past. Whereas optimal system parameters change quite quickly from one time period to another, optimal portfolio mixes change very slowly (as do optimal f values). Generally, the correlations between market systems tend to remain constant. This is good news to a trader who has found the optimal portfolio mix, the optimal diversification among market systems.

Modern portfolio theory embodies concepts that have been employed successfully by money managers for the last few decades in the stock market. Very little has been done to apply this toward trading futures using a trading system. This is unfortunate, because the concepts of modern portfolio theory can actually do more to enhance a portfolio of futures market systems than they can to enhance a portfolio of individual stocks (since stocks tend to be much more positively correlated to each other than do futures market systems). It is also quite rare that a stock concept be transported to the futures arena. Usually, it is the other way around. We begin our discussion by dealing with stocks; later we show how the same ideas can be employed in futures.

THE MARKOWITZ MODEL

The basic concepts of modern portfolio theory emanate from a monograph written by Dr. Harry Markowitz.[1] Essentially, Markowitz proposed that sound portfolio management has to do with composition, not individual stock selection (as is more commonly practiced).

Markowitz argued that diversification is effective only to the extent that the correlation coefficient between the markets involved is negative. Recall the linear correlation coefficient from Chapter 1. If we have a portfolio composed of one stock, our best diversification is obtained if we choose another stock such that the correlation between the two stock prices is as low as possible. The net result would be that the portfolio, as a whole (composed of these two stocks with negative correlation), would have less variation in price than either one of the stocks alone (see Figure 6–1).

---

[1] *Portfolio Selection—Efficient Diversification of Investments*, Dr. Harry Markowitz, Yale University Press, New Haven, Conn., 1959.

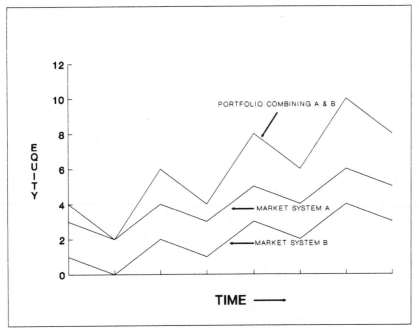

Figure 6-1   A portfolio of two positively correlated market systems—a poor choice.

The portfolio shown in Figure 6–1 (the combination of market systems A and B) will have variance at least has high as the individual market systems since the market systems have a correlation of + 1.00 to each other.

The portfolio shown in Figure 6–2 (the combination of market systems A and C) will have less variance than either market system A or market system C since there is a negative correlation between market systems A and C.

Markowitz proposed that investors act in a rational manner and, given the choice, would opt for a portfolio with the same return as the one they have, but with less risk, or opt for a portfolio with a higher return than the one they have but with the same risk. Further, for a given level of risk there is an optimal portfolio with the highest yield; likewise, for a given yield there is an optimal portfolio with the lowest risk. Investors with portfolios where the yield could be increased with no resultant increase in risk or investors with portfolios where the risk could be lowered with no resultant decrease in yield are said to have *inefficient* portfolios.

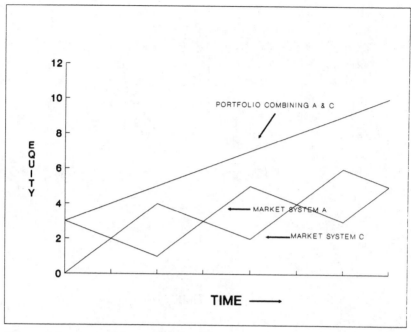

Figure 6-2 A portfolio of two negatively correlated market systems—a good choice.

Figure 6–3 shows all of the available portfolios under a given study. If you hold portfolio C, you would be better off with portfolio A, as you would have the same return with less risk, or portfolio B, where you would have more return with the same risk.

In describing this, Markowitz described what is called the *efficient frontier*. This is the set of portfolios that lie on the upper and left sides of the graph. These are portfolios where the yield can no longer be increased without increasing the risk and the risk cannot be lowered without lowering the yield. Portfolios lying on the efficient frontier are said to be *efficient* portfolios (see Figure 6–4).

Portfolios lying high up and off to the right and low down and to the left are generally not very well diversified among very many issues. Portfolios lying in the middle of the efficient frontier are usually very well diversified. Which portfolio a particular investor chooses is a function of the investor's risk aversion, his willingness to assume risk. In the Markowitz model, any portfolio that lies upon the efficient frontier is said to be a good portfolio choice; where on the efficient frontier is a matter of personal preference (later on, we'll see that there is an exact optimal spot on the efficient frontier).

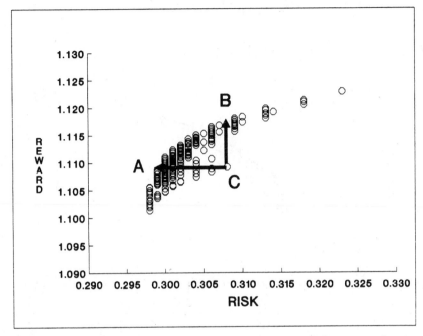

Figure 6-3 Risk/reward relationships for various portfolios according to modern portfolio theory.

In Markowitz's work, risk was quantified for the first time. He described risk as the variation in a portfolio's returns, a definition many people have challenged. As we prove later, though, from a purely mathematical perspective this definition is in fact correct.

CAPITAL ASSET PRICING THEORY

In the world of stock analysis, the individual intercorrelations of the different stocks are not measured. Rather what is generally measured is the individual stock's beta,[2] its correlation to a market average as a whole. The concept of separating risk into two distinct elements, market risk (*beta*) and specific risk (i.e., risk specific to that particular stock, termed *alpha*) was introduced during a period where there was

[2] The mathematical definition of beta often differs from one beta ranking service to the next, with no universal acceptance as to the exact mathematics involved. Therefore, no exact formula for beta will be given here. Suffice to say, it is the correlation of an individual stock to the market as a whole.

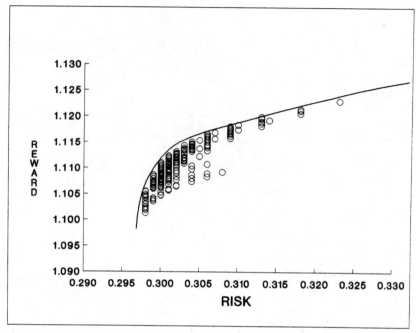

Figure 6-4   The efficient frontier.

much academic concern regarding portfolio management, a period that was instigated by the Markowitz concepts. Now that risk was segregated into two parts by stock portfolio managers, it became obvious that diversification reduced the nonmarket (alpha) element of risk.

Here we are discussing what is now known as *capital asset pricing theory*, which was promulgated for the most part by William F. Sharpe. Under these concepts, the risk portion of the Markowitz risk versus return tradeoff curve, the variation in returns, is replaced by beta, the total market risk.

Imagine that we are drawing a line from left to right, beginning on the left at the risk-free interest rate (zero on the X axis, risk, and that point on the Y axis, return, that represents the yield). We draw the line straight through that point on the efficient frontier which corresponds to a beta of 1—i.e., a portfolio which performs exactly the same as the market (generally the S&P 500 stock index is used as this particular point along the efficient frontier)[3]—and continue that line on up and to the right. This can be seen in Figure 6–5.

[3] According to Sharpe, not just the stock averages, but rather an index of all assets (stocks, options, bonds, real estate) would be less risky than simply the stock averages, since there would be less variance in returns of the sum of all of these assets.

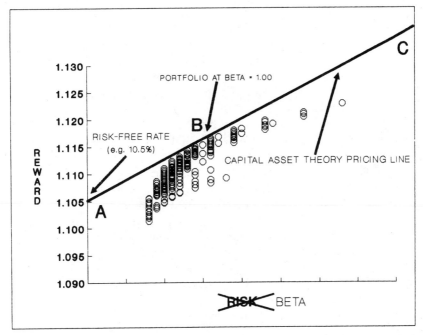

Figure 6-5   Relationship between reward and beta according to capital asset pricing theory.

Unlike the Markowitz model, which adjusts the risk/reward tradeoff by moving up or down the efficient frontier of *alternative portfolios of different securities*, under capital asset pricing theory the risk/reward tradeoff is adjusted by borrowing or lending against a *single fully diversified portfolio* (the market as a whole). It is important to realize that under capital asset pricing theory the market, or its surrogate stock price index, is seen as the ultimate limit of efficient diversification.[4]

Under the capital asset pricing theory, risk can be reduced and return enhanced beyond the efficient frontier by being on the capital asset theory line between points A and B. This would represent having a certain percentage in a fully diversified stock portfolio (the whole market) and a percentage of capital invested at the current risk-free rate (T-bills). This is accomplished by placing some assets in the whole market (portfolio B) and the remainder in a risk-free vehicle. The proportion in which this is done determines where on line segment AB the investor will be. Notice that a portfolio at any point along line

[4] This is so because the percentage effect of the individual alphas of the stocks comprising the portfolio (the market) would be small, since there are so many stocks in the portfolio.

segment AB gets a better return for the same level of risk than do those portfolios directly below the line. Those portfolios directly below line segment AB represent being 100% invested in less risky portfolios than portfolio B, with no assets in a risk-free vehicle. Obviously being on line segment AB is superior to any of those portfolios directly below, since the investor has a greater return for the same level of risk.

Also, we can increase our return for a given level of risk beyond the efficient frontier by being on the line between points B and C. This represents having all of our trading capital invested in the market and borrowing to invest more.[5]

However, as Latane and Tuttle[6] pointed out, the variance of returns causes the straight-line risk/reward tradeoff of the capital asset pricing theory to curve downward, much like the f curve discussed in Chapter 4. In other words, at some point you pay a price for borrowing more to invest in a portfolio that contains risk. Latane and Tuttle have shown that there is an optimal point along the capital asset pricing line (since this line rounds over and back down and is not in fact straight) where the line peaks out. This point, called q, is defined as:

$$q = \frac{\text{Dollars of investment in a portfolio}}{\text{Dollars of investor's own resources}}$$

So *q measures the proportion of an investor's equity placed in fluctuating return assets.* If q is less than 1, then $1 - q$ of the investor's resources are placed in a riskless investment. If q is greater than 1, then $q - 1$ of the investor's resources are borrowed.

As an example, if q = .4, then 40% of the investor's resources are placed in a fluctuating asset and 60% are placed in a risk-free asset. If q = 1.5, then for every dollar the investor has invested in a fluctuating asset he should borrow an additional 50 cents to further invest in the fluctuating asset.

Latane and Tuttle have shown that we can approximate the optimal q, which they call q * , by:

$$q^* = (R - I)/(S^2)$$

---

[5] Actually, this assumes being able to borrow at the risk-free rate, which is unlikely. Most likely you would have to borrow at a rate greater than the current risk-free rate, and therefore line segment BC would be shallower than line segment AB (i.e., BC would have less slope, be more horizontal, than AC). The effect of this is that the rate of return gained to risk assumed would be lower.

[6] "Criteria for Portfolio Building," Henry Latane and Donald Tuttle, *Journal of Finance* 22, September, 1967, pp. 362–363.

where: R = The return from the portfolio.

   I = The risk-free rate (generally the 90-day T-bill rate).

   S = The standard deviation of returns of the portfolio.

In other words, the optimal level of leverage can be paraphrased as *the ratio of expected excess returns from the portfolio to the variance of the portfolio.* Using the concept of optimal q may be of use to a fund manager looking to invest in an index fund.

Now let's return to the realm of futures. The Markowitz model utilizes the intercorrelations of individual stocks (among their prices), which are measured by the different stocks' betas. In futures, this would not be applicable, since to calculate a beta you need an index, an average of prices. Of course you could use something like the CRB Index, but the technique would still be awkward compared to its stock counterpart. The reason for this is that there is a vast difference between, say, orange juice prices and Eurodollars. The two are not really comparable, whereas with two individual stocks there is far more similarity.

TRANSPORTING PORTFOLIO
CONCEPTS TO FUTURES

Yet the Markowitz model can be applied to futures and it can be applied in a far purer version than by using betas. We can actually measure the intercorrelations of the various futures, which is exactly what betas try to do indirectly. When modern portfolio theory was in its infancy, the computational aspect was a great consideration (which promulgated the use of betas). However, with today's computers the enormous number crunching involved is hardly a consideration.

The question arises, "If we are measuring the intercorrelation of prices, what if we have two systems on the same market that are negatively correlated?" In other words, suppose we have systems A and Z. There is a perfect negative correlation between the two. When A is in a drawdown, B is in a drawup and vice versa. Isn't this really an ideal diversification?

What we really want to measure, then, is not the intercorrelations of prices of the markets we're using. Rather, we want to *measure the intercorrelations of daily equity changes among the different market systems.*

Yet this is still an apples-and-oranges comparison. Say that two of the market systems which we are going to examine the intercorrelations are both trading the same market, yet one of the systems has an optimal f corresponding to one contract per every \$2,000 in account equity, while the other system has an optimal f corresponding to one contract per every \$10,000 in account equity.

To overcome this and incorporate the optimal f's of the various market systems under consideration, as well as to account for fixed fractional trading, we convert the daily equity changes for a given market system into daily HPRs. The HPR in this context is how much a particular market made or lost for a given day on a 1-contract basis relative to what the optimal f for that system is. Here is how this can be solved. Say the market system with an optimal f of \$2,000 made \$100 on a given day. The HPR for that market system for that day is then 1.05. To find the daily HPR:

Daily HPR = (A/B) + 1

where: A = Dollars made or lost that day.

B = Optimal f in dollars.

So we begin by converting the daily dollar gains and losses for the market systems we are looking at into daily HPRs relative to the optimal f in dollars for a given market system. In so doing, we make quantity irrelevant. In the example just cited, where the daily HPR is 1.05, we made 5% that day on that money. This is 5% regardless then of whether we had on 1 contract or 1,000 contracts.

Now we are ready to begin comparing different portfolios. The trick here is to compare every possible portfolio combination, starting with portfolios of one market system (for every market system under consideration, N) to portfolios of N market systems.

As an example, suppose we are looking at market systems A, B, and C. Every combination would be:

A
B
C
A B
A C
B C
A B C

But we do not stop there. For each combination, we must figure each percentage allocation as well. To do so we need to have a minimum percentage increment. The following example, continued from the earlier example of portfolios A, B, and C, illustrates this with a minimum portfolio allocation of 10% (.10):

A		100%		
B		100%		
C		100%		
A B		90%	10%	
		80%	20%	
		70%	30%	
		60%	40%	
		50%	50%	
		40%	60%	
		30%	70%	
		20%	80%	
		10%	90%	
A C		90%	10%	
		80%	20%	
		70%	30%	
		60%	40%	
		50%	50%	
		40%	60%	
		30%	70%	
		20%	80%	
		10%	90%	
B C		90%	10%	
		80%	20%	
		70%	30%	
		60%	40%	
		50%	50%	
		40%	60%	
		30%	70%	
		20%	80%	
		10%	90%	
A B C		80%	10%	10%
		70%	20%	10%
		70%	10%	20%
		60%	30%	10%
		60%	20%	20%
		60%	10%	30%
		50%	40%	10%

50%	30%	20%
50%	20%	30%
50%	10%	40%
40%	50%	10%
40%	40%	20%
40%	30%	30%
40%	20%	40%
40%	10%	50%
30%	60%	10%
30%	50%	20%
30%	40%	30%
30%	30%	40%
30%	20%	50%
30%	10%	60%
20%	70%	10%
20%	60%	20%
20%	50%	30%
20%	40%	40%
20%	30%	50%
20%	20%	60%
20%	10%	70%
10%	80%	10%
10%	70%	20%
10%	60%	30%
10%	50%	40%
10%	40%	50%
10%	30%	60%
10%	20%	70%
10%	10%	80%

As you can see there are 66 such combinations and percentage allocations (CPAs) for 3 elements with a 10% percentage increment. Many of
these CPAs are unacceptable right from the start because they have far
too high a percentage in any one market system for our preference. Say
we want to place a constraint that no more than 50% of an account's
funds be allocated to any given market system. In this case, our entire
possible list of CPAs (again with a 10% increment) would be:

A	B	50%	50%
A	C	50%	50%

B	C		50%	50%	
A	B	C	50%	40%	10%
			50%	30%	20%
			50%	20%	30%
			50%	10%	40%
			40%	50%	10%
			40%	40%	20%
			40%	30%	30%
			40%	20%	40%
			40%	10%	50%
			30%	50%	20%
			30%	40%	30%
			30%	30%	40%
			30%	20%	50%
			20%	50%	30%
			20%	40%	40%
			20%	30%	50%
			10%	50%	40%
			10%	40%	50%

For each CPA we go through each day and compute a net HPR for that day. The net HPR for a given day is the sum of each market system's HPR for that day times the system's percentage allocation. For example, suppose for systems A, B, and C we are looking at percentage allocations of 10%, 50%, 40% respectively. Further, suppose that the individual HPRs for those market systems for that day are .9, 1.4, and 1.05 respectively. Then the net HPR for the day is:

$$\text{Net HPR} = (.9 * .1) + (1.4 * .5) + (1.05 * .4)$$
$$= .09 + .7 + .42$$
$$= 1.21$$

To summarize to this point:

1. Convert the daily equity changes of a given market system to a daily HPR. Equity change means the net change in open and closed equity from yesterday.

2. Figure the net HPR for each day of each CPA.

The first necessary tabulation is that of the average daily net HPR for each CPA. This comprises the reward or Y axis of the Markowitz model. The second necessary tabulation is that of the standard deviation of the daily net HPRs for a given CPA, specifically the population standard deviation. This measure corresponds to the risk or X axis of the Markowitz model. (At this point it should be mentioned that a program is provided in Appendix F that does all of this. Also in Appendix F you will find a sample of the output generated by this program. Examine the output while you are reading this to better follow what is going on here.) From these first two tabulations we can find our efficient frontier. We have effectively incorporated various markets, systems, and f factors, and we can now see *quantitatively* what our best CPAs are (i.e., which CPAs lie along the efficient frontier).

THE GEOMETRIC MEAN PORTFOLIO STRATEGY

Which particular point on the efficient frontier you decide to be on (i.e., which particular efficient CPA) is a function of your own risk-aversion preference, at least according to the Markowitz model. However, there is an optimal point to be at on the efficient frontier, and the problem of finding this point is mathematically solvable.

If you choose that CPA which shows the highest geometric mean of the HPRs, you will arrive at the optimal CPA! Recall from Chapter 3 that we can estimate the geometric mean from the arithmetic mean HPR and the population standard deviation of the HPRs (both of which are calculations we already have, as they are the X and Y axes for the Markowitz model!). *The CPA with the highest geometric mean is the CPA that will maximize the growth of the portfolio value over the long run. Furthermore, it will minimize the time required to reach a specified level of equity.* Of course, this is predicated on the ratio of the arithmetic average HPR and the standard deviation remaining relatively the same (which there is a strong tendency in favor of).

Like the idea of optimal f itself, selecting the portfolio with the highest geometric mean is an exercise in asymptotic dominance. What is meant here is that over the next day, week, month, year, and so on, the portfolio with the highest geometric mean (like the optimal f value) may not have a higher growth rate than all other alternative portfolios tested (or any other value of f). However, in the long run, that is, as time approaches infinity, this portfolio (or value for f) will provide the greatest geometric growth rate, with a probability approaching 1. This strategy, of selecting the portfolio with the highest geometric mean, maximizes the probability of the portfolio being more valuable than under any other alternative portfolio selection strategy.

Interestingly, then, the proof that variance of returns is the best measure of risk, as Markowitz contended, can be arrived at indirectly here. Wealth maximization is a function of the risk/reward tradeoff. This mathematical relationship is expressed by the geometric mean, which you will recall from Chapter 3 is estimated as:

EGM = ((arithmetic mean^2) – (standard deviation^2))^(1/2)

which is the same as:

EGM = ((arithmetic mean^2) – variance)^(1/2)

This, per the Markowitz model, is the same as:

EGM = ((reward^2) – risk)^(1/2)

Hence we can state that:

risk = variance

where variance means variance in arithmetic average HPRs, holding period returns. Simply stated, risk equals the variance in returns.

Thus Markowitz's contention that the variance is a good estimate of a portfolio's risk is mathematically correct for the most part. Hence, one of the major complaints against modern portfolio theory—namely, that variance is a poor measure of risk—is, as we have just seen, simply not valid.

At this point, there may be some question as to how you implement this portfolio approach on a day-to-day basis. Again, an example will be used to illustrate.

Suppose our optimal CPA calls for us to be in 3 different market systems. (Rarely will the optimal be more than 3 to 5 different market systems. After this amount the correlation coefficients of the different market systems begin to "swamp" together. Usually the optimals are 2 to 4 market systems.) In this case, suppose the percentage allocation is 10%, 50%, and 40%. If you were looking at a $50,000 account, your account would be "subdivided" into three accounts of $5,000, $25,000, and $20,000 for each market system A, B, and C respectively. Then for each market system's subaccount balance you would figure how many contracts you could trade. Let's say that the f factors dictated the following:

Market system A, 1 contract per $5,000 in account equity.

Market system B, 1 contract per $2,500 in account equity.

Market system C, 1 contract per $2,000 in account equity.

You would then be trading 1 contract for market system A ($5,000/$5,000), 10 contracts for market system B ($25,000/$2,500) and 10 contracts for market system C ($20,000/$2,000).

Each day, as the total equity in the account changes, all subaccounts are recapitalized. What this means is: Suppose that the next day this $50,000 account dropped to $40,000. Since we recapitalize the subaccounts each day, we then have $4,500 for market system subaccount A, $22,500 for market system subaccount B, and $18,000 for market system subaccount C. Thus, we would trade 0 contracts the next day on market system A ($4,500/$5,000 = .9, or, since we always floor to the integer, 0), 9 contracts for market system B ($22,500/$2,500), and 9 contracts for system C ($18,000/$2,000). We always recapitalize the subaccounts each day, regardless of whether there was a profit or a loss. Do not be confused. Subaccount, as used here, is a mental construct.

Another way of doing this that will give us the same answers, and is perhaps easier to understand, is to divide a market system's optimal f amount by its percentage allocation. This gives us a dollar amount by which we then divide the entire account equity to know how many contracts to trade. Since the account equity changes daily, we recapitalize this daily to the new total account equity. In the example we have cited, market system A, at an f value of 1 contract per $5,000 in account equity and a percentage allocation of 10%, yields 1 contract per $50,000 in total account equity ($5,000/.10). Market system B, at an f value of 1 contract per $2,500 in account equity and a percentage allocation of 50%, yields 1 contract per $5,000 in total account equity ($2,500/.50). Market system C, at an f value of 1 contract per $2,000 in account equity and a percentage allocation of 40%, yields 1 contract per $5,000 in total account equity ($2,000/.40). Thus, if we had $50,000 in total account equity, we would trade 1 contract for market system A, 10 contracts for market system B, and 10 contracts for market system C.[7]

---

[7] Note that all we are really doing in effect is a fractional f for each separate market system. (Fractional f was discussed in Chapter 4.) In so doing, we have a portfolio being traded at the optimal f where the components are at fractional f's. If we were to trade the components at the full f value, we would most likely find ourselves too far to the right of the composite f curve for the portfolio as a whole. Also, to not recapitalize the subaccounts, that is, to use a separate bankroll for each market system, generally underperforms the idea of operating from a single bankroll as described here.

Tomorrow we would do the same thing. Let's say our total account equity got up to $59,000. In this case, dividing $59,000 into $50,000 yields 1.18, which floored to the integer is 1, so we would trade 1 contract for market system A. For market system B, we would trade 11 contracts ($59,000/$5,000 = 11.8, which floored to the integer = 11). For market system C we would also be trading 11 contracts, since system C also trades 1 contract for every $5,000 in total account equity.

Suppose we have a trade on from market system C yesterday, and we are long 10 contracts. We do not need to go in and add another today to bring us up to 11 contracts. Rather the amounts we are calculating using the equity as of the most recent close mark-to-market is for new positions only. So, for tomorrow, since we have 10 contracts on, if we get stopped out of this trade (or exit it on a profit target), we will be going 11 contracts on a new trade if one should occur.

How long a time period should you look at when calculating the optimal portfolios? As with the question "How long a time period should you look at to determine the optimal f for a given market system?" there is no definitive answer. Again, the more back data you use, the better your result should be; that is, the more closely should the near optimal portfolios in the future resemble what your study concluded were the near optimal portfolios. However, correlations do change, albeit slowly. One of the problems with using too long a time period is that there will be a tendency to use what were yesterday's hot markets. For instance, if you ran this program in 1983 over 5 years of back data you would most likely have one of the precious metals show very clearly as being a part of the optimal portfolio, but the precious metals did very poorly for most trading systems for quite a few years after the 1980–1981 markets. So you see, in determining the optimal portfolio of the future there is a tradeoff between using too much past history and too little.

Finally, the question arises, "How often should you rerun this entire procedure of finding the optimal portfolio?" Ideally, you should run it continuously. However, rarely will the portfolio composition change. Realistically, you should probably run it about every three months. Even running this program every three months, you are still highly likely to arrive at the same optimal portfolio composition, or one very similar to it, that you arrived at before.

You may be wondering at this point why we don't just take each market system's optimal f in dollars and divide the account equity by that to know how many contracts to trade for each market system. In our $50,000 account example, for market systems A, B, and C we have f values in dollars of $5,000, $2,500, and $2,000 respectively. So we are discussing trading 10 contracts for market system A ($50,000/$5,000),

20 contracts for market system B ($50,000/$2,500) and 25 contracts for market system C ($50,000/$2,000).

This is a valid question the answer to which is that to manage an account in this fashion, even if the markets are uncorrelated, eventually will cause enormous drawdowns, far greater in both depth and frequency than the drawdowns of the individual market systems. Furthermore, by managing an account in this fashion you most likely have put yourself too far out to the right of the f curve of the portfolio as a whole. Recall that the least a historical drawdown may be in terms of percent equity retracement is a value equivalent to the f for that given market system. That is the *least* the drawdown may be. If two market systems go into a drawdown phase simultaneously, you can see that the results could be disastrous if an account were managed this way. (See important notes on using the Div.C Program and Optimal Portfolios in Appendix F for a more thorough discussion of this situation.)

Often, when you construct a portfolio of market systems along these principles, you will end up not trading very many contracts in some market systems. For example, if the optimal f for a particular market works out to be $3,500 per contract, and the optimal portfolio construction calls for 10% of the funds to be allocated to this market system, then you will only be trading one contract of this particular market system for every $35,000 in equity. If you have a $50,000 account, that means you will only be looking to trade one contract at the moment for this particular market system until and if your account equity reaches $70,000.

That, however, is the way you should do it. As soon as you start to trade two contracts and you have less than $70,000 in your account, you have moved to the right of the peak of the f curve of the composite, the whole portfolio. Recall that there is no benefit to be gained by going to the right of the peak, and you pay a price to do so. You can expect your drawdowns to be more severe, and you can expect to make less money than trading per the prescribed formula. This takes discipline.

Do not get the idea that the only way to diversify an account is the way presented in this chapter. That is not true. What is presented in this chapter is one intelligent way to diversify your account, taking the intercorrelations of the daily equity changes of the different market systems and their respective f values into consideration. It is not the only way to accomplish this. Yet it is an intelligent starting point, as well as an introduction to the concepts of portfolio management.

What if you are using a system that trades all of the markets, yet is only in a given market for a small fraction of the year? That is, what if you are only in anywhere from 1 to, say, 4 markets at a time, yet you don't know what those markets will be, or how they will be correlated.

What can you do? For example, suppose your system has you trade only the 3 or 4 markets of highest volatility at any given time, measured by some proprietary measurement of volatility that you have constructed. Obviously you have no control over being in negatively correlated market systems (let's say it could have you in all the currencies at once which tend to have high correlations). Is there a way to structure such a scenario within the total portfolio approach?

Fortunately, there is. Although the correlations of the different markets will not be taken into account, we can make sure that we are not too far to the right of the peak of the *composite* f curve for any combination of market systems that might come up. The way we would do this is to figure the *maximum* number of market systems we may be in at any one time. For the sake of illustration, let us assume that this is 5 markets. Dividing 100% by 5 yields 20% (1.00/5 = .2). Since we know our optimal f's for each possible market system (in terms of dollars to allocate per trade), it is simply a matter of dividing each of these by .2.

As long as we never take on more than 5 market systems, we are operating at the optimal f for the composite, the portfolio of market systems. If we are in less than 5 market systems, that's all right. It may appear that we do not have enough contracts on, but at least we are doing this correctly. If we are in more than 1 but less than 6 commodities, then regardless of how positively correlated they are, we do not have to worry about being farther to the right of the composite, the portfolio's f curve, than the optimal value. Furthermore, by managing an account that trades this way we are consistent in our exposure on each trade, whether we have only 1 market on or the maximum. We will always be to the left of the peak of the f curve of the composite, the portfolio, unless either (a) we have more than the maximum allotted number of market systems on, or (b) we are in the maximum allotted number of market systems and their correlation coefficient (of daily equity changes) is + 1.00 (in which case we are right at the peak of the f curve).

THE SEVERITY OF DRAWDOWN

We know that if we are using the optimal f when fixed fractional trading, we can expect substantial drawdowns in terms of percentage equity retracements. In this chapter we have discussed how diversification can greatly buffer the drawdowns. This it does, but do not expect that you can eliminate drawdown.

Many traders have the mistaken impression that drawdown in terms of equity retracement is not as severe as it is. For instance, I can think of a system on bonds which, when traded on a 1-contract basis, made $86,460 and drew down $2,890 over the test period of January 1982 to June 1989. One would think, then, that the drawdown wouldn't have been too bad on a fixed fractional basis. Well, let's take a look. The optimal f was .85, meaning that the drawdown, if one were trading at the optimal f over the historic test period, would have been at least 85% equity retracement. In fact it was 87.84%! Most people could never handle that. Yet that was the "best" mathematical route to take. In fact, trading at the optimal f value over this test period would have resulted in a gain in excess of 10 trillion dollars. This is no more attainable in real life than my hurling a brick across Lake Erie, yet it demonstrates the enormous power of using the optimal f as well as the concomitant drawdowns to expect.

We have seen in this chapter that drawdown can be partially eliminated through effective diversification. Here again, many people have the mistaken impression that drawdown can be completely eliminated if they diversify effectively enough. I do not want to leave you with that thought. It is true that drawdowns can be buffered to an extent through effective diversification, but they can never be completely eliminated. *Do not be deluded.* No matter how good the systems employed are, no matter how effectively you diversify, you will still encounter substantial drawdowns. The reason is that no matter how uncorrelated your market systems are, a period comes when most or all of the market systems in your portfolio zig in unison against you when they should be zagging. You will have enormous difficulty finding a portfolio with at least five years of historical data to it, and all market systems employing the optimal f, that had any less than a 30% drawdown in terms of equity retracement! This is true no matter how many market systems you employ. It is difficult to put together a portfolio in which all market systems are trading at the half f amounts that has only 30% of its equity erased at one point over a five-year test. These are the facts of life. This is the manifestation of Murphy's famous law. If you want to be in this game and do it mathematically correctly, expect to be nailed for equity retracements of from 30% to 95%. Withstanding these takes enormous discipline. Very few people can emotionally handle it.

Most brokerage firms will not even look at a CTA (commodity trading adviser, who manages the commodity accounts of others) who has historically had a 30% drawdown, nor will they promote a futures pool or fund that has had such a drawdown.[8] Think about that. If you are not at the optimal f, or where you believe it will be in the future, you are

---

[8] Throughout the text, when we refer to drawdown we are referring to an equity curve that, when plotted, would be plotted at the close of each day and be comprised of the

simply diluting the potential of the system. If you have your money in any kind of a managed arrangement and it is not being traded at near optimal amounts, you are being charged a management fee on money that really isn't going toward trading. If the manager is trading $50,000 of yours with as many contracts as a $5,000 account trading at the optimal f, then you are paying that manager to manage $45,000 for nothing. You, the client, would be far better off having the adviser only manage $5,000, trade it at the optimal or near optimal amounts (which will probably seem terribly aggressive), go through the equity swings and come out ahead of the $50,000 account trading the same number of contracts as the $5,000 account. Your gain is that you are not charged an administrative fee on the $45,000 difference and you can put that money to work elsewhere. Remember that when you dilute f, when you trade less contracts than the optimal f calls for, you are reducing your drawdown arithmetically, but your are also reducing your returns geometrically. Why commit funds to futures trading that aren't necessary simply to flatten out the equity curve at the expense of your bottom line profits. *You can diversify cheaply somewhere else.*

Why dilute a system's potential? So that you can emotionally handle the equity retracements? Why not recognize the fallacy of this and vow to live through the roller coaster equity retracements?

Stock fund managers compare their returns to the returns of the S&P 500 over a period. Given the mechanics of capital asset pricing theory this is understandable. People tend to look at managed futures funds on an absolute return basis versus the return of some riskless asset, such as the yield they could get on Treasury Bills. People also look at their returns on managed futures funds on a comparative basis (i.e., compared to other futures fund managers). In the world of stocks there has been a great tendency towards *closet indexing*, trying to have most of the assets under management mimic the S&P index, while only trading

---

current cumulative closed equity plus the mark-to-market equity of any open positions. Drawdown is then expressed as the greatest percentage retracement figured along that line. However, the drawdown published and tracked by many brokerage firms, rating services, and so on, is not quite the same and tends to understate the drawdown relative to our definition. The way many of these entities calculate drawdown is by plotting the equity curve line on a month by month or quarter by quarter basis. This tends to understate the actual drawdown as we have described it (being calculated at the close of each day). The latter way of calculating it, month by month or quarter by quarter, can never yield more of a drawdown than the day by day method. Hence, the day by day method is more realistic, because it is both a more conservative estimate of what to expect and a more realistic one (since it is what you would have experienced on a day by day basis). Who looks at their account equity only at the end of the month or end of the quarter anyhow?

a small portion of the assets under any active management to try and outperform the averages, figuring at worst to only slightly underperform the averages if the active part of the portfolio fails. Managed money in futures has been going a similar route. The funds are diluted by not trading as many contracts as the optimal f would imply. Here there is closet indexing in trying to mimic the return of Treasury Bills, the reason being: If money under management by a futures adviser can get twice the return of Treasury Bills, why take the money away from the manager? There is also closet indexing in managed futures funds when the advisers trade in many more markets than the mathematically optimal number in an attempt to catch any big moves that may develop in any market. This, too, is closet indexing because managing an account this way (i.e., spreading an account thinly among all the markets) is really an attempt to mimic the activity of the average futures fund manager. The purpose here is to be no worse than average. Here, the average futures fund manager's performance is the index.

Perhaps the clients are partly to blame for this, too. How many clients would stick with a futures adviser who lost 85% of their equity? The clients also tend to put too much money with a CTA. Rather than taking $10,000 of pure risk capital, they put the entire $100,000 of their liquid net worth with him. This is simply greed and ignorance at work.

The correct recipe calls for clients to commit only pure risk capital, money they can afford to lose, and expect to see an almost complete equity retracement at some point in time, and perhaps more than once. The adviser, on the other hand, should not dilute the potential profitability of that account by trading only a fraction of the quantities mathematically called for, or trade in more markets than is mathematically optimal. The adviser must be willing to make nonconsensus bets for the client and not worry about trying to get performance equivalent to the yield of Treasury Bills or be in the middle or upper percentile of futures fund managers. There is enormous potential in the futures markets; that is what the client is seeking and paying the adviser to pursue.

7

Covering the Periphery

A SUMMARY OF THE QUANTITATIVE APPROACH

This chapter touches a few bases that have not been covered in the text but are important and illuminating in terms of money management ideas. Before we get to that, however, a quick summary of what we have covered so far in this text is in order.

First, you must be decision oriented (i.e., you must find a system with a positive mathematical expectation *in the future*). Second, you must determine if dependency exists or not between the stream of trades generated by a system. It appears from most testing that dependency among system trades does not exist. Since you are assuming nothing in assuming that dependency does not exist (i.e., if you assume dependency and act on it and are wrong, it is costly; if you assume independence, and are wrong, it does not cost as much), you know that you are best off to trade a fixed fraction of your stake. When you do so, each trade is allocated the same percentage of account equity. Third, you must find what the optimal percentage is for a given distribution of trades. The technique detailed in Chapter 4 will find your optimal f for any given distribution of trades. Fourth and finally, you need to combine various market systems and their respective optimal f's together and find the optimal weightings to maximize growth and minimize downside.

TOUGHER THAN IT LOOKS

Since this is a book primarily for futures traders and account managers, let's take the typical managed futures account. Generally the account manager's fee structure is in two parts. The first part, the administrative fee, is charged at the beginning of a quarter, for that quarter, and usually is for about ½% of the account's total equity per month, or 1½% for the quarter. Some managers do not have administrative fees. The second part of the fee structure is the incentive fee. The incentive fee is charged at the end of the quarter and usually runs about 15% to 25% (depending on how the manager has structured it) of new high equity, accounting further for any withdrawals or additions to the account. New high equity is the highest ending quarterly equity an account has seen since it has been under the guidance of a particular manager.

When we consider management fees, commissions, and slippage (which quite often are more than management fees, incidentally) and interest earned on cash in the account, we can approximate what kind of a percentage return we must really make, if we want to make P% at the end of a quarter, by the formula:

$$((A + P + M)/B) - 1$$

where: $A = 1 + ((\text{Total expected commissions and slippage for the quarter} - \text{Interest earned for the quarter})/E)$

$E = $ Account equity at the beginning of the quarter before administrative fees are deducted.

$P = $ The percentage gain we desire for the investor as a bottom line gain at the end of the quarter.

$B = 1 - \text{administrative fee}$.

$H = $ The high equity mark, beyond which the investor is charged an incentive fee on profits.

$C = P - ((H/E) - 1)$. This variable must be floored to zero (i.e., if $C < 0$ then $C = O$).

$M = (C/(1 - \text{incentive fee})) - C$. This variable reflects how much extra must be made to offset the incentive fee.

Commissions, slippage, and interest earned must all be estimated for the quarter. Hence, our final answer is itself an estimation of how much we must make to return P% to the investor. Our final answer will only be as accurate as our estimations for commissions, slippage, and interest earned. This equation can also be used to judge the effect a change in commissions, interest rates, or different fee structures would have on performance.

Consider this example. Suppose you have or are managing a $50,000 account. You estimate the account will make 2 round trades per week for the next quarter, and each trade will be for about 7 contracts. You are paying $25 commissions per contract per trade and you estimate slippage at another $25 per contract per trade. Further, you estimate earning $1,000 in interest in the account over the next quarter. Assume the account has just been opened, so that the new high equity equals the amount the account was opened with, $50,000. The fee structure calls for an up-front quarterly administrative fee of 1½% and a 15% management fee on new high equity. If the desired return at the end of the quarter is 10%, then here is how much really needs to be made:

$P = .1$

$E = 50,000$

$H = 50,000$

$A = 1 + (((7 * (25 + 25) * 12 \text{ weeks}) - 1,000)/50,000)$

$\quad = 1 + ((4,200 - 1,000)/50,000)$

$\quad = 1 + (3,200/50,000)$

$\quad = 1 + .064$

$\quad = 1.064$

$B = 1 - .015$

$\quad = .985$

$C = .1 - ((50,000/50,000) - 1)$

$\quad = .1 - (1 - 1)$

$\quad = .1 - 0$

$\quad = .1$

$M = (.1/(1 - .15)) - .1$

$\quad = (.1/.85) - .1$

$\quad = .117647 - .1$

$\quad = .017647$

So,

$$((A + P + M)/B) - 1 = ((1.064 + .1 + .017647)/.985) - 1$$
$$= (1.181647/.985) - 1$$
$$= 1.199641624 - 1$$
$$= .199641624$$

In other words, in order for the investor to see a 10% net return at the end of the quarter he or she needs to really make in excess of 19.96%. For this account to grow to $55,000, it must make almost a 20% return this quarter!

Now suppose a tough quarter is encountered and the $50,000 account goes down to $45,000. With all other constraints the same as just described, and if we want to get this account up to $55,000, a 22.22% gain, what we must really make is:

$P = .2222$

$E = 45,000$

$H = 50,000$

$A = 1 + (((7 * (25 + 25) * 12 \text{ weeks}) - 1,000)/45,000)$

$\quad = 1 + ((4,200 - 1,000)/45,000)$

$\quad = 1 + (3,200/45,000)$

$\quad = 1 + .0711$

$\quad = 1.0711$

$B = 1 - .015$

$\quad = .985$

$C = .2222 - ((50,000/45,000) - 1)$

$\quad = .2222 - (1.1111 - 1)$

$\quad = .2222 - .1111$

$\quad = .1111$

$M = (.1111/(1 - .15)) - .1111$

$\quad = (.1111/.85) - .1111$

$\quad = .1307058824 - .1111$

$\quad = .0196058824$

So,

$$((A + P + M)/B) - 1 = ((1.0711 + .2222 + .0196058824)/.985) - 1$$
$$= (1.312905882/.985) - 1$$
$$= 1.332899373 - 1$$
$$= .332899373$$

As can be seen, in such a case the account must make in excess of 33% to go from $45,000 to $55,000 in one quarter.

Sometimes the administrative fee is not charged up front; that is, it is charged at the end of the quarter rather than at the beginning of the quarter. In such a case, our formula becomes:

$$A + ((M + P) * (1 + \text{administrative fee})) - 1$$

For our two examples, then, we need to make 18.34117% and 31.65329706% respectively. However, this equation tells us what we need to make if the administrative fee is charged *before* the incentive fee. When the incentive fee is charged before the administrative fee, and both charges occur at the end of a quarter, the formula becomes:

$$A + M + (P * (1 + \text{administrative fee})) - 1$$

which, in reference to our two examples, means we must make 18.3147% and 31.62388824% respectively.

All of these equations bear out a distressing point—managing money is tougher than it looks. For the investor, the game is almost equally tough should she choose not to have her account professionally managed. In such a case, the formula for percent gain required in order to net a gain of P% is given by:

$$A + P - 1$$

In our two examples this would result in gains needed of $1.064 + .1 - 1 = 16.4\%$ (versus 19.96% for a managed account) and $1.0711 + .2222 - 1 = 29.33\%$ (versus 33.29% for a managed account). Clearly, whether money is professionally managed or not, the scenario is tougher than it looks, and it is easy to see how investors and managers delude themselves into thinking it is easier than it really is. That is dangerous—the mathematics of the situation dictate that we must make every effort to perform at optimum levels.

SCALE TRADING SYSTEMS
(TACTICAL TRADING SYSTEMS)

Lately, there has been a great deal of interest in what are called "scale trading" or "tactical trading" systems. Essentially, these systems take a position and immediately place an order for taking profits, usually a small distance away from their entry price. If the market moves adversely for them before hitting their profit objective, the traders of such systems will add to their already losing positions, usually adding more contracts than the original position, and moving their profit objective down as well. They will keep on doing this until ultimately their profit objective is met and they will net out a small gain. This is akin to the martingale idea of betting. Here is an example of how these systems tend to work:

1. The trader buys 1 bond at 9800 and places an order to take profits on this one contract at 9916 or better, for a profit of $1,500 before commissions and fees.

2. Suppose that the 9916 is not seen; rather, the market trades down to 9700. Here the trader buys 2 more bonds at 9700 and changes the profit-taking order to sell 3 bonds at 9727 or better, leaving roughly a $1,500 profit on the net of all contracts before commissions and fees.

3. Now suppose the market trades down to 9600 before 9727 is seen. The position is underwater to the tune of $4,000. The trader now may buy 4 contracts at 9600 and changes the profit target to selling 7 bonds at 9625 or better for roughly a $1,500 profit net on all contracts before commissions and fees.

Returning to Chapter 3 regarding martingale-type systems, we see that the problem is the ceiling on how many contracts/bets may be assumed, because of either house limits or undercapitalization. Although house limits are not a consideration in the markets (with the exception of those markets where the position limit rules come into play), undercapitalization is a problem. In a prolonged adverse move, the trader will have lots of contracts on (meaning lots of required initial margin *plus* the maintenance of the contracts that are underwater) and if the target isn't hit will have to add on yet more contracts. Everyone has a breaking point with these types of systems. Either people don't have the capital to continue to add to the positions or emotionally there is some level of heat at which they will be unable to add to their already losing position.

There are two possible methods to get around the undercapitalization problem. The first is to have virtually unlimited capital (and trade in markets with no position limits). The second is to trade those markets that have a boundary as to how far an adverse move against you can go. Although no market has an upside limit (with the *possible* exception of some credit instruments), every market has a downside limit of zero. Therefore, it makes sense to trade a system like this on a severely depressed market, at or near 0, where even if that market should decline to zero, you still have the capitalization to carry the full position. A good example might be sugar at below 3 cents per pound. These situations are not very common. Since you are looking to repeatedly make small profits with 100% reliability, you'll have to live a long time or have virtually unlimited capital to do it trading markets where you have the capitalization to carry longs all the way to 0 if necessary.

Furthermore, since it takes virtually unlimited capital to trade this way, and since it is the goal of each attempt to net out a small profit, you can never experience geometric growth because you can never have more than 1 attempt running simultaneously.

As a final consideration, recall that the sum of a series of negative expectancy bets must be a negative expectancy. Unless you are entering these trades based on some trading system that has a proven positive mathematical expectation on a one-contract basis you are asking for trouble. Just like the gambler betting à la martingale on red or black in roulette, you may win the majority of the time (i.e., the trade will work out for a small net profit), but when you lose it will be for an enormous amount. To trade a scale or tactical type of system, whereby you are entering on an arbitrary basis (i.e., entering because the gambling scheme has you entering rather than by a proven entry technique with a positive mathematical expectation on a one-contract basis), is akin to betting à la martingale on a negative expectancy basis. Remember, due to commissions, slippage, and fees, simply entering a market arbitrarily causes a negative expectation. A negative expectation, if you will recall from Chapter 1, no matter how small, guarantees eventual ruin. Therefore, to trade a scale or tactical system, making your entries and exits based upon such a gambling scheme, will mathematically guarantee eventual ruin. You may make profits for a long time in the meantime, yet these systems are simply not mathematically sound in the long run.

A trader is better off seeking a system that makes profits on a basis other than depending upon any type of gambling progression or scheme. There are other good systems out there, so to trade scale or tactical systems, which as you have seen are mathematically unsound, makes no sense at all.

OLD AXIOMS THAT CAN STAND ON THEIR OWN

Since we're in the key of adding to losing positions, we might as well acknowledge that there is a lot to be said for the following age-old axioms:

"Never average down."

"Never meet a margin call."

"If you must lighten up, liquidate your worst position."

These adages are not new. Yet they make a great deal of sense and should always be adhered to. They make logical sense by the same argument we just discussed in opposing scale or tactical types of systems.

To those three adages I would add one more:

"Always know your positions and your equity."

I won't elaborate much on this except to say that it is akin to playing a game where you're not paying attention. To not pay attention is to invite mistakes.

AVOIDING AND HANDLING MISTAKES

Suppose you are the shortstop for the Cleveland Indians. There are no outs, and runners are on first and third. The batter hits a one-hopper to you. Do you just throw it to first and throw him out? Do you throw to second and go for the double-play? No! The play is at the plate. You should have known this before the batter stepped into the batter's box. You should have said to yourself, "The play is at the plate unless I catch a line drive, in which case I then look over to third to see if the man on third has gone back to the bag."

It is the same thing in the markets. You must know going into today what your positions and equity are. This way you will know how many contracts to take on a trade that your system may have you take today, and so you have a backstop, in that if you have made a mistake you will be made aware of it. This is a heads-up business.

Since we're discussing avoiding mistakes, I might throw in another adage, which is:

"The first mistake is usually the cheapest mistake."

You can put that in the bank. As a system trader you probably know how, all too often, a simple mistake that is not remedied quickly tends to cascade into multiple mistakes.

For example, suppose you are trading a system that would have you exit your current position at the market on the open tomorrow. Say you want to play it fast and loose; you think the market is going to continue moving in your favor after the open. The market opens and—guess what?—the open was the best price you could have had all day. You're still in the position and it's moving against you. You should be out of this position, but now you're underwater on it. Your system at this point is putting on another trade in the opposite direction, and with the optimal f factor, you should be putting that trade on with more contracts if you were strictly following the system. Instead of being in sync with the system, you're still holding onto the old trade, hoping that it comes back to the open so you can catch up with the system.

Forget it, it won't. The first mistake is the cheapest mistake *especially for system traders!* In the markets, with the unavoidable emotional drain, mistakes are not only common, you can count on them. When a mistake is made, shoulder the consequences (i.e., take the immediate loss) and immediately get back in line with the system.

TAKING PROFITS

A common, classic error is not taking profits out of an account. Recall that in a compounding function the earlier in the process that you withdraw funds, the greater the adverse effect on the compounding function. Yet at some point you must begin withdrawing at least a portion of your winnings. When you do this later in the compounding function, the effect is not so severe. You should do this if for no other reason than that, if the account blows up, you then have the capital to establish a new account. This makes sense from a mathematical stand-point. The edge that a trading system has over the markets shifts over time (the distribution of the stream of profits and losses that a trading system generates is non-stationary). Some months are better than others, some years are better than others. If you have racked up a substantial gain, it only makes sense to salt some away so that, if the edge should move severely against you for some period, you have enough to come back with.

A LAST LOOK AT DRAWDOWN

In Chapter 4 we blasted drawdown, relegating it to the heap of useless measures. The purpose was to get you away from looking at drawdown as the measure of risk that it so mistakenly is regarded as being. Yet there are a couple of uses for keeping track of the drawdown. The first of these is that if drawdown is exceeded it may be a really good idea to pack it in with that system for a while and wait until the system goes back to a new equity high. Here we are talking about drawdown being exceeded on a 1-contract basis (assuming, of course, that the drawdown we are comparing the current 1-contract drawdown against is derived from at least 5 years of back data and at least 30 trades). If a system is going to blow up, it is going to exceed the historical drawdown. Of course, it may be just exceeding the historical drawdown and about ready to go into a terrific drawup, but you don't know that. If you don't want to be in a system when it blows up then vow to get out if the maximum historical drawdown is ever exceeded, and not get back into trading the system until it completely earns back that drawdown amount (i.e., goes to new equity highs on a 1-contract basis). The second use of drawdown is that if the historical drawdown is exceeded, this may indicate some heretofore undetected dependence in that particular market system that can possibly be exploited.

On another topic, there is no reason in the world not to be getting interest on the funds in your account—someone is. Always have excess funds placed into treasuries or some type of a money market sweep. Remember the equations in "Tougher Than It Looks"? Even though we are talking about a relatively small percentage gain compared to what we're trying to make trading the futures, we need every edge we can get, and interest on our funds is just one small benefit we should be taking advantage of.

REGARDING REPORTS

Now for a very important point for system traders. *Always be flat going into a report.* Another old adage but well worth repeating. So many systems that come out of the computer looking so good blow up in real time solely as a result of report days. The problem here is one of illiquidity. Let's say you are entering on a stop order. If it is the initial impact of the report that propels prices to and through your stop point, then you are very likely to suffer extreme slippage on the entry. If the report propels prices to and through a protective stop for a position you are carrying into the report, the same thing can happen. There is also the chance of lock-limit situations against you due to a report. Another common report-day occurrence is wide-swinging, volatile, high-volume days where the computer guys and system traders tend to get whipsawed to death. It just doesn't pay to be in the markets in that kind of an environment. Sure, on occasion you'll watch your system be in line with the report on a trade that you passed and as a result you'll have to forego some big profits. But, by and large, if a system is any good it usually is best in a somewhat quiet, more normal kind of market.

Consider a system that historically has greater than 50% winning trades. It is illogical to trade such systems on report days. Logically, you have to assume fifty-fifty probabilities coming into a report. It can go either way—for you or against you. If you have a system that has greater than 50% accuracy, why be in there on days when this percentage is dropped down to fifty-fifty? Trade the more normal days and take advantage of that higher percentage your system gives you. Why risk getting whipped to death on one crazy day?

Although this is not following the system to the letter, since historically the computer doesn't know a report day from any other day, you'll find you are light-years ahead to go flat into a report, and stay out until the froth in the market caused by the report has dissipated. By doing so, you can often actually improve the real-time results of a system and drastically lower the total slippage. In the end, you raise your mathematical expectation.

What reports to sit out is a difficult question that changes over time. You have to pay attention to the markets and what the big reports are at that time. This is the kind of work you should do well in advance of the reports, when you have time away from the grind of the markets. That way, you can know in advance what days that week you will be sitting out of what markets. This is not the kind of thing you want to be doing five minutes before the open of trading on a day when a report is due out.

AVOIDING CATASTROPHE

One of the big problems with trading is when the unexpected adverse event occurs. You are short orange juice and an unexpected freeze hits Florida overnight or a stock you are short is bought out. Anything can happen.

Fortunately there are options. One of the nice things about long options is the limited liability. Your liability is limited to the price you paid for the option if you are long. Yet trading options is for most traders far more difficult than trading stocks or futures. This is so because options decay in price over time. Yet there is a way we can use options in our trading to limit our liability in trading futures or stocks to a pre-determined amount.

Say we are trading coffee. In the summer months, coffee is very vulnerable to a quick upward burst in price due to a freeze in South America. If we want to trade coffee in the summer and protect ourselves from getting trapped on a short position, we can buy a call on coffee for every futures position we are trading. Now, if we are short and the market moves adversely against us, once coffee gets up to the strike price of our call (assuming we are doing this with out-the-money options) we are covered on the futures for any further advances against our short position.

We are using this technique simply as insurance. We can use it in any market that has options, and we can do it with puts, calls, or both. Just in case things get away from us, we have an escape hatch in the form of the options. Say we buy an out-the-money put and an out-the-money call. In any event, we are protected if the price of the futures runs outside the boundaries of these strike prices. Although the options are decaying against us continuously, we have effectively put a cap, a limit, on the extent of any catastrophic risk we may encounter in that market while we have those options.

And while we are on the topic of escape hatches and avoiding catastrophic losses, it's a good idea to have a set of contingency plans already in place should the unexpected happen. What is meant here is getting caught in a bad spot with positions on. Even if you're sitting out reports, it's possible to be in a position that you cannot get out of. This usually happens due to lock-limit situations. You should have a set of contingency plans laid out in case such a thing happens.

For instance, suppose you are long T-bonds, and some news event comes up that will severely hit the bond market. If it's during market hours, you can get out in the market itself, unless it's lock-limit against you. You should find out if you can buy puts in the options market (to protect yourself) if the bonds are lock-limit down or calls if you are short and the market is lock-limit up. You should know this in advance. What if it's the middle of the night? Can you cover or at least spread against your position in Singapore or London? You should have all of this planned out in advance so that if the unexpected disaster happens you can go to your plans and know what to do. You will be able to react to the situation immediately, without having to think, hesitate, or stall.

Again, it all gets down to being prepared. Risk is minimized by being prepared. Whether it is what to do if you make a mistake, or if the markets blow up in your face, or if there is a big report due out in ten minutes, by being prepared you can eliminate a great deal of the risk, not to mention the emotional benefits preparedness allows you in the marketplace. That alone will help eliminate even more mistakes.

THE NON-STATIONARY DISTRIBUTION
OF SYSTEM TRADES

On several occasions throughout the text, mention has been made of the fact that the profit and loss stream of trades generated by a trading system resembles that of a non-stationary distribution. Not only does the profit and loss stream of trades generated by a trading system resemble that of a non-stationary distribution, the changes in prices of commodities (and stocks) also resemble a non-stationary distribution. This is true whether we are looking at daily, weekly, monthly, yearly, or minute-to-minute fluctuations in prices! Is it any wonder, then, that market researchers have had such a difficult time pinning down exactly what kind of distribution is at work in price changes (as well as the stream of P&L's generated by trading systems).

Figure 7–1 bears out this phenomenon. Here you see a series of identical stationary distributions. Yet, as they move around through time, the composite distribution (the bold line) has a flatter top as well as thicker tails (so that the composite distribution resembles the *student's* distribution). This is what we are wrestling with when we look at the profit and loss stream of trades generated by a trading system or the changes in prices of the commodities or stocks themselves. What's more, the distributions in Figure 7–1 do not change shape (with respect to skewness or kurtosis), whereas in reality the distributions not only move around, they also change their shape.

The fact that the stream of profits and losses from trading systems appear as non-stationary distributions is the main reason why systems go into up and down phases. Many people have the mistaken impression that this is because the parameters being used in the system have changed. Yet such is rarely the case. Usually, when a system goes into a down phase, the performance of the system at any parameter value suffers. So it's not so much that systems go into drawdowns because the parameters have changed as it is that the distribution of the stream of profits and losses generated by the system (at any parameter value) has changed to an unfavorable state.

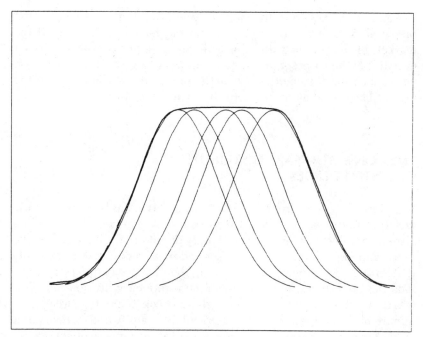

Figure 7-1   A series of identical non-stationary distributions.

Recall that a stream of data, such as we are discussing, can be non-stationary and independent. That is, the outcome of each event in the stream is independent of the previous outcomes. Throughout the text, we have addressed the stream as being independent and stationary. How, then, can we tell when the distributions are changing into favorable or unfavorable shapes or positions?

Fortunately, this last question can be answered. Although there are no valid statistical techniques that will tell us in advance when a distribution will become favorable or unfavorable,[1] there are valid techniques that tell us *as early as possible* that the distribution has shifted favorably or unfavorably. Thus, the damage done or opportunity lost can be minimized.

We have avoided categorizing the distribution of the stream of profits and losses generated by a trading system as a non-stationary distribution. Rather, we have treated this stream as a stationary distribution. This has kept things simple enough so that all of the bases we have

[1] This assumes independence between the events comprising the distribution as well as that there is no causal relationship, or no *known* causal relationship, between the current distribution's shape and location and any prior shape and location.

covered thus far could be readily understood. What we have covered throughout this text is also directly applicable to a non-stationary distribution. However, the tools for monitoring a non-stationary distribution add a new dimension to what we have covered—not that they alter what we have covered in this text; rather, they make the concepts that we have covered more powerful by showing us the most opportune times to apply them, as well as when to change the markets and systems that we are monitoring. To adequately discuss the statistical techniques for early detection of change in a non-stationary distribution would require an entire text, and is therefore beyond the scope of this one.

UPSIDE POTENTIAL

Consider the upside potential of using optimal f on a positive mathematical expectancy situation, where you are properly diversified (so that the drawdowns experienced take the minimal time to recover from). Start out with a mere $5,000, and double it. If you have a halfway decent system, this shouldn't be beyond the realm of possibility. With optimal f, going from $10,000 to $20,000 is the same exercise as going from $5,000 to $10,000 (just as going from $500,000 to $1,000,000 is exactly the same exercise—exactly the same trades). The only thing that can trip you up is liquidity, yet markets today can handle enormous quantities. Liquidity should be no problem whatsoever for all but the largest fund managers. If you can double $5,000, you can double $500,000. It is effectively the same exercise. Starting with $5,000 let's see what happens if we double it eight times:

	$5,000
1st doubling	$10,000
2nd doubling	$20,000
3rd doubling	$40,000
4th doubling	$80,000
5th doubling	$160,000
6th doubling	$320,000
7th doubling	$640,000
8th doubling	$1,280,000

Most people do not comprehend how fast a geometric progression grows. This is what the techniques in this book (like optimal f) maximize. Now you know what market systems to combine together in what percents, and how many contracts to trade for each market system so that the geometric growth rates are optimized in the mathematically correct fashion.

Finally, remember that just as bear markets come and go in stocks, so do drawdowns come and go in futures systems. If you are a trader, then you know that your account exists in one of two states. Either you are at equity highs, or you are in drawdown. Since equity highs are not sustainable forever, savor those moments when you are at them. Further, you should recognize that equity highs are followed by drawdowns just as night follows day, and should learn to be comfortable with this fact.

We must learn to be able to live in an environment that is characterized by being in a drawdown most of the time. We must learn to be able to live in a state of always wondering when the current drawdown will end and new equity highs be seen again.

APPENDIX A

Using a Negative Mathematical Expectation Market System

In Chapter 3 mention was made of the keystone money-management rule, that being that for an independent trials process, where you have only one game or market system going, you must have a positive mathematical expectation. If you do not have a positive mathematical expectation in a single-game case, then no money-management strategy can create one.

When you have more than one game or market system running concurrently, such as when you are trading a portfolio of market systems, the rules are different. Now, a game with a negative mathematical expectation may be an ideal candidate for inclusion, provided its negative correlation to the other market systems in the portfolio is strong enough.

Consider, for the sake of simplicity, the two-to-one coin-toss example once more. If a coin is tossed and comes up heads, you win $2; if the coin comes up tails, you lose $1. You know that your mathematical expectation in such a game is fifty cents. Further, the optimal f in this situation is .25, and yields a geometric mean of 1.0607.

Now let's consider a different game, whereby if we lose on a coin toss we lose $1.10, and if we win we only win $.90. Such a game has a negative mathematical expectation, that being − .10. If this were the only game we were to play, then there is no money-management strategy that we could employ to turn it into a positive expectation game. If we continue to play, it is simply a matter of time until we are completely wiped out, with a probability that approaches certainty. Obviously, for such a scenario there is no optimal f, and hence there is no geometric mean, either.

Say we play both games simultaneously. Further, assume that in the second game we win on heads and lose on tails.

	Game 1	Game 2	Composite
Heads	+2	+.9	+2.9
Tails	−1	−1.1	−2.1

Here, the two games are positively correlated—they either both win or both lose. The mathematical expectation is forty cents, compared to fifty cents for the straight two-to-one game. The optimal f on the composite is .14, yielding a geometric mean of 1.013, versus the geometric mean of the straight two-to-one game of 1.0607.

Now let's look at what happens if we win on tails on the second game. This will make the linear correlation coefficient between the two games negative.

	Game 1	Game 2	Composite
Heads	+2	−1.1	+.9
Tails	−1	+.9	−.1

For this game the mathematical expectation is again forty cents. However, the optimal f is .44, which yields a geometric mean of 1.666!

Remember that the geometric mean is the growth factor per play. In the last scenario, the geometric mean, the growth factor, is more than ten times greater than the straight two-to-one coin toss, yet it is obtained by combining the straight two-to-one coin toss with a negative expectation game! Such is the importance of the linear correlation of returns.

Programming the Functions Described in the Text

Listed in this appendix are programs in both BASIC and the C language. Some are in both languages, and some are in just one of the languages. As for the programs in BASIC, I have tried to make them as generic as possible, to run on as many different machines, operating systems, and dialects of BASIC as possible with only slight modifications, if any, required. The BASIC programs can be run in the BASICA or GWBASIC interpreter environment for the IBM PC® or compatibles under PC or MS DOS version 2.0 or higher. These Basic interpreters are provided with your computer.

The C programs were written for the the IBM PC and compatibles using PC or MS-DOS® version 2.0 or higher and the Microsoft® C Compiler version 5.0, using the large library. Again, with only slight modifications these programs should run on any computer, operating system, or C Compiler.

First, we see a short program in BASIC that performs a number of functions that have been discussed in the text. Essentially, in this program the user will key in the individual profits and losses from a series of system trades or bets, and the program will return the optimal f, risk of ruin at a user-specified level for R3 and R6, linear correlation coefficient, Z score, geometric mean, geometric average trade, and terminal wealth relative, as well as how much would have actually been made if the system had traded at the optimal f amount (on an integer-bet basis). There is lots of room for embellishments in the code if you like. For instance, you may want the program to read from a file of individual profits and losses, or you may want to add more calculations to the output.

As for the individual calculations, the main variables used are:

TCONT The total number of trades.

TRAX(X) The individual trade profits and losses from trade number 1 through TCONT.

BL The biggest loss.

AW The average win.

LW the average loss.

The geometric average trade is calculated on line 1060. The risk of ruin, R3, is calculated on line 750, and R6 is calculated on lines 590–700. Linear correlation is in lines 870–930. The terminal wealth relative, geometric mean, and optimal f are calculated in lines 990–1060. The optimal f is also optionally calculated via parabolic interpolation in lines 1130–1300. The total amount that would have been made if you had traded the sequence at the optimal f is figured in 1070–1110. Finally, the runs test, or Z score, is calculated in line 1350.

This program is presented not so much to use or embellish as is, but rather so that you may see how the individual parts work. For example, you may want to know how to program up finding the optimal f via parabolic interpolation. That can be studied in this program, as can other calculations that have been covered in the text. The program is shown first in BASIC, and later the same program is shown in C (this program can also be run on the Microsoft Quickc Compiler).

Cash.BAS Program (in BASIC)

```
10 REM CASH.BAS, A PROGRAM TO DEMONSTRATE SOME OF THE CONCEPTS
20 REM EXPLAINED IN THE TEXT
100 CLS
110 LOCATE 1,1
120 INPUT"DO YOU WISH TO FIND f VIA PARABOLIC INTERPOLATION (Y/N)";FPARB$
130 IF FPARB$="y" THEN FPARB$="Y" ELSE IF FPARB$="n" THEN FPARB$="N"
140 IF FPARB$><"Y" AND FPARB$><"N" THEN 110
150 DIM TRAX(1000) 'ALLOWS UP TO 1000 TRADES - BUT YOU CAN DIM IT TO MORE
160 DEF FNCHINT(X)=INT(X+.5) 'ROUNDS TO NEAREST INTEGER,
                            'NOT RESTRICTED TO <32,000
170 PRINT
180 PRINT "INPUT THE VALUES FOR THE BETS/TRADES YOU WISH TO COMPUTE"
190 PRINT "INPUT AN X WHEN FINISHED."
200 PRINT
210 FLAG%=0:TCONT=1
220 WHILE FLAG%=0
230 INPUT"", X$
240 IF X$="X" OR X$="x" THEN FLAG%=1:TCONT=TCONT-1
250 IF X$<>"X" AND X$<>"x" THEN TRAX(TCONT)=VAL(X$):TCONT=TCONT+1
260 WEND
270 PRINT
280 PRINT "YOU INPUT A TOTAL"TCONT"BETS/TRADES"
290 INPUT "PERCENT OF ACCOUNT DEPLETION TILL RUIN ";DEPLE
300 IF DEPLE>1 THEN DEPLE=DEPLE/100
310 WT=0:BL=999999!:FOR Y=1 TO TCONT:IF TRAX(Y)<BL THEN BL=TRAX(Y)
```

```
320 IF TRAX(Y)>0 THEN WT=WT+1
330 NEXT
340 GOSUB 850
350 GOSUB 1310
360 PRINT
370 INPUT "OUTPUT DEVICE (1. Screen  2. Printer  3.File) ";IOO%
380 IF IOO%=1 THEN PRTR$="SCRN:" ELSE IF IOO%=2 THEN PRTR$="PRN"
        ELSE IF IOO%<>3 THEN GOTO 370
390 IF IOO%=3 THEN INPUT "FILENAME FOR OUTPUT ",PRTR$
400 OPEN PRTR$ FOR OUTPUT AS #1
410 'NOW OUTPUT THE RESULTS
420 CLS
430 PRINT#1, "FOR THE FOLLOWING BETS/TRADES:"
440 FOR X=1 TO TCONT
450 PRINT#1, TRAX(X)
460 NEXT
470 PRINT#1," "
480 IF GEOMEAN#<=0 OR TRUEF<=0 THEN GOTO 550
490 PRINT#1,"GEOMETRIC AVERAGE TRADE =";
500 PRINT #1, USING "$$#####,.##";(GEOMEAN#-1)*ABS(BL/TRUEF)
510 PRINT #1,"GEOMETRIC MEAN =";
520 PRINT #1, USING"###.####";GEOMEAN#
530 PRINT #1,"TERMINAL WEALTH RELATIVE =";
540 PRINT #1, USING "#############,.###";TWR#
550 IF TRUEF<=0 THEN GOTO 1370
560 PRINT#1, "TRUE OPTIMAL f ="FNCHINT(TRUEF*100)/100"OR 1 CONTRACT
                FOR EVERY";
570 PRINT #1, USING"$$#####,.##";ABS(BL/TRUEF);
580 IF FPARB$><"Y" THEN PRINT#1,"" ELSE PRINT#1," ITERATIVE PASSES ="PCOUNT%
590 RA=WT/TCONT
600 VAF=((AW/ABS(BL/TRUEF))*RA)-((ABS(AL/ABS(BL/TRUEF))*(1-RA))
610 FAL=((RA*((AW/ABS(BL/TRUEF))^2))+((1-RA)*((AL/ABS(BL/TRUEF))^2)))^(1/2)
620 PAF=.5*(1+(VAF/FAL))
630 FAN=0:N=1
640 X=1:Y=0:FAP=1
650 WHY=1/X:IF X=1 THEN WHY=DEPLE
660 UAL=WHY/FAL
670 SEA=((((ABS(BL/TRUEF)/X)+ABS(BL/TRUEF))-((1-WHY)*ABS(BL/TRUEF)))
        /ABS(BL/TRUEF))/FAL
680 Y=1-((((((1-PAF)/PAF)^UAL)-1)/((((1-PAF)/PAF)^SEA)-1))
690 IF X<=N THEN FAP=FAP*Y:X=X+1:GOTO 650
700 FAN=FAN+FAP:IF FAP>.00001 THEN N=N+1:GOTO 640
710 PRINT#1,"PERCENT OF ACCOUNT DEPLETION TILL RUIN ";DEPLE*100"%"
720 PRINT#1,"RISK OF RUIN (FIXED FRACTION)    = ";
730 PRINT #1, USING"#.#####";FAN
740 PRINT#1,"RISK OF RUIN (CONSTANT CONTRACT) = ";
750 PRINT #1, USING"#.#####";((1-PAF)/PAF)^(DEPLE/FAL)
760 PRINT#1,"EVERY";
770 PRINT #1, USING"$$######,";YUNG;
780 PRINT#1," OF INITIAL EQUITY GREW TO";
790 PRINT #1, USING"$$###############,";(ACCU#)+(YUNG)
800 PRINT#1,"Z SCORE =";
810 PRINT #1, USING"###.####";ZSCORE
820 PRINT#1,"LINEAR CORRELATION = ";
830 PRINT #1, USING"##.####";PEARSON
840 GOTO 1370
850 'PERFORM MAIN CALCULATIONS
860 PEARSON=0:GEOMEAN#=0:TWR#=0:TRUEF=0:IF TCONT<2 OR BL>=0 THEN RETURN
870 PEAR1=0:FOR X=1 TO TCONT:PEAR1=PEAR1+TRAX(X):NEXT:
880 XBAR=(PEAR1-TRAX(TCONT))/(TCONT-1)
890 YBAR=(PEAR1-TRAX(1))/(TCONT-1):SIGXY=0:SIGY=0:SIGXQ=0:SIGYQ=0
900 FOR X=1 TO (TCONT-1):SIGXY=SIGXY+((TRAX(X)-XBAR)*(TRAX(X+1)-YBAR))
910 SIGXQ=SIGXQ+((TRAX(X)-XBAR)*(TRAX(X)-XBAR))
920 SIGYQ=SIGYQ+((TRAX(X+1)-YBAR)*(TRAX(X+1)-YBAR)):NEXT
930 IF (SIGXQ=0 OR SIGYQ=0) THEN GOTO 940 ELSE PEARSON=SIGXY/(SQR(SIGXQ)*
        SQR(SIGYQ))
940 AW=0:AL=0:WCNX=0:LCNX=0:FOR X=1 TO TCONT
950 IF TRAX(X)>0 THEN AW=AW+TRAX(X):WCNX=WCNX+1
960 IF TRAX(X)<=0 THEN LW=LW+TRAX(X):LCNX=LCNX+1
970 NEXT:AW=AW/WCNX:LW=LW/LCNX
980 F=.01:F2=0:TWR2#=0
990 'START INTO THE LOOP THROUGH TRADES
1000 TWR#=1:HPR#=1:IF F>1 THEN F=1
1010 FOR X=1 TO TCONT
```

```
1020 HPR#=(1+(F*(TRAX(X)/ABS(BL)))):TWR#=TWR#*HPR#
1030 NEXT
1040 IF TWR#>TWR2# THEN TWR2#=TWR#:F2=F:F=F+.01:IF F2<.999 THEN GOTO 990
1050 IF TWR#<=TWR2# OR F2>=.999 THEN TWR#=TWR2#:TRUEF=F2
1060 GEOMEAN#=TWR#^(1/TCONT)
1070 YUNG=ABS(BL/TRUEF)
1080 ACCU#=0:KON%=1:FOR X=1 TO TCONT:KON=INT(ACCU#/YUNG)
1090 IF KON<1 THEN KON=1
1100 ACCU#=ACCU#+(TRAX(X)*KON)
1110 NEXT
1120 IF FPARB$="N" THEN RETURN
1130 'PARABOLIC INTERPOLATION
1140 TOLERANCE=.005:PCOUNT%=0
1150 PT1=0:PT3=1:P3X=0:P1X=0:PT2=1-TOLERANCE
1160 TWTEMP#=1
1170 PCOUNT%=PCOUNT%+1
1180 TWTEMP#=1
1190 FOR X=1 TO TCONT:HPR#=(1+(PT2*(TRAX(X)/ABS(BL))))
1200 TWTEMP#=TWTEMP#*HPR#:NEXT
1210 P2X=TWTEMP#^(1/TCONT)
1220 X=((PT2-PT1)*(P2X-P3X)-(PT2-PT3)*(P2X-P1X))
1230 IF X=0 THEN X=.00001
1240 ABSCISSA=PT2-.5*((((PT2-PT1)^2)*(P2X-P3X)-((PT2-PT3)^2)*(P2X-P1X))/X)
1250 TPT2=PT2
1260 IF ABS(ABSCISSA-TPT2)<=TOLERANCE THEN TRUEF=TPT2:RETURN
1270 IF ABSCISSA>TPT2 THEN PT1=PT2:P1X=P2X
1280 IF ABSCISSA<TPT2 THEN PT3=PT2:P3X=P2X
1290 PT2=ABSCISSA
1300 GOTO 1170
1310 'NOW DO RUNS TEST
1320 RNS=1:FOR X=2 TO TCONT
1330 IF (TRAX(X)>0 AND TRAX(X-1)<=0) OR (TRAX(X)<=0 AND
               TRAX(X-1)>0) THEN RNS=RNS+1
1340 NEXT
1350 ZSCORE=(TCONT*(RNS-.5)-(2*WT*(TCONT-WT)))/SQR(((2*WT*(TCONT-WT))*
               ((2*WT*(TCONT-WT))-TCONT))/(TCONT-1))
1360 RETURN
1370 'END/RESTART PROMPT
1380 PRINT
1390 INPUT "HIT <ENTER> TO INPUT NEW TRADES, OR <E>ND  ",BRCH$
1400 IF BRCH$="E" OR BRCH$="e" THEN END
1410 IF BRCH$="" OR BRCH$=" " THEN RUN
1420 GOTO 1370
```

Cash.C Program (in C)

```c
/* cash.c - a program to demonstrate some of the */
/* functions described in the book.  This is the */
/* same thing as cash.bas, only written in C     */

#include<stdio.h>
#include<stdlib.h>
#include<math.h>
#include<string.h>
#include<graph.h>
#include<conio.h>
#include<dos.h>
#include<process.h>

#define MAXCHLEN 80

static double  accu_dbl             = 0.0;
static float   al                   = 0.0;
static float   aw                   = 0.0;
static float   bl                   = 0.0;
static char    fparb_str[MAXCHLEN]  = "\0";
static double  geomean_dbl          = 0.0;
static int     pcount_int           = 0;
static float   pearson              = 0.0;
static int     tcont                = 0;
static float   trax[1001];


static float   truef                = 0.0;
```

```
static double   twr_dbl            = 0.0;
static int      wt                 = 0;
static int      x                  = 0;
static float    xfl                = 0.0;
static float    yung               = 0.0;
static float    zscore             = 0.0;

FILE *file_no[15];

static void io();
static void calculs();
static void runstest();
static float   fround();

void main()
{
  int      brch;

  do {
    io();
    printf("\n\nHIT <ENTER> TO INPUT NEW TRADES,OR <E>ND  ");
    do {
      flushall();
      brch = getche();
    } while (brch != 'E' && brch != 'e' && brch != '\015');
  } while (brch != 'E' && brch != 'e');
  exit(0);
}


static float   fround(xx)
float    xx;
{
  return((float)((long)(xx + 0.5)));
}
static void io()
{
  float    deple;
  float    fal;
  float    fan;
  float    fap;
  int      flag_int;
  int      n;
  float    paf;
  char     prtr_str[MAXCHLEN];
  float    ra;
  float    sea;
  char     str[MAXCHLEN];
  float    ual;
  float    vaf;
  float    why;
  float    xx;
  int      y;
  float    yy;
  int      ioo;

  _clearscreen(_GCLEARSCREEN);
  do {
    _settextposition(1, 1);
    printf("%s%s", "DO YOU WISH TO FIND f VIA PARABOLIC
                INTERPOLATION (Y/N)" , "? ");
    scanf("%s", fparb_str);
    if (!(strcmp(fparb_str, "y")))
      strcpy(fparb_str, "Y");
    else if (!(strcmp(fparb_str, "n")))
      strcpy(fparb_str, "N");
  } while (strcmpne(fparb_str, "Y") && strcmpne(fparb_str, "N"));
  printf("\n");
  printf("%s\n", "INPUT THE VALUES FOR THE BETS/TRADES YOU WISH TO COMPUTE");
  printf("%s\n", "INPUT X WHEN FINISHED.");
  printf("\n");
  flag_int = 0;
  tcont = 1;
  flushall();
```

```
while (flag_int == 0) {
  printf("");
  gets(str);
  if (!(strcmp(str, "x") && strcmp(str, "X"))) {
    flag_int = 1;
    tcont--;
  } else {
    trax[tcont] = atof(str);
    tcont++;
  }
}
printf("\n");
printf("%s%d%s\n", "YOU INPUT A TOTAL ", tcont, " BETS/TRADES");
printf("%s%s", "PERCENT OF ACCOUNT DEPLETION TILL RUIN " , "?   ");
scanf("%f", &deple);
if (deple > 1.0)
  deple /= 100.0;
wt = 0;
bl = 999999.9;
for (y = 1; y <= tcont; y++) {
  if (trax[y] < bl)
    bl = trax[y];
  if (trax[y] > 0)
    wt++;
}
calculs();
runstest();
printf("\n");
ioo = 0;
while (ioo < 1 || ioo > 3) {
  printf("OUTPUT DEVICE (1. Screen  2. Printer  3.File) ?  ");
  scanf("%d", &ioo);
}
if (ioo == 2)
  strcpy(prtr_str, "PRN");
if (ioo == 3) {
  printf("FILENAME FOR OUTPUT   ");
  scanf("%s", prtr_str);
}
/* NOW OUTPUT THE RESULTS*/
_clearscreen(_GCLEARSCREEN);
ra = wt / (float)tcont;
/* HERE IS RISK OF RUIN CALCS */
vaf = ((aw / fabs(bl / truef)) * ra) - (fabs(al / fabs(bl
      / truef)) * (1 - ra));
fal = pow((double)((ra * (pow((aw / fabs(bl / truef)), (double)2.0))) +
      ((1 - ra) * (pow((al / fabs(bl / truef)), (double)2.0)))),
      (double)(1.0 / 2.0));
paf = 0.5 * (1 + (vaf / fal));
fan = 0.0;
n = 1;
do {
  x = 1;
  yy = 0.0;
  fap = 1.0;
  while (x <= n) {
    why = 1.0 / x;
    if (x == 1)
      why = deple;
    ual = why / fal;
    sea = (((((fabs(bl / truef) / x) + fabs(bl / truef)) - ((1 - why) *
          fabs(bl / truef))) / fabs(bl / truef)) / fal;
    yy = 1 - ((pow((double)((1 - paf) / paf), (double) ual) - 1) / ((
          pow((double)((1 - paf) / paf) , (double)sea)) - 1));
    fap *= yy;
    x++;
  }
  fan += fap;
  n++;
} while (fap > .000001);
if (ioo > 1) {
  if ((file_no[1] = fopen(prtr_str, "w")) == NULL)
    exit(0);
  fprintf(file_no[1], "%s\n", "FOR THE FOLLOWING BETS/TRADES:");
```

```
      for (x = 1; x <= tcont; x++) {
        fprintf(file_no[1], "%f\n", trax[x]);
      }
      fprintf(file_no[1], "%s\n", " ");
      if (!((geomean_dbl <= 0) || (truef <= 0))) {
        fprintf(file_no[1], "%s", "GEOMETRIC AVERAGE TRADE = ");
        fprintf(file_no[1], "$%8.2f\n", (geomean_dbl - 1) * fabs(bl / truef));
        fprintf(file_no[1], "%s", "GEOMETRIC MEAN = ");
        fprintf(file_no[1], "%3.7f\n", geomean_dbl);
        fprintf(file_no[1], "%s", "TERMINAL WEALTH RELATIVE = ");
        fprintf(file_no[1], "%17.3f\n", twr_dbl);
      }
      if (!(truef <= 0)) {
        fprintf(file_no[1], "%s %3.2f %s", "TRUE OPTIMAL f =", truef, "OR
                1 CONTRACT FOR EVERY ");
        fprintf(file_no[1], "$%9.2f", fabs(bl / truef));
        if (strcmpne(fparb_str, "Y"))
          fprintf(file_no[1], "%s\n", "");
        else
          fprintf(file_no[1], "%s %d\n", " ITERATIVE PASSES =", pcount_int);
        fprintf(file_no[1], "%s%3.0f%s\n", "PERCENT OF ACCOUNT DEPLETION TILL
                RUIN ", deple * 100 , "%");
        fprintf(file_no[1], "%s", "RISK OF RUIN (FIXED FRACTION)    = ");
        fprintf(file_no[1], "%7.5f\n", fan);
        fprintf(file_no[1], "%s", "RISK OF RUIN (CONSTANT CONTRACT) = ");
        fprintf(file_no[1], "%7.5f\n", pow((double)((1 - paf) / paf),
                (double)(deple / fal)));
        fprintf(file_no[1], "%s", "EVERY ");
        fprintf(file_no[1], "$%6.0f", yung);
        fprintf(file_no[1], "%s", " OF INITIAL EQUITY GREW TO ");
        fprintf(file_no[1], "$%17.0f\n", (accu_dbl + yung ));
        fprintf(file_no[1], "%s", "Z SCORE = ");
        fprintf(file_no[1], "%7.4f\n", zscore);
        fprintf(file_no[1], "%s", "LINEAR CORRELATION = ");
        fprintf(file_no[1], "%6.4f\n", pearson);
      }
      fcloseall();
    }
    if (ioo == 1) {
      printf("%s\n", "FOR THE FOLLOWING BETS/TRADES:");
      for (x = 1; x <= tcont; x++) {
        printf("%f\n", trax[x]);
      }
      printf("%s\n", " ");
      if (!((geomean_dbl <= 0) || (truef <= 0))) {
        printf("%s", "GEOMETRIC AVERAGE TRADE = ");
        printf("$%8.2f\n", (geomean_dbl - 1) * fabs(bl / truef));
        printf("%s", "GEOMETRIC MEAN = ");
        printf("%3.7f\n", geomean_dbl);
        printf("%s", "TERMINAL WEALTH RELATIVE = ");
        printf("%17.3f\n", twr_dbl);
      }
      if (!(truef <= 0)) {
        printf("%s %3.2f %s", "TRUE OPTIMAL f =", truef, "OR 1 CONTRACT
                FOR EVERY ");
        printf("$%9.2f", fabs(bl / truef));
        if (strcmpne(fparb_str, "Y"))
          printf("%s\n", "");
        else
          printf("%s %d\n", " ITERATIVE PASSES =", pcount_int);
        printf("%s%3.0f%s\n", "PERCENT OF ACCOUNT DEPLETION TILL RUIN ",
                deple * 100 , "%");
        printf("%s", "RISK OF RUIN (FIXED FRACTION)    = ");
        printf("%7.5f\n", fan);
        printf("%s", "RISK OF RUIN (CONSTANT CONTRACT) = ");
        printf("%7.5f\n", pow((double)((1 - paf) / paf), (double)(deple / fal)));
        printf("%s", "EVERY ");
        printf("$%6.0f", yung);
        printf("%s", " OF INITIAL EQUITY GREW TO ");
        printf("$%17.0f\n", (accu_dbl + yung ));
        printf("%s", "Z SCORE = ");
        printf("%7.4f\n", zscore);
        printf("%s", "LINEAR CORRELATION = ");
        printf("%6.4f\n", pearson);
```

```
        }
      }
}


static void calculs()
{
    float    abscissa;
    float    f;
    float    f2;
    double   hpr_dbl;
    float    kon;
    int      kon_int;
    float    lcnx;
    float    lw;
    float    p1x;
    float    p2x;
    float    p3x;
    float    pearl;
    float    pt1;
    float    pt2;
    float    pt3;
    float    sigxq;
    float    sigxy;
    float    sigy;
    float    sigyq;
    float    tolerance;
    float    tpt2;
    double   twr2_dbl;
    double   twtemp_dbl;
    float    wcnx;
    float    xbar;
    float    ybar;
/* PERFORM MAIN CALCULATIONS*/
pearson = 0.0;
geomean_dbl = 0.0;
twr_dbl = 0.0;
truef = 0.0;
if ((tcont < 2) || (b1 >= 0) )
  return;
pearl = 0.0;
for (x = 1; x <= tcont; x++) {
  pearl = pearl + trax[x];
}
xbar = (pearl - trax[tcont]) / (tcont - 1);
ybar = (pearl - trax[1]) / (tcont - 1);
sigxy = 0.0;
sigy = 0.0;
sigxq = 0.0;
sigyq = 0.0;
for (x = 1; x <= (tcont - 1); x++) {
  sigxy = sigxy + ((trax[x] - xbar) * (trax[x+1] - ybar));
  sigxq = sigxq + ((trax[x] - xbar) * (trax[x] - xbar));
  sigyq = sigyq + ((trax[x+1] - ybar) * (trax[x+1] - ybar));
}
if (!(((sigxq == 0) || (sigyq == 0))))
  pearson = sigxy / (sqrt(sigxq) * sqrt(sigyq));
aw = 0.0;
al = 0.0;
wcnx = 0.0;
lcnx = 0.0;
for (x = 1; x <= tcont; x++) {
  if (trax[x] > 0) {
    aw += trax[x];
    wcnx++;
  }
  if (trax[x] <= 0) {
    lw += trax[x];
    lcnx++;
  }
}
aw /= wcnx;
lw /= lcnx;
f = 0.01;
```

```
f2 = 0.0;
twr2_dbl = 0.0;
do { /* START INTO THE LOOP THROUGH TRADES */
  twr_dbl = 1.0;
  hpr_dbl = 1.0;
  if (f > 1)
    f = 1.0;
  for (x = 1; x <= tcont; x++) {
    hpr_dbl = (1 + (f * (trax[x] / fabs(bl))));
    twr_dbl *= hpr_dbl;
  }
  if (!(twr_dbl > twr2_dbl))
    break;
  twr2_dbl = twr_dbl;
  f2 = f;
  f += 0.01;
} while (f2 < 0.999);
if ((twr_dbl <= twr2_dbl) || (f2 >= 0.999)) {
  twr_dbl = twr2_dbl;
  truef = f2;
}
geomean_dbl = pow(twr_dbl, (double)(1.0 / (double)tcont));
yung = fabs(bl / truef);
accu_dbl = 0.0;
kon_int = 1;
for (x = 1; x <= tcont; x++) {
  kon = (double)((long)(accu_dbl / yung));
  if (kon < 1)
    kon = (double)(1);
  accu_dbl = accu_dbl  + (trax[x] * kon);
}
if (!(strcmp(fparb_str, "N")))
  return;
/* PARABOLIC INTERPOLATION*/
tolerance = 0.005;
pcount_int = 0;
pt1 = 0.0;
pt3 = 1.0;
p3x = 0.0;
p1x = 0.0;
pt2 = 1.0 - tolerance;
twtemp_dbl = 1.0;
while (1) {
  pcount_int += 1;
  twtemp_dbl = 1.0;
  for (x = 1; x <= tcont; x++) {
    hpr_dbl = (1 + (pt2 * (trax[x] / fabs(bl))));
    twtemp_dbl *= hpr_dbl;
  }

  p2x = pow(twtemp_dbl, (double)(1.0 / (double)tcont));
  xfl = (((pt2 - pt1) * (p2x - p3x)) - ((pt2 - pt3) * (p2x - p1x)));
  if (xfl == 0)
    xfl = 0.00001;
  abscissa = pt2 - (0.5 * ((((pow((double)(pt2 - pt1), (double)2.0)) *
      (p2x - p3x)) - ((pow((double)(pt2 - pt3), (double)2.0)) * (p2x -
      p1x))) / xfl));
  tpt2 = pt2;
  if (fabs(abscissa - tpt2) <= tolerance) {
    truef = tpt2;
    return;
  }
  if (abscissa > tpt2) {
    pt1 = pt2;
    p1x = p2x;
  }
  if (abscissa < tpt2) {
    pt3 = pt2;
    p3x = p2x;
  }
  pt2 = abscissa;
}
}
```

```
static void runstest()
{
  float    rns;
  /* NOW DO RUNS TEST*/
  rns = 1.0;
  for (x = 2; x <= tcont; x++) {
    if (((trax[x] > 0) && (trax[x-1] <= 0)) || ((trax[x] <= 0) &&
          (trax[x-1] > 0)))
      rns = rns + 1;
  }
  zscore = ((tcont * (rns - 0.5)) - (2 * wt * (tcont - wt))) / sqrt(((2 * wt *
          (tcont - wt)) * ((2 * wt * (tcont - wt)) - tcont)) / (tcont - 1));
}


int  strcmpne(s1, s2)
char *s1, *s2;
{
  if (strcmp(s1, s2) == 0)
    return(0);
  return(1);
}
```

APPENDIX C

The Cumulative Normal Distribution

The Cumulative Normal Distribution, sometimes referred to as the Cumulative Normal Density Function, gives most people trouble. The function can be found in many statistics books, usually in the form of tables. Yet tables are awkward to use from a programming standpoint. Therefore, here is a function that will approximate the Cumulative Normal Distribution about as accurately as any published tables. Here the variable A is the input, and N(A) the output:

$C = 1 - Z * (1.330274 * Y^5 - 1.821256 * Y^4 + 1.781478 * Y^3 - .356538 * Y^2 + .3193815 * Y)$

If A > or = to 0 then N(A) = C.

If A < 0 then N(A) = 1 - C.

where: $Y = 1/(1 + .2316419 * abs(A))$.

abs(A) = The absolute value of A.

$Z = .3989423 * exp(-(A^2)/2)$.

exp(A) = The exponential function of A, available in most statistics books or hand-held calculators.

APPENDIX D

The Calendar

In many programming applications it is necessary to perform some type of calendar manipulation. Whether it is to calculate what day of the week a particular date is or how many days there are between two dates, programmers need a set of algorithms to perform such calendar manipulations. Options calculations, Gann calculations, and other types of market-oriented programming routinely need to manipulate dates of the calendar. Our applications in this book rely quite heavily on the ability to do this.

First, a little background on the calendar itself is in order. The length of the year is not exactly 365 days, and the amount left over after 365 has been subtracted is not a simple fraction of a day (i.e., it is an irrational number). Mathematically speaking, the day and the year are therefore incommensurable with each other.

Generally speaking, there are two types of years. The first, the sidereal year, is the amount of time it takes the earth to return to a given position with respect to the stars. The sidereal year is roughly 365.2564 days. The second type of year is the solar year, or tropical year. The solar year is the time it takes the earth to return to the vernal equinox, the point where the ecliptic crosses the celestial equator. Recall that the angle of the earth's axis changes throughout the year. Midsummer is defined as the moment when the angle between the direction of the Sun and the Earth's axis takes a minimum value. Therefore, we say that the solar or tropical year is the time it takes the earth's axis to return to a given point, to have made one complete cycle. Unfortunately, a complete cycle of the tilt of the Earth's axis does not take exactly the same length of time as it takes the Earth to return to a given point with respect to the stars. The solar year is roughly 365.2422 days. This means that the solar year differs from the sidereal year by about one part in

26,000. Therefore, 13,000 years ago the stars of the winter sky were out during midsummer and vice versa.

From civilization's point of view, the solar or tropical year is the one of importance, as it tells farmers when to plant and keeps religious holidays in the same season; as a side-benefit, governments can collect an extra year of taxes every 26,000 years!

The Romans had different numbers of days in a year at different times. The dates rapidly drifted out of synchronization with the seasons (which follow the tropical year). In 46 B.C. Julius Caesar decreed that there would be a 445-day year in order to catch up, and defined a calendar that would then be more accurate. This calendar later became known as the Julian calendar. According to the Julian calendar, each year would be 365 days in length, and every fourth year would be a leap year, (i.e., an extra day would be added). This would bring the average length of a year to 365.25 days.

The last four months of the year (September, October, November, December) still bear essentially their original names from this calendar. In those days, the year was considered to have begun in March. The name of the fifth month, Quintilis, was changed to honor Julius Caesar, and in English today we call it July. Augustus Caesar, who later carried out more calendar reforms, renamed August after himself. Not to be outdone by Julius, Augustus also transferred a day from February in order to make August last as long as July. That is why February, which used to have 29 days every year and 30 on leap years, now has 1 day less (February was the shortest and also the month that took the leap-year day as it was the last month of the year and the leap-year day was, in effect, added on to the end of the year), and both July and August have 31 days each, back to back. The Julian calendar was much more accurate than any of its predecessors. However, it was out of step with the tropical year, as it was roughly .0078 days too long every year. Naturally, this didn't cause a problem for quite a few years.

From its inception to the early 16th century, the Julian calendar accumulated a little more than 12 extra days, which was enough to cause serious concern. Interestingly enough the concern was not about drift relative to the seasons from an agricultural point of view, but rather that the calendar had gotten out of step, by about ten days, with the date at which Easter had occurred at the time of a religious council 1250 years earlier. The Pope at that time, regarded as the authority on the matter, was Gregory XIII. He solicited the advice of astronomers as to how best to remedy the situation. One of the astronomers polled was Copernicus. The reply that Copernicus gave Pope Gregory XIII was that more time was needed to study the matter, meaning that the tropical year was not known with any greater accuracy at that time

than 365.25 days. Later, astronomers at the Vatican itself would determine the tropical year to a greater degree of accuracy.

On October 15th, 1582, Gregory issued a bull (a proclamation) to
remedy the situation. First, the ten extra days that had accumulated in
the last 1,250 years would be exorcised, pulled from existence. Many
citizens objected to losing this time from their lives, and were upset by
the commercial complications that arose (is a full month's rent due for
the month that the days were pulled from?). Further, the 1582 proclamation set forth a newer, more accurate calendar, now known as (what
else) the Gregorian calendar. Essentially it is the Julian calendar, but
"century years" (1700, 1800, and so on), which were leap years, no
longer would be, unless they were divisible by 400. Therefore, under the
old Julian calendar the year 1900 would be a leap year, but since it is a
century year, under the Gregorian calendar it would not be a leap year.
The year 2000 is divisible by 400, so it will be a leap year. The next
century year after the year 2000 to be a leap year will be 2400.

Many countries adopted the Gregorian calendar as soon as it was
promulgated. However, Great Britain did not; hence the American
colonies did not adopt it until 1752, when 11 days were skipped. George
Washington's birthday was really February 11, 1732, not February 22,
as we now celebrate it. When Alaska was annexed, its calendar, too, had
to be changed over to the Gregorian.

The Gregorian calendar has an average length of 365.2425 days,
differing from the actual tropical year by roughly .0003 days, and
therefore takes about 3,000 years to get out of step by 1 day.[1]

From a programming standpoint, calendar manipulation is accomplished by converting from a standard YYMMDD format, such as
680523, for May 23, 1968, to what is known as the Julian Day Number,
2440000. Julian Day Numbers follow sequentially; there is no distinction between days, months, and years; rather, every day that passes
adds 1 to the Julian Day Number. The calendar can be manipulated
more easily this way if we have two functions, one to convert the
YYMMDD format to the Julian Day Number, and another to convert
the Julian Day Number to YYMMDD. Therefore, if we want to know
how many days elapsed between two dates, we convert the two dates to
their Julian Day Numbers, then obtain the difference to get our result.

---

[1] The earth's rate of rotation is actually slowing down at a rate of approximately
.0000000391 seconds per day. Therefore, each year, tropical or sidereal, requires pro-
gressively fewer rotations of the earth, or days. This fact is not accounted for in this
discussion because it takes over 70,021 years for the length of a day to gain 1 second.
However, it is interesting to note that a son who lives to be as old as his father was when his
father died has actually lived longer than his father.

If we want to know, for instance, what date is X days from day such-and-such, we convert such-and-such to its Julian Day Number, add X to it, then convert the sum back to YYMMDD format.

Days of the week, the third essential function for calendar manipulation, are easily found by adding 1 to the Julian Day Number, then dividing the result by 7 and taking the remainder. Thus, 0 corresponds to Sunday, 1 to Monday, . . . , and 6 to Saturday. With this function, you can not only answer questions such as what day of the week a particular date is, or whether it was a weekday or weekend, you can also determine how many weekdays or weekends there were between two dates, or what date is X weekdays or weekends from a given date, and so on.

The three essential functions are shown here first in BASIC (BASICA) as subroutines. Note that in the BASIC versions no allowances are made for the differences between the Gregorian and Julian calendars (i.e., Gregorian is assumed prior to October 15, 1582). This should suffice for most working purposes, as there is little need for using dates prior to October 15, 1582. In the C versions such allowances are made, but could be worked out, if a programmer so desired, to give the program less code and faster execution time.

Calendar Manipulation Program (in BASIC)

```
10 REM CNVRT YYMMDD TO JULIAN - INPUT X AND OUTPUT JU#
20 YMD$=STR$(X)
30 YMD$=RIGHT$(YMD$,6)
40 YY#=1900+VAL(LEFT$(YMD$,2))
50 IF VAL(MID$(YMD$,3,2))>2 THEN JY#=YY#:JM#=1+VAL(MID$(YMD$,3,2))
60 IF VAL(MID$(YMD$,3,2))<3 THEN JY#=YY#-1:JM#=13+VAL(MID$(YMD$,3,2))
70 ID#=VAL(RIGHT$(YMD$,2))
80 JU#=INT(365.25*JY#)+INT(30.6001*JM#)+ID#+1720995#
90 JA#=INT(.01*JY#)
100 JU#=JU#+2-JA#+INT(.25*JA#)
110 RETURN


10 REM INPUT JULIAN# AND OUTPUT YMD$
20 JB#=JULIAN#+1+(INT(((JULIAN#-1867216!)-.25)/36524.25))
      -INT(.25*(INT(((JULIAN#-1867216!)-.25)/36524.25)))+1524
30 JC#=INT(6680+((JB#-2439970!)-122.1)/365.25)
40 JD#=365*JC#+INT(.25*JC#):JE#=INT((JB#-JD#)/30.6001)
50 ID#=JB#-JD#-INT(30.6001*JE#):MM#=JE#-1:IF MM#>12 THEN MM#=MM#-12
60 YY#=JC#-4715:IF (MM#>2) THEN YY#=YY#-1
70 IF YY#<0 THEN YY#=YY#-1
80 ID$=STR$(ID#)
90 IF LEFT$(ID$,1)=" " THEN ID$=RIGHT$(ID$,LEN(ID$)-1):GOTO 90
100 IF LEN(ID$)<2 THEN ID$="0"+ID$
110 MM$=STR$(MM#)
120 IF LEFT$(MM$,1)=" " THEN MM$=RIGHT$(MM$,(LEN(MM$)-1)):GOTO 120
130 IF LEN(MM$)<2 THEN MM$="0"+MM$
140 YMD$=RIGHT$(STR$(YY#),2)+MM$+ID$
150 RETURN


10 REM DAY OF THE WEEK ROUTINE
11 REM INPUT X#, THE JULIAN DAY AND OUTPUT X%, THE DAY OF THE WEEK 0-6
20 X#=JU#+1:X#=(X#/7)-INT(X#/7):X%=CINT(X#*7)
30 RETURN
```

Next we see the three essential functions in C. Allowances are made for dates prior to October 15, 1582.

```c
unsigned long  toyymmdd(x) /* converts julian to YYMMDD */
unsigned long  x;
{
    long igreg, jalpha, ja, jb, jc, jd, je, id, mm, yy, q;

    igreg = 2299161;
    /* Gregorian Calendar Adopted October 15, 1582 */
    if (x >= igreg) {
        jalpha = (((x - 1867216) - .25) / 36524.25);
        q = (.25 * jalpha);
        ja = x + 1 + jalpha - q;
    } else {
        ja = x;
    }
    jb = ja + 1524;
    jc = 6680 + ((jb - 2439870) - 122.1) / 365.25;
    q = .25 * jc;
    jd = 365 * jc + q;
    je = (jb - jd) / 30.6001;
    q = (30.6001 * je);
    id = jb - jd - q;
    mm = je - 1;
    if (mm > 12)
        mm = mm - 12;
    yy = jc - 4715;
    if (mm > 2)
        yy--;
    if (yy <= 0)
        yy--;
    yy = yy - 1900;
    return((unsigned long)((yy * 10000) + (mm * 100) + id));
}

unsigned  dayofweek(x)
/* catches julian day x, returns day of the week 0-6 */
unsigned long  (x);
{
    x++;
    return((unsigned int)(x % 7));
}
```

Calendar Manipulation Program (in C)

```c
unsigned long  tojul(x) /* converts YYMMDD to julian */
unsigned long  (x);
{
    float    day, month, year, igreg, julday, ja, jy, jm;

    igreg = (float)(15 + 31 * (10 + 12 * 1582));
    /* Gregorian Calendar Adopted October 15, 1582 */
    year = (float)((int)(x / 10000));
    month = (float)((int)((x / 100) - ((x / 10000) * 100)));
    day = (float)((int)(x - (year * 10000) - (month * 100)));
    year += 1900.0;
    if (year < 0.0)
        year++;
    if (month > 2.0) {
        jy = year;
        jm = month + 1.0;
    } else {
        jy = year - 1.0;
        jm = month + 13.0;
    }
    julday = (float)((unsigned long)(365.25 * jy));
    julday += ((float)((unsigned long)(30.6001 * jm)));
    julday += ((float)(day + 1720995));
```

```
        if ((day + 31 * (month + 12 * year)) >= igreg) {
            ja = (float)((unsigned long)(.01 * jy));
            julday += (2.0 - ja);
            julday += (.25 * ja);
        }
        return((unsigned long)(julday));
    }
```

APPENDIX E

Options Calculations

Next, we have a program that incorporates not only the aforementioned calendar calculations and Cumulative Normal Distribution Function, but also the mathematics for option pricing models. This program, a shortened and uncommercialized version of *The Precision Options Analyst* is courtesy of my good friend Joe Bristor of Sacramento, California. The commercial version performs in color and with far more features. Although this shortened version will run, it is provided to show how to calculate the fair (theoretical) values of options for commodities and stocks, as well as the computer code for such. Joe's program is terrific in that many of the equations involved are from Lawrence MacMillan's classic work *Options as a Strategic Investment* (see the bibliography and suggested reading near the end of this book).

I am grateful to Joe for allowing me to amend the code for this program to include a technique for finding the optimal f of a fair value for an option. Furthermore, I have incorporated into this code the method of finding the optimal mandated exit date. I have added these portions of code so that you may better see how the technique is performed. Note that when you run this program, if you select option number 1, "Fair Market Values & Optimal f," the program will tie up your computer for quite a few hours. The process of finding the optimal f and optimal mandated exit date for an option is very slow. Furthermore, the process can be a bit quirky in that you may not get an optimal f and mandated exit date if the optimal geometric mean is less than 1 or if the optimal f is less than 0 or greater than 1. Nevertheless, I have put this code in here for you to have a starting point if this avenue interests you. Perhaps you can improve the code's speed and efficiency.

Finally, you will notice in the code that the program calculates HPRs for all dates up to and including the mandated exit date. This assumes

206

you do not know exactly on what date you will exit the option between now and the mandated exit date, but do know that you will be out of the position by the mandated exit date. Also notice that the date returned by this process as the optimal exit date means you should *exit on the close of trading on the optimal exit date.*

Excerpts from the manual to the software follow, so that you will know how to answer the prompts that the program asks of you, and so that you may see the math involved in the program. Later on, the shortened version of the program itself is presented in BASIC. What follows now are excerpts from the manual for *The Precision Options Analyst.*

The Precision Options Analyst

The program utilizes the Black-Scholes stock option pricing model, which was introduced in early 1973, right around the time that listed options began trading. Black-Scholes is widely accepted as the standard option pricing model since it is relatively easy to employ, has a large number of adherents, and is remarkably accurate. The formula is as follows:

Call Option Price = (P * N(D1)) − ((E(− (R * T))) * (S * N(D2)))

where: $D1 = \dfrac{(\ln(P/S) + (R + ((V^{(1/2)})12)) * T)}{V * (T^{(1/2)})}$

$D2 = D1 − (V * (T^{(1/2)}))$

P = Price of the underlying instrument, adjusted for dividends per share where ex-date is prior to option expiration, if applicable.

S = Strike price.

T = Time remaining until expiration, as a percent of a year.

R = Current risk-free interest rate.

V = Volatility expressed as an annual standard deviation.

ln = Natural logarithm.

E(X) = The exponential function.

N(X) = Cumulative Normal Density Function.

Black went on to make the model applicable to the evaluation of premiums on commodity futures contracts.

Call Option Price = $E(-(R*T))*((P*N(D1))-(S*N(D2)))$

where: $D1 = \dfrac{(\ln(P/S) + (((V^2)*T)/2))}{V*(T^{(1/2)})}$

$D2 = D1 - (V*(T^{(1/2)}))$

P = Commodity price.

S = Strike price.

T = Time remaining until expiration, as a percent of a year.

R = Current risk-free interest rate.

V = Volatility expressed as an annual standard deviation.

ln = Natural logarithm.

E(X) = The exponential function.

N(X) = Cumulative Normal Density Function.

Put prices can be derived from the theoretical call prices given by these formulas. The next formula assumes that the value of puts will be maintained relative to the value of the corresponding call with the same strike price and same expiration date by the arbitrage process. This formula is one of a class of put pricing formulas, known as *conversion methods*, that are widely regarded as being reliable, accurate models.

Put option price = $(((C + S - P + G)*W) + Z)/W$

P = Underlying instrument price.

S = Strike price.

C = Fair call value for corresponding strike price and expiration date.

G = Dividends per share, in dollars, where ex-date is prior to expiration, if applicable.

W = Dollars per point, or 1 in the case of stocks.

Z = Carrying charges.

Put prices can also be found using the pricing models but modified for puts. Here, for the Black-Scholes stock option pricing model:

Put option price = (P * N(D2)) − (E(R * T) * (S * N(D1)))

where: $D1 = \dfrac{-(\ln(P/S) + (R + ((V^2)/2)) * T)}{V * (T^{(1/2)})}$

D2 = − (D1 − (V * (T^(1/2))))

P = Price of the underlying instrument, adjusted for dividends per share where ex-date is prior to option expiration, if applicable.

S = Strike price.

T = Time remaining until expiration, as a percent of a year.

R = Current risk-free interest rate.

V = Volatility expressed as an annual standard deviation.

ln = Natural logarithm.

E(X) = The exponential function.

N(X) = Cumulative Normal Density Function.

The modified Black commodity options formula for puts is:

Put option price = − E(− (R * T)) * ((P * N(D1)) − (S * N(D2)))

where: $D1 = \dfrac{-(\ln(P/S) + (((V^2) * T)/2))}{V * (T^{(1/2)})}$

D2 = − (D1 − (V * (T^(1/2))))

P = Commodity price.

S = Strike price.

T = Time remaining until expiration, as a percent of a year.

R = Current risk-free interest rate.

V = Volatility expressed as an annual standard deviation.

ln = Natural logarithm.

E(X) = The exponential function.

N(X) = Cumulative Normal Density Function.

If you were to take the first derivative of the change in an options price with respect to the change in the price of the underlying instrument, you would obtain what is called the delta (also known as the hedge ratio). It is the delta that tells us the amount by which we can expect the options price to change for a small change in the underlying price. One of the conveniences these models perform for the user is the exact calculation of the delta (without having to perform the calculus).

Call option delta = $N(D1)$

Put option delta = $N(-D1)$

Another important point should be made regarding these models. In the event that the fair price, as presented by these models, is less than the difference between the underlying price and the strike price (with respect to calls) then the fair call option price equals the difference between the underlying price and the strike price. In such cases, the delta = 1. With puts, the same is true if the fair put option price is less than the difference between the strike price and the underlying price.

Carrying charges also are figured:

Simple interest = $S * R * T$

Compound interest, present worth = $S * (1 - ((1 + R)^{\wedge}(-T)))$

where: S = Strike price (for the stock model) or the initial margin (for the commodity model).

R = Current risk-free interest rate.

T = Time remaining until expiration, as a percent of a year.

Features

–The Black-Scholes models for stock options as well as the Fisher Black model for commodity options.

–Calculation of implied volatility through an iterative process.

–User-specified carrying charge calculations. The user can select to use the simple interest formula or the compound interest, present worth formula.

–Analysis of arbitrage positions. The user can see how far prices are out of line in relation to the mathematical models, as well as where prices are relative to other options.

–Fair value tables. The user can hold all variables constant and print tables where only one factor changes (such as the days left to expiration, the price of the underlying instrument, or the strike price).

–Expected return analysis. This feature allows the user to see statistically what the chances are of the underlying instrument being above or below a certain price by date of expiration. This provides the user a "window" within which prices will most likely fall upon expiration.

–The Cumulative Normal Density Function can be approximated from a fifth order polynomial or it can be approximated by what is known as an infinite series expansion process (the details of which will not be discussed here).

Running the Program

You will first be prompted to enter today's date, which will be called the "System Date." You will calculate values based on the close of trading on the system date. In other words, if tomorrow is the last day of trading in an option and trading is closed for today, then there is only one market day left to trade the option in; hence you would enter today's date as the system date and all calculations would proceed assuming one day was left in which to trade the option.

Next, you will be prompted as to select either the Black-Scholes stock option model or the Fisher Black commodity option model. Then select either simple interest or compound interest, present worth for the carrying charge calculation. Both the stock and commodity option models employ a carrying charge calculation. Since simple interest is more commonly used, it is included as a selection. However, the compound interest, present worth method is more accurate and is the preferred choice.

Next, select what type of Cumulative Normal Density Function calculation you would like employed. Here you have two choices: Either approximate the function with a fifth-order polynomial or use a looping process known as infinite series expansion. In most instances, the choice you make has no noticeable effect on the prices, but both methods are included.

Finally, select how you would like the put values calculated—with the conversion method or with a pricing model. Under the conversion method, the put is calculated by taking the calculated price of the call with the same strike and expiration, and then calculating what the put value must be if the arbitrageurs have worked it to be in line with the call value. Calculating the puts with a pricing model is different, in that the call value is not computed—rather, the put value is calculated totally independently of the call value by modifying the call option fair pricing formulas to price puts. This is an important selection and you should work with both until you learn which method is applicable to the options you want to concentrate on.

The Main Prompts

Now the main page will appear. At the top is the system date as well as what day of the week it is. Also displayed is your choice of model as well as the carrying charge computation, Cumulative Normal Distribution calculation method, and put calculation methods.

Nine selections are available. If you choose selection 8, Reset Parameters, you will return to the point we just came from (i.e., you will be prompted for a new system date, model type, carrying charge calculation, and so on). You will then be returned to the menu.

Anytime you want to print the results of a study on the printer, simply press the <SHIFT> and <PRT SC> keys simultaneously. Otherwise, all output is always to the screen.

One of the most important inputs in an option pricing model is that of the volatility of the underlying instrument. Volatility is expressed as an annual standard deviation in prices. However, the preferred method of determining volatility is by letting the marketplace itself dictate what the volatility is. If we know what the price of a call option is, then by using the fair pricing models we can determine what the marketplace implies the volatility is. This method is known as *implied volatility*. As you use it, you will notice that it changes little on a day-to-day basis for a given underlying instrument. Once you have chosen selection 7, Calculate Implied Volatility, and have answered the prompting questions that this function will ask you, the program will then calculate the implied volatility. It does this by what is known as an iterative process. In other words, the assumption is made that 50% is the implied volatility. All variables are run through the model and the model yields an option price. If the option price is greater than the market price the system knows that the volatility assumption (50%) is too great, and that the correct answer lies between 0 and 50. It chooses the halfway point (25%) and tries again. If the answer the model yields is less than the market price of the call, the system knows that the correct answer lies between 25% and 50%. This process is carried out until the volatility assumption input to the model yields the same fair value as the market value of the given call.

In using implied volatility, it is important that you use the nearest out-the-money or in-the-money option. Use an active option. Going deep in-the-money or deep out-the-money will yield inaccurate results. Furthermore, you can use call or put options in this determination of implied volatility. Many professional options traders use the two or four most accurate call options of a given underlying instrument and average the implied volatilities. Some keep a moving average (generally 10–21 days) of the implied volatility.

Now choose selection number 1, Fair Market Valuations. Here you are given what the fair value for a given option is, as well as the delta. You will be required to input the volatility here, so if you do not have a volatility percentage, you will want to calculate the implied volatility before choosing this selection. Once the fair value is calculated, you can then calculate the optimal f amount for either the put or the call of that strike and expiration by the technique that was introduced in Chapter 4. Remember, if your optimal f amount returned by the program is less than or equal to zero, it is a bad bet and the option should not be bought. If the optimal f returned by the program is greater than 1.00, the program is telling you to borrow money to purchase more options than the equity in your account would allow. Of course, as was discussed in Chapter 4, it may be a good idea to be to the left of the optimal f peak of the curve and hence not borrow, but trade within the bounds of which you feel comfortable.

Suppose you wanted to calculate the fair value of the puts and calls on an option for a given strike price and you wanted to keep all the input variables the same, but you wanted to increment the strike price by, say, five points. Selection 5, Fair Value Tables, will do this. You can elect to vary either the strike price (to print up fair value tables similar to the market prices published in the newspapers) or you can choose to vary the underlying price (to create tables of fair options prices for various underlying prices the next day). Not only are the fair values printed in the table, so you can see how they change, so are the deltas, so you can see how they can be expected to change as well.

What if you wanted to keep everything constant except the number of days to expiration? By selecting number 6, Decay Over Time, you can achieve exactly that. Again, the deltas are displayed so you can see how they change as well. If you've ever wondered how a six-month option will fare compared to one with three months to go on it, try out this function.

If you're curious about the possibilities of an underlying instrument being above or below a certain point by expiration, then try selection number 4, Expected Return Analysis. This function will also give you an upper and lower "window" that the underlying instrument should remain in until expiration. This is expressed as the current price plus or minus (one standard deviation multiplied by the square root of the percentage of a year remaining until expiration).

Finally, you are given a way to assess option premiums other than by the theoretical models. Selections 2 and 3, the Arbitrage Analysis, allow you to look at option values relative to other options of the same underlying security.

Here is a brief synopsis of the basic arbitrage plays. A conversion is simply buying the underlying instrument, buying a put and selling a call with the same strike and expiration as the put. This is a riskless transaction to the arbitrageur. If the conversion can be done at a profit, it is indicative of a call, being overvalued relative to the put (or vice versa; the put can be undervalued relative to the call). This would seem to imply that the sentiment in this particular underlying instrument is bullish. A reversal is the opposite of a conversion. A box measures options premiums across four separate legs, two puts and two calls. This method uses identical expirations for all four legs, but there are two different strikes involved. The potential profit in a box indicates that the premiums are out of line—in a more efficient market a box would not show a profit.

Other Prompts

Whenever you choose selections 1 through 7, you will be prompted with some of the following prompts. Which ones appear is a function of which option model you are using as well as which function you have selected.

By <S>trike or <U>nderlying

This prompt appears only if you have selected Fair Value Tables. You are asked if you want the strike price to be incremented or the underlying price incremented in the table (the one not chosen will remain constant). Answer with S or U. Note that either upper- or lowercase will do throughout the program.

Underlying Price

Strike Price

Price in Question

Starting Strike Price

Underlying Start Price

Call Price

Put Price

These are all prompts for prices that will appear at various times. You cannot enter fractions; all input must be decimal.

Increment Strike Price

Increment Underlying Price

These prompts appear with the Fair Value Tables option. They appear after you have answered the Starting Strike Price or Underlying Start Price prompt. This answer is the amount you want the initial value to be increased by at each row of the table. For instance, if you are printing up a fair value table, you start with an underlying price of 200, and you want to increment the price by 5 (200, 205, 210, 215, and so on), you will answer 5 at this prompt.

Expiration Date (YYMMDD)

Here you simply input the last two digits of the year, the month, and the day. For example, if we want to key in October 9, 1988, as the expiration date, we answer this prompt with 881009. Notice that the program automatically calculates the exact number of days to expiration for you by comparing the expiration date you have just entered to the system date you entered previously.

Volatility

Here you simply place the volatility generated by function 7, Calculate Implied Volatility. For example, if volatility on the underlying instrument is 13.12%, you would simply enter 13.12.

Short Term Rates

Generally you should use the recent 90 day T-Bill rate. Remember: Always enter all of your answers to every prompt in decimal. Do *not* enter with a percent (%) sign. That is, if the recent 90 day T-Bill rate is 8½%, you will enter 8.5 (notice how you express this—as 8.5 and *not* .085).

Dividends Per Share in Dollars

If you are using the stock model, you will encounter this one. You should enter the dollar amount of any dividends between now and the expiration date of the option. Only enter if the dividends ex-date precedes the expiration date of the option. Do *not* enter with a dollar sign. Since dividends play such a small part in determining options prices, you can get by with an entry of 0 here if you do not have a ready answer, as it will not affect the output too much (naturally the higher the dividend you are omitting, the greater will be the effect on the output). If the stock is paying 75 cents per share dividend and the ex-date precedes the options expiration date, you will enter .75.

Margin Per Contract

If you are using the commodity model you will encounter this one. Enter the initial margin requirement, *without* a dollar sign.

Dollars Per Full Point

If you are using the commodity model you will encounter this one, too. If you are doing, say, Soybeans, you would enter 50. Again, do not prefix your answer with a dollar sign.

No. Days to Skip

This is essentially the "increment amount" when you are using selection 6, Decay Over Time. You should put in the number of days you want to skip for each row in the table. For example, if you want to have each row be one full week into the future, you would enter 7 at this prompt. You must pick a whole number, and it must be 1 or greater.

For <P>ut or <C>alls

Answer with either P or C (either uppercase or lowercase, it doesn't matter). This prompt only appears when you are doing implied volatilities; it is asking you whether you want to find the implied volatility of a put or a call.

Minimum Tick in Decimal

Here, you want to answer with the smallest increment the underlying instrument is traded in, in decimal. For instance, if you were working with T-Bonds, which are traded in 32nds, you would enter .03125.

Now, here is the code to the shortened version of *The Precision Options Analyst*:

```
                OPTIONS.BAS Program (in BASIC)
10 REM OPTIONS.BAS, A PROGRAM TO SHOW THE MATH OF OPTION MODELS
1000 DIM NUTHR(250),GPH(17,5),GIG$(80),NT$(10,2)
         :ZACH$="
1010 CLS
1020 PRINT "System Date (YYMMDD) ":LOCATE 1,23:INPUT DE$
1030 ED$=DE$:GOSUB 1040:GOSUB 1240:JL=JU#:GOSUB 1280:GOTO 1090
1040 REM CNVRT YYMMDD TO JULIAN
1050 YY#=1900+VAL(LEFT$(ED$,2)):IF VAL(MID$(ED$,3,2))>2
         THEN JY#=YY#:JM#=1+VAL(MID$(ED$,3,2))
1060 IF VAL(MID$(ED$,3,2))<3 THEN JY#=YY#-1
         :JM#=13+VAL(MID$(ED$,3,2))
1070 ID#=VAL(RIGHT$(ED$,2)):JU#=INT(365.25*JY#)+INT(30.6001*JM#)
         +ID#+1720995#:JA#=INT(.01*JY#)
         :JU#=JU#+2-JA#+INT(.25*JA#)
1080 RETURN
1090 ZA$="...................................."
1100 PRINT:PRINT"Carrying Charge Calculations:"
         :PRINT "<S>imple Interest"
         :PRINT"<C>ompound Interest, Present Worth"
         :LOCATE 12,1:PRINT CHR$(219)
1110 CC$=INKEY$:IF CC$="" THEN 1110
1120 IF ASC(CC$)>90 THEN CC$=CHR$(ASC(CC$)-32)
1130 IF CC$<>"S" AND CC$<>"C" THEN 1110
1140 LOCATE 12,1:PRINT CC$:LOCATE 14,1
         :PRINT "Cumulative Normal Distribution:"
         :PRINT"<F>ifth Order Polynomial"
         :PRINT"<I>nfinite Series Expansion"
         :LOCATE 17,1
         :PRINT CHR$(219)
1150 FI$=INKEY$:IF FI$="" THEN 1150
1160 IF ASC(FI$)>90 THEN FI$=CHR$(ASC(FI$)-32)
1170 IF FI$<>"F" AND FI$<>"I" THEN 1150
1180 LOCATE 17,1:PRINT FI$
1190 LOCATE 19,1:PRINT "Put Calculation:"
         :PRINT"<C>onversion Method"
         :PRINT"<P>ricing Models":LOCATE 22,1:PRINT CHR$(219)
1200 PTY$=INKEY$:IF PTY$="" THEN 1200
1210 IF ASC(PTY$)>90 THEN PTY$=CHR$(ASC(PTY$)-32)
1220 IF PTY$<>"C" AND PTY$<>"P" THEN 1200
1230 LOCATE 22,1:PRINT PTY$:GOTO 1340
1240 REM DAY OF THE WEEK ROUTINE
1250 X#=JU#+1:X#=(X#/7)-INT(X#/7):X%=CINT(X#*7)
1260 IF X%=0 THEN D$="Sunday" ELSE IF X%=1 THEN D$="Monday"
         ELSE IF X%=2 THEN D$="Tuesday" ELSE IF X%=3 THEN
         D$="Wednesday" ELSE IF X%=4 THEN D$="Thursday"
         ELSE IF X%=5 THEN D$="Friday" ELSE IF X%=6 THEN
         D$="Saturday"
1270 RETURN
1280 REM WHICH MODEL ?
1290 PRINT:PRINT:PRINT "SELECT:":PRINT"<S>tock Option Model"
         :PRINT "<C>ommodity Option Model"
         :LOCATE 7,1:PRINT CHR$(219)
1300 CM$=INKEY$:IF CM$="" THEN 1300
1310 IF ASC(CM$)>90 THEN CM$=CHR$(ASC(CM$)-32)
1320 IF CM$<>"S" AND CM$<>"C" THEN 1300
1330 LOCATE 7,1:PRINT CM$:RETURN
1340 GOSUB 3590:PRINT "System Date is "D$", "DE$
1350 IF CM$="S" THEN PRINT "Black-Scholes Stock Option Model"
1360 IF CM$="C" THEN PRINT "Black Commodity Option Model     "
1370 IF CC$="S" THEN PRINT "Simple Interest"
1380 IF CC$="C" THEN PRINT "Compound Interest, Present Worth"
1390 IF FI$="F" THEN PRINT "Fifth Order Polynomial" ELSE IF
         FI$="I" THEN PRINT "Infinite Series Expansion"
1400 IF PTY$="C" THEN PRINT"Conversion Put Calculation" ELSE
         PRINT "Pricing Model Put Calculation"
1410 PRINT ZA$:PRINT "Select:"
1420 PRINT "<1> = Fair Market Values & Optimal f"
1430 PRINT "<2> = Arbitrage Analysis - Conversions"
```

```
1440 PRINT "<3> = Arbitrage Analysis - Boxes"
1450 PRINT "<4> = Expected Return Analysis"
1460 PRINT "<5> = Fair Value Tables"
1470 PRINT "<6> = Decay Over Time"
1480 PRINT "<7> = Calculate Implied Volatility"
1490 PRINT "<8> = Reset Parameters"
1500 PRINT "<0> = End"
1510 PRINT:PRINT ZA$
1520 LOCATE 7,9:PRINT CHR$(219)
1530 O$=INKEY$:LOCATE 7,9:PRINT O$;
1540 OO$=" ":IF O$="6" THEN O$="10"
1550 IF O$<"5" THEN 1630
1560 LOCATE 1,42:PRINT "By <S>trike or <U>nderlying ?"
          :LOCATE 3,42:PRINT CHR$(219)
1570 OO$=INKEY$:IF OO$="" THEN 1570
1580 IF OO$="s" THEN OO$="S"
1590 IF OO$="u" THEN OO$="U"
1600 LOCATE 3,42:PRINT OO$:IF OO$="S" THEN O$="5"
1610 IF OO$="U" THEN O$="6"
1620 IF OO$<"U" AND OO$<"S" THEN 1570 ELSE GOSUB 3630
1630 IF O$="1" OR O$="2" OR O$="3" OR O$="4" OR O$="5" OR
          O$="6" OR O$="7" OR O$="10" THEN 1670
1640 IF O$="8" THEN GOSUB 3610:GOTO 1020
1650 IF O$="0" THEN 3580
1660 GOTO 1520
1670 REM MAIN CONTROL
1680 LOCATE 1,42:PRINT"Input the Following:"
1690 ZEB=3
1700 LOCATE ZEB,42:IF O$<"3" AND O$<"6" THEN INPUT "Underlying
          Price       ",UU:IF UU<=0 THEN 1700 ELSE ZEB=ZEB+1
1710 LOCATE ZEB,42:IF O$="4" THEN INPUT"Price in
          Question          ",E:ZEB=ZEB+1
1720 LOCATE ZEB,42:IF O$="5" THEN INPUT"Starting Strike
          Price       ",E:ZEB=ZEB+1
1730 LOCATE ZEB,42:IF O$="5" THEN INPUT"Increment Strike
          Price       ",IC:ZEB=ZEB+1
1740 LOCATE ZEB,42:IF O$="6" THEN INPUT"Underlying Start
          Price       ",UU:ZEB=ZEB+1
1750 LOCATE ZEB,42:IF O$="6" THEN INPUT"Inc. Underlying
          Price by   ",IC:ZEB=ZEB+1
1760 LOCATE ZEB,42:IF O$<"4" AND O$<"5" THEN INPUT "Strike
          Price       ",E:ZEB=ZEB+1
1770 LOCATE ZEB,42:IF O$="3" THEN INPUT"Second Strike
          Price       ",EC:ZEB=ZEB+1
1780 LOCATE ZEB,42:IF O$<"3" THEN INPUT"Expiration
          Date (YYMMDD)  ",ED$:ZEB=ZEB+1
1790 IF VAL(ED$)<VAL(DE$) THEN 1780
1800 LOCATE ZEB,42:IF O$<"3" THEN GOSUB 1050:TD=JU#-JL
          :TY=TD/365:PRINT "Days to Expiration      "TD:ZEB=ZEB+1
1810 LOCATE ZEB,42:IF O$<"7" AND O$<"2" AND O$<"3" THEN INPUT
          "Volatility              ",SD:ZEB=ZEB+1
1820 SP=SD/100
1830 LOCATE ZEB,42:IF O$<"4" AND O$<"3" THEN INPUT"Short
          Term Rates       ",RA:ZEB=ZEB+1
1840 RP=RA/100
1850 IF O$="3" OR CM$="C" THEN U=UU
1860 LOCATE ZEB,42:IF O$="2" THEN
          INPUT"Call Price                ",C:ZEB=ZEB+1
          :LOCATE ZEB,42 :INPUT"Put Price          ",PU
          :ZEB=ZEB+1
1870 LOCATE ZEB,42:IF O$="3" THEN
          PRINT"For Strike Price"E:ZEB=ZEB+1:LOCATE ZEB,42
          :INPUT"Call Price          ",C:ZEB=ZEB+1
          :LOCATE ZEB,42:INPUT"Put Price            ",PU
          :ZEB=ZEB+1
1880 LOCATE ZEB,42:IF O$="3" THEN PRINT"For Strike
          Price"EC:ZEB=ZEB+1:LOCATE ZEB,42
1890 IF O$="3" THEN INPUT"Call Price              ",C1
          :ZEB=ZEB+1:LOCATE ZEB,42:INPUT"Put
          Price         ",P1:ZEB=ZEB+1
1900 LOCATE ZEB,42
1910 IF O$="7" THEN INPUT "For <P>ut or <C>all       ",PYUK$
          :IF ASC(PYUK$)>90 THEN PYUK$=CHR$(ASC(PYUK$)-32)
1920 IF O$="7" AND PYUK$<"P" AND PYUK$<"C" THEN 1900 ELSE
          IF O$="7" THEN ZEB=ZEB+1
```

```
1930 LOCATE ZEB,42:IF O$><"3" AND CM$><"C" THEN
          INPUT "Dividends per Share in $   ",DA$:DA=VAL(DA$)
          :U=UU-DA:LOCATE ZEB,67:PRINT DA:ZEB=ZEB+1
1940 DPP=E:LOCATE ZEB,42:IF O$><"4" AND O$><"3" AND CM$><"S"
          THEN INPUT"Margin per Contract        ",DPP:ZEB=ZEB+1
1950 DX=1:LOCATE ZEB,42:IF O$><"4" AND CM$><"S" THEN
          INPUT"Dollars per Full Point      ",DX:ZEB=ZEB+1
1960 IF CM$="S" THEN DX=100:DPP=E*100
1970 IF O$="7" AND PYUK$="C" THEN LOCATE ZEB,42:INPUT"Call
          Price                  ",C:ZEB=ZEB+1
1980 IF O$="7" AND PYUK$="P" THEN LOCATE ZEB,42:INPUT"Put
          Price                  ",C:ZEB=ZEB+1
1990 IF O$="1" THEN LOCATE ZEB,41:PRINT ZA$:ZEB=ZEB+2
2000 IF O$="7" THEN LOCATE ZEB,41:PRINT ZA$:GOTO 2590
2010 LOCATE ZEB,41:IF O$="4" THEN PRINT ZA$:ZEB=ZEB+2:GOTO 2310
2020 IF O$="2" THEN ZEB=ZEB+1:GOTO 2240
2030 IF O$="3" THEN ZEB=ZEB+1:GOTO 2370
2040 IF O$="5" THEN 2420
2050 IF O$="6" THEN 2720
2060 IF O$="10" THEN LOCATE ZEB,42:INPUT"No. Days to
          Skip             ",IC:ZEB=ZEB+1:GOTO 2870
2070 REM
2080 GOSUB 3060
2090 PR=INT((PR*1000)+.5)/1000
2100 ZEB=ZEB-1:LOCATE ZEB,42:PRINT "Fair Market Call
          Value ="PR:ZEB=ZEB+1:PRCALL=PR
2110 N1=INT(N1*1000)/1000
2120 LOCATE ZEB,42:PRINT "Delta                    ="N1:ZEB=ZEB+1
2130 GOSUB 3290
2140 PR=INT((PR*1000)+.5)/1000
2150 LOCATE ZEB,42:PRINT "Fair Market Put Value  ="PR
          :ZEB=ZEB+1:PRPUT=PR
2160 N1=INT(N1*1000)/1000
2170 LOCATE ZEB,42:PRINT "Delta                    ="N1:ZEB=ZEB+1
2180 GOSUB 4010
2190 ZEB=ZEB+1
2200 LOCATE ZEB,42:PRINT "Press Any Key to Continue...";
2210 LOCATE ZEB,71:O$=INKEY$:IF O$="" THEN 2210
2220 PR=0:E=0:U=0:UU=0:DA=0:DX=0:RP=0:RY=0:RA=0:TY=0:Z=0:ZZ=0
          :N=0:C=0:DPP=0:PU=0:SD=0:TD=0:IC=0:IB=0:EC=0:N1=0
          :N2=0:CA=0:ZEB=0
2230 O$="":GOSUB 3630:GOTO 1520
2240 REM CONVERSION
2250 LOCATE ZEB,41:PRINT ZA$:ZEB=ZEB+1
2260 CA=RP*TY*DPP:IF CC$="C" THEN CA=DPP*(1-((1+RP)^(-TY)))
2270 PR=((E+C-UU+DA-PU)*DX)-CA:PR=INT(PR*100)/100
2280 LOCATE ZEB,42:PRINT"Conversion at $"PR:ZEB=ZEB+2
2290 PR=((-E-C+UU-DA+PU)*DX)+CA:PR=INT(PR*100)/100
2300 LOCATE ZEB,42:PRINT"Reversal at    $"PR:ZEB=ZEB+2:GOTO 2190
2310 Z=(LOG(E/U))/(SP*(TY^.5)):GOSUB 3510
2320 LOCATE ZEB,42:PRINT"Probability <"E" by "ED$" is"
          (INT(N*1000)/1000)*100"%":ZEB=ZEB+2
2330 LOCATE ZEB,42:PRINT"Probability >"E" by "ED$" is"
          (1-(INT(N*1000)/1000))*100"%":ZEB=ZEB+2
2340 UH=U*EXP(SP*(TY^.5)):UL=U+(U-UH):UH=INT(UH*100)/100
          :UL=INT(UL*100)/100
2350 LOCATE ZEB,42:PRINT"One Std Dev Targets at Expiration
          Are:":ZEB=ZEB+1:LOCATE ZEB,42:PRINT UH"      "UL:ZEB=ZEB+2
2360 GOTO 2190
2370 LOCATE ZEB,41:PRINT ZA$:ZEB=ZEB+1
2380 LOCATE ZEB,42:PRINT"Arbitrage Analysis - Boxes":ZEB=ZEB+2
2390 X=ABS(ABS(E-EC)-ABS((C-C1)-(PU-P1))):X=INT(X*100)/100:X=X*DX
2400 LOCATE ZEB,42:PRINT "Riskless Profit = $"X
2410 ZEB=ZEB+2:GOTO 2190
2420 GOSUB 3630:LOCATE 3,41:PRINT"Strike":LOCATE 3,59:PRINT "Fair"
          :LOCATE 3,73:PRINT"Fair"
2430 LOCATE 4,41:PRINT "Price":LOCATE 4,51:PRINT "Delta"
          :LOCATE 4,66:PRINT"Delta"
2440 LOCATE 4,59:PRINT"Call":LOCATE 4,73:PRINT "Put"
2450 LOCATE 1,42:PRINT "Current Price is"UU:LOCATE 1,69
          :PRINT"Exp. "ED$
2460 ST=5
2470 IB=E:FOR E=IB TO (IB+(IC*16)) STEP IC
2480 ST=ST+1
2490 LOCATE ST,41:PRINT INT((E*1000)+.5)/1000
```

```
2500 GOSUB 3060
2510 PR=INT((PR*1000)+.5)/1000:N1=INT((N1*1000)+.5)/1000
2520 LOCATE ST,59:PRINT PR:LOCATE ST,51:PRINT N1
2530 GOSUB 3290
2540 PR=INT((PR*1000)+.5)/1000:N1=INT((N1*1000)+.5)/1000
2550 LOCATE ST,73:PRINT PR:LOCATE ST,66:PRINT N1
2560 NEXT E
2570 ZEB=ST+1
2580 GOTO 2210
2590 REM IMPLIED VOLATILTIY SUBTNE
2600 VP=0
2610 HI=1:LO=0:SP=.5
2620 VP=VP+1
2630 IF PYUK$="C" THEN GOSUB 3060 ELSE IF PYUK$="P" THEN GOSUB 3290
2640 PR=INT((PR*1000)+.5)/1000
2650 IF VP>999 THEN 2680
2660 IF PR>C THEN HI=SP:SP=((SP+LO)/2):GOTO 2620
2670 IF PR<C THEN LO=SP:SP=((SP+HI)/2):GOTO 2620
2680 SP=SP*100
2690 SP=INT((SP*1000)+.5)/1000
2700 IF O$="X" THEN RETURN
2710 ZEB=ZEB+2:LOCATE ZEB,42:PRINT"Implied Volatility is"SP"%"
     :ZEB=ZEB+2:GOTO 2190
2720 GOSUB 3630:LOCATE 4,41:PRINT"Price":LOCATE 3,59:PRINT"Fair"
     :LOCATE 3,73:PRINT"Fair":LOCATE 4,51:PRINT"Delta"
     :LOCATE 4,66:PRINT"Delta":LOCATE 1,42:PRINT "Strike
     Price is"E:LOCATE 2,42:PRINT"Expires "ED$:LOCATE 3,41
     :PRINT"Market"
2730 LOCATE 4,59:PRINT"Call":LOCATE 4,73:PRINT"Put"
2740 ST=5
2750 IB=UU:FOR UU=IB TO(IB+(IC*16)) STEP IC
2760 ST=ST+1
2770 U=UU-DA:IF O$="3" OR CM$="C" THEN U=UU
2780 LOCATE ST,41:PRINT INT((UU*1000)+.5)/1000
2790 GOSUB 3060
2800 PR=INT((PR*1000)+.5)/1000:N1=INT((N1*1000)+.5)/1000
2810 LOCATE ST,59:PRINT PR:LOCATE ST,51:PRINT N1
2820 GOSUB 3290
2830 PR=INT((PR*1000)+.5)/1000:N1=INT((N1*1000)+.5)/1000
2840 LOCATE ST,73:PRINT PR:LOCATE ST,66:PRINT N1
2850 NEXT UU
2860 ZEB=ST+1:GOTO 2210
2870 GOSUB 3630:LOCATE 4,41:PRINT"Price":LOCATE 3,59:PRINT"Fair"
     :LOCATE 3,73:PRINT"Fair":LOCATE 4,51:PRINT"Delta"
     :LOCATE 4,66:PRINT"Delta":LOCATE 1,42
     :PRINT "Strike ="E"  Underlying ="UU:LOCATE 2,42
     :PRINT"Expires "ED$
2880 LOCATE 4,59:PRINT"Call":LOCATE 4,73:PRINT"Put"
2890 ST=5
2900 IB=TD:FOR TD=IB TO (IB-(IC*16)) STEP -IC:TY=TD/365:IF TY<=0
     THEN TY=.0000001:GOTO 3050
2910 ST=ST+1:JN#=JL+(IB-TD):JX#=INT(((JN#-1867216#)-.25)/36524.25)
     :JX#=JN#+1+JX#-INT(.25*JX#)+1524
2920 JC#=INT(6680+((JX#-2439870#)-122.1)/365.25)
     :JD#=365*JC#+INT(.25*JC#):JE#=INT((JX#-JD#)/30.6001)
     :IDJ#=JX#-JD#-INT(30.6001*JE#):MM#=JE#-1
     :IF MM#>12 THEN MM#=MM#-12
2930 YN#=JC#-4715:IF MM#>2 THEN YN#=YN#-1
2940 IF YN#<=0 THEN YN#=YN#-1
2950 ID$=RIGHT$(STR$(IDJ#),(LEN(STR$(IDJ#))-1)):IF LEN(ID$)<2
     THEN ID$="0"+ID$
2960 MO$=RIGHT$(STR$(MM#),(LEN(STR$(MM#))-1)):IF LEN(MO$)<2
     THEN MO$="0"+MO$
2970 DB$=RIGHT$(STR$(YN#),2)+MO$+ID$:LOCATE ST,41:PRINT
     INT((VAL(DB$)*1000)+.5)/1000
2980 GOSUB 3060
2990 PR=INT((PR*1000)+.5)/1000:N1=INT((N1*1000)+.5)/1000
3000 LOCATE ST,59:PRINT PR:LOCATE ST,51:PRINT N1
3010 GOSUB 3290
3020 PR=INT((PR*1000)+.5)/1000:N1=INT((N1*1000)+.5)/1000
3030 LOCATE ST,73:PRINT PR:LOCATE ST,66:PRINT N1
3040 NEXT TD
3050 ZEB=ST+1:GOTO 2210
3060 REM CALL EVALUATION SUBTNE
```

```
3070 IF CM$="C" THEN 3180
3080 IF TY=0 THEN N=0:GOTO 3110
3090 Z=(LOG(U/E)+((RP+((SP^2)/2))*TY))/(SP*(TY^.5))
3100 GOSUB 3510
3110 N1=N:IF TY=0 THEN N=0:GOTO 3140
3120 Z=((LOG(U/E)+((RP+((SP^2)/2))*TY))/(SP*(TY^.5)))-(SP*(TY^.5))
3130 GOSUB 3510
3140 N2=N
3150 PR=(U*N1)-(EXP(-(RP*TY))*(E*N2))
3160 IF PR<(U-E) THEN N1=1:PR=U-E
3170 RETURN
3180 REM HERE IS BLACK-SCHOLES MODIFIED FOR FUTURES OPTIONS
3190 IF TY=0 THEN N=0:GOTO 3220
3200 Z=(LOG(U/E)+(((SP^2)*TY)/2))/(SP*(TY^.5))
3210 GOSUB 3510
3220 N1=N:IF TY=0 THEN N=0:GOTO 3250
3230 Z=((LOG(U/E)+(((SP^2)*TY)/2))/(SP*(TY^.5)))-(SP*(TY^.5))
3240 GOSUB 3510
3250 N2=N
3260 PR=EXP(-(RP*TY))*((U*N1)-(E*N2))
3270 IF PR<(U-E) THEN N1=1:PR=U-E
3280 RETURN
3290 REM PUT EVAL ROUTINE - FINDS FAIR VALUE VIA THE CONVERSION METHOD
3300 REM COMPUTES FAIR CALL(NOT ADJ FOR DIVS) + STRIKE - UNDLYNG + DIVS
3310 REM THEN MULTUPLIES THE WHOLE THING BY $ PER PT, ADDS CARRYING CHGS
3320 REM THEN DIVIDES WHOLE THING BY $ PER POINT
3330 CA=RP*TY*DPP:IF CC$="C" THEN CA=DPP*(1-((1+RP)^(-TY)))
3340 IF O$<>"6" THEN U=UU
3350 IF PTY$="P" THEN 3380
3360 GOSUB 3060
3370 PR=(((PR+E-UU+DA)*DX)-CA)/DX:IF TY=0 THEN N=0:GOTO 3410
3380 IF CM$="S" THEN Z=-((LOG(U/E)+((RP+((SP^2)/2))*TY))
       /(SP*(TY^.5)))
3390 IF CM$="C" THEN Z=-((LOG(U/E)+(((SP^2)*TY)/2))
       /(SP*(TY^.5)))
3400 GOSUB 3510
3410 N1=N:IF PTY$="C" THEN 3500
3420 IF TY=0 THEN N=0:GOTO 3460
3430 IF CM$="S" THEN Z=-((LOG(U/E)+((RP+((SP^2)/2))*TY))
       /(SP*(TY^.5)))-(SP*(TY^.5))
3440 IF CM$="C" THEN Z=-((((LOG(U/E)+(((SP^2)*TY)/2))
       /(SP*(TY^.5))))
       -(SP*(TY^.5)))
3450 GOSUB 3510
3460 N2=N
3470 IF CM$="C" THEN PR=-(EXP(-RP*TY))*(U*N1-E*N2)
3480 IF CM$="S" THEN PR=-((U*N2)-(EXP((RP*TY))*(E*N1)))
3490 IF PR<E-U THEN PR=E-U:N1=1
3500 RETURN
3510 REM CUMULATIVE NORMAL DISTRIBUTION R'UTINE BY 5TH ORDER POLYNOMIAL
3520 IF FI$="I" THEN 3680
3530 ZZ=.3989423*EXP((-(Z^2))/2)
3540 Y=1/(1+(ABS(Z)*.2316419))
3550 N=1-(ZZ*((1.330274*Y^5)-(1.821256*Y^4)+(1.781478*Y^3)
       -(.3565638*Y^2)+(.3193815*Y)))
3560 IF Z<0 THEN N=1-N
3570 RETURN
3580 CLS:END
3590 FOR X=24 TO 1 STEP -1:LOCATE X,1
       :PRINT"                                            :";
3600 NEXT:LOCATE 1,1:RETURN
3610 FOR X=1 TO 24:LOCATE X,1
       :PRINT"                                            ";
3620 NEXT:LOCATE 1,1:RETURN
3630 FOR X=1 TO 24:LOCATE X,41
       :PRINT"                                            ";
3640 NEXT:LOCATE 1,1:RETURN
3650 ZEB=23
3660 LOCATE ZEB,1:O$=INKEY$:IF O$="" THEN 3660
3670 CLS:PR=0:E=0:U=0:UU=0:DA=0:DX=0:RP=0:RY=0:RA=0:TY=0:Z=0:ZZ=0
       :N=0:C=0:DPP=0:PU=0:SD=0:TD=0:IC=0:IB=0:EC=0:N1=0:N2=0
       :CA=0:ZEB=0:PYUK$="":GOTO 1340
3680 REM CUMULATIVE NORMAL DISTRIBUTION ROUTINE BY INFINITE SERIES EXPANSION
3690 IF Z>4 THEN 3840
3700 IF Z<-4 THEN 3860
```

```
3710 ZZ=ABS(Z)/SQR(2)
3720 N%=0
3730 S=ZZ
3740 T=ZZ
3750 REM START LOOPING
3760 N%=N%+1
3770 H=S
3780 T=2*T*(ZZ^2)/(1+(2*N%))
3790 S=T+H
3800 IF(T>.000001*S) THEN 3750
3810 EEE=S*EXP(-ZZ^2)/SQR(3.14159)
3820 IF Z<0 THEN N=.5-EEE ELSE N=.5+EEE
3830 RETURN
3840 N=1
3850 RETURN
3860 N=0
3870 RETURN
3880 REM INPUT JULIAN# AND OUTPUT YMD$
3890 JB#=JULIAN#+1+(INT(((JULIAN#-1867216!)-.25)/36524.25))
        -INT(.25*(INT(((JULIAN#-1867216!)-.25)/36524.25)))+1524
3900 JC#=INT(6680+((JB#-2439870!)-122.1)/365.25)
3910 JD#=365*JC#+INT(.25*JC#):JE#=INT((JB#-JD#)/30.6001)
        :ID#=JB#-JD#-INT(30.6001*JE#):MM#=JE#-1
        :IF MM#>12 THEN MM#=MM#-12
3920 YY#=JC#-4715:IF (MM#>2) THEN YY#=YY#-1
3930 IF YY#<0 THEN YY#=YY#-1
3940 ID$=STR$(ID#)
3950 IF LEFT$(ID$,1)=" " THEN ID$=RIGHT$(ID$,LEN(ID$)-1):GOTO 3950
3960 IF LEN(ID$)<2 THEN ID$="0"+ID$
3970 MM$=STR$(MM#)
3980 IF LEFT$(MM$,1)=" " THEN MM$=RIGHT$(MM$,(LEN(MM$)-1)):GOTO 3980
3990 IF LEN(MM$)<2 THEN MM$="0"+MM$
4000 YMD$=RIGHT$(STR$(YY#),2)+MM$+ID$:RETURN
4010 ZEB=ZEB+1:LSTDAY#=JU#:LOCATE ZEB,42:INPUT "FIND OPTIMAL f
        FOR <P>ut or <C>all ",PYUK$:IF ASC(PYUK$)>90 THEN
        PYUK$=CHR$(ASC(PYUK$)-32)
4020 ZEB=ZEB+1:LOCATE ZEB,42:INPUT "COMM. PER CONTRACT (1
        SIDE) $",COMMIS:COMMIS=COMMIS/DX
4030 ZEB=ZEB+1
4040 LOCATE ZEB,42:INPUT "MINIMUM TICK IN DECIMAL ",MINTICK
4050 ZEB=ZEB+1:LOCATE ZEB,42:PRINT "WAIT"
4060 WSTDAY#=JU#:ED$=DE$:GOSUB 1040:FSTDAY#=JU#:CURPRC=UU
4070 TROOF=0:TRUEF=0:TGEO=0:NSTDAY#=FSTDAY#+1:WHILE NSTDAY#<=WSTDAY#
4080 X%=CINT((((NSTDAY#+1)/7)-INT((NSTDAY#+1)/7))*7):IF X%=0 OR
        X%=6 THEN NSTDAY#=NSTDAY#+1:GOTO 4080
4090 GOSUB 4210:IF P2X>TGEO THEN TGEO=P2X:TROOF=TRUEF:MSTDAY#=NSTDAY#
4100 NSTDAY#=NSTDAY#+1
4110 WEND
4120 IF TGEO<=1.0 OR TROOF<=0 OR TROOF>1 THEN 4190
4130 LOCATE ZEB,42:PRINT "GEOMETRIC MEAN ="TGEO
4140 ZEB=ZEB+1:LOCATE ZEB,42:PRINT"OPTIMAL f ="TROOF
4150 ZEB=ZEB+1:LOCATE ZEB,42
4160 IF PYUK$="C" AND TROOF>0 THEN PRINT "OR 1 CONTRACT
        PER";USING"$$######,.##";(PRCALL*DX)/TROOF
4170 IF PYUK$="P" AND TROOF>0 THEN PRINT "OR 1 CONTRACT
        PER";USING"$$######,.##";(PRPUT*DX)/TROOF
4180 JULIAN#=MSTDAY#:GOSUB 4650:ZEB=ZEB+1:LOCATE ZEB,42:PRINT
        "OPTIMAL EXIT IS "YMD$
4190 ZEB=ZEB+1
4200 RETURN
4210 REM PARABOLIC INTERPOLATION
4220 TOLERANCE=.005:PCOUNT%=0
4230 PT1=0:PT3=1:P3X=0:P1X=0:PT2=1-TOLERANCE
4240 PCOUNT%=PCOUNT%+1
4250 TWTEMP#=1:TCONT=0
4260 GOSUB 4370
4270 P2X=TWTEMP#
4280 X=((PT2-PT1)*(P2X-P3X)-(PT2-PT3)*(P2X-P1X))
4290 IF X=0 THEN X=.00001
4300 ABSCISSA=PT2-.5*((((PT2-PT1)^2)*(P2X-P3X)-((PT2-PT3)^2)
        *(P2X-P1X))/X)
4310 TPT2=PT2
4320 IF ABS(ABSCISSA-TPT2)<=TOLERANCE THEN TRUEF=TPT2:RETURN
4330 IF ABSCISSA>TPT2 THEN PT1=PT2:P1X=P2X
```

```
4340 IF ABSCISSA<TPT2 THEN PT3=PT2:P3X=P2X
4350 PT2=ABSCISSA
4360 GOTO 4240
4370 REM LOOP THROUGH WEEKDAYS AND PRICES OF -3 TO +3 STD DEVS,
4380 REM GET HPRS & GEOMEANS
4390 XSTDAY#=NSTDAY#
4400 X%=CINT((((XSTDAY#+1)/7)-INT(((XSTDAY#+1)/7))*7)
          REM WHAT DAY OF THE WEEK IS XSTDAY#
4410 IF X%=0 OR X%=6 THEN 4620
4420 TY=(XSTDAY#-FSTDAY#+1)/365
4430 LOPRC=CURPRC-3*((CURPRC*EXP(SP*(TY^(1/2))))-CURPRC)
          REM 1 STD DEV BELOW
4440 LOPRC=INT(LOPRC/MINTICK)*MINTICK REM ROUND IT DOWN TO THE TICK
4450 HIPRC=CURPRC+3*((CURPRC*EXP(SP*(TY^(1/2))))-CURPRC)
          REM 1 STD DEV ABOVE
4460 HIPRC=(INT(HIPRC/MINTICK)*MINTICK)+MINTICK REM ROUND IT UP TO THE TICK
4470 FOR UU=LOPRC TO HIPRC STEP MINTICK
4480 IF CM$><"C" THEN U=UU-DA ELSE U=UU
4485 TY=(XSTDAY#-FSTDAY#+1)/365
4490 TCONT=TCONT+1:IF TY=0 THEN PROB=0:GOTO 4530
4500 Z=LOG(U/CURPRC)/(SP*(TY^(1/2)))
4510 GOSUB 3510  REM CALCULATE PROBABILITY
4520 IF U<=CURPRC THEN PROB=N ELSE PROB=1-N
4530 TY=(LSTDAY#-XSTDAY#)/365
4540 IF PYUK$="C" THEN GOSUB 3060
4550 IF PYUK$="P" THEN GOSUB 3120
4560 ON ERROR GOTO 0
4570 IF (PR-COMMIS)<0 THEN X=0 ELSE X=PR-COMMIS
4580 IF PYUK$="C" THEN HPR=1+(PT2*((X/(PRCALL+COMMIS))-1))
4590 IF PYUK$="P" THEN HPR=1+(PT2*((X/(PRPUT+COMMIS))-1))
4595 IF HPR<=0 THEN HPR=0 ELSE HPR=HPR^PROB
4600 TWTEMP#=TWTEMP#*HPR
4610 NEXT
4620 XSTDAY#=XSTDAY#+1
4630 RETURN
4640 REM END OF OPTIMAL F ROUTINE
4650 REM INPUT JULIAN# AND OUTPUT YMD$
4660 JB#=JULIAN#+1+(INT(((JULIAN#-1867216!)-.25)/36524.25))
          -INT(.25*(INT(((JULIAN#-1867216!)-.25)/36524.25)))+1524
4670 JC#=INT(6680+((JB#-2439870!)-122.1)/365.25)
4680 JD#=365*JC#+INT(.25*JC#):JE=INT((JB#-JD#)/30.6001)
          :ID#=JB#-JD#-INT(30.6001*JE#):MM#=JE#-1
          :IF MM#>12 THEN MM#=MM#-12
4690 YY#=JC#-4715:IF (MM#>2) THEN YY#=YY#-1
4700 REM
4710 IF YY#<0 THEN YY#=YY#-1
4720 ID$=STR$(ID#)
4730 IF LEFT$(ID$,1)=" " THEN ID$=RIGHT$(ID$,LEN(ID$)-1):GOTO 4730
4740 IF LEN(ID$)<2 THEN ID$="0"+ID$
4750 MM$=STR$(MM#)
4760 IF LEFT$(MM$,1)=" " THEN MM$=RIGHT$(MM$,(LEN(MM$)-1)):GOTO 4760
4770 IF LEN(MM$)<2 THEN MM$="0"+MM$
4780 YMD$=RIGHT$(STR$(YY#),2)+MM$+ID$:RETURN
```

APPENDIX F

The Portfolio Program

Next is the program DIV.C, the portfolio program. This is the program that was discussed in Chapter 6; it will take the daily trade profits and losses from a file and compute the intercorrelations of the different daily equity curves of different market systems. The program is set up to simulate this as if you were trading the systems on a fixed fractional basis. The end result is an output file that shows you how best to diversify your account equity among the different market systems.

Shown first is the input data file to this program. The code for the program is provided in C, and you can alter it to suit the input file you want to use. The function **gitvarbls()** is the function in the C program that reads this input file; should you want to use a different input file format you will have to adjust **gitvarbls()** accordingly.

The input file's first line is simply the date and time stamp that the file was created on. The next line contains the name of the system. Line 3 is the contract name, the market that the program is run on. Lines 2 and 3 are appended together within the program and comprise the actual name for the market system. The following two lines are the parameter inputs. Next come the start and end dates. Note that it is necessary here to have a space between the words "START DATE:" and the date itself, "770926", as well as between the words "END DATE:" and the date itself, "780621". Lastly there is a line for how much commissions and slippage per trade there is, followed by a page heading that is four lines deep. After this heading, we go into the actual data.

The actual data exists as one line for each day. The width of the line is not important to the program as it reads each line. What is important is that there be whitespace (a blank or a tab) between each column, or item, on the line. In the columns, the data is presented as the date in YYMMDD format; the position, either L, F, or S for long, flat, or short respectively; and the price at which the system went long, flat, or short accordingly. This last column is followed by a column for the close on the given date. If the position is not flat, then the next column, the open equity, contains the appropriate amount or else a 0. Next is the drawdown, the maximum drawdown seen thus far in the run. This is followed by the cumulative running open + closed equity column and finally, the last column, the change from yesterday's cumulative running open + closed equity column. Note that not all of this information is used by the program. The only columns that the program uses are the first column, the date, and the last column, the daily net change in open + closed equity. The input file ends with a blank line followed again by the date and time stamp that the file was completed on.

Finally, note that this run assumes you are trading one contract straight through. The program internally converts this to trading on a fixed fractional basis.

Input File to DIV.C Program

```
08-07-1989 09:53:13
SYSTEM A
TBONDS
PARAM1 = 0    PARAM2 = 0    PARAM3 = 0
PARAM4 = 0    PARAM5 = 0    PARAM6 = 0
START DATE: 770926    END DATE: 780621
SLIPPAGE & COMMISSIONS PER TRADE:   $50.00
```

DATE	POS	FROM	CLOSE	OPEN EQ IN $$	DRAWDOWN IN $$	OPEN+CLOSED EQ IN $$	CHANGE IN $$
770927	L	10209	10209	0	0	0	0
770928	F	10208	10208	0	-80	-80	-80
770929	F	10208	10210	0	-80	-80	0
770930	S	10207	10207	0	-80	-80	0
771003	S	10207	10200	220	-80	140	220
771004	S	10207	10203	130	-80	50	-90
771005	S	10207	10202	160	-80	80	30
771006	S	10207	10128	340	-80	260	180
771007	S	10207	10121	560	-80	480	220
771010	S	10207	10119	630	-80	550	70
771011	S	10207	10106	1,030	-80	950	400
771012	F	10100	10029	0	-80	1,080	130
771013	L	10102	10031	-90	-90	990	-90
771014	L	10102	10107	160	-90	1,240	250
771017	L	10102	10102	0	-90	1,080	-160
771018	L	10102	10100	-60	-90	1,020	-60
771019	L	10102	10107	160	-90	1,240	220
771020	L	10102	10109	220	-90	1,300	60
771021	L	10102	10107	160	-90	1,240	-60
771024	L	10102	10107	160	-90	1,240	0
771025	S	10103	10100	100	-90	1,230	-10
771026	S	10103	10030	160	-90	1,290	60
771027	S	10103	10030	160	-90	1,290	0
771028	L	10028	10027	-31	-90	1,279	-11
771031	L	10028	10010	-561	-561	749	-530
771101	L	10028	9931	-901	-901	409	-340
771102	L	10028	9930	-931	-931	379	-30
771103	L	10028	9931	-901	-931	409	30
771104	L	10028	10008	-621	-931	689	280
771107	L	10028	10010	-311	-931	999	310
771108	L	10028	10023	-151	-931	1,159	160

DATE	POS	FROM	CLOSE	OPEN EQ IN $$	DRAWDOWN IN $$	OPEN+CLOSED EQ IN $$	CHANGE IN $$
771109	F	10023	10022	0	-931	1,110	-49
771110	L	10023	10024	30	-931	1,140	30
771111	L	10023	10108	530	-931	1,640	500
771114	F	10100	10100	0	-931	1,340	-300
.	.	.	.	.	.	.	.
.	.	.	.	.	.	.	.
.	.	.	.	.	.	.	.
.	.	.	.	.	.	.	.
.	.	.	.	.	.	.	.
780523	F	9511	9502	0	-1,020	2,940	0
780524	S	9429	9426	100	-1,020	3,040	100
780525	S	9429	9420	280	-1,020	3,220	180
780526	S	9427	9418	350	-1,020	3,290	70
780530	S	9429	9415	440	-1,020	3,380	90
780531	F	9417	9413	0	-1,020	3,270	-110
780601	F	9417	9418	0	-1,020	3,270	0
780602	F	9417	9428	0	-1,020	3,270	0
780605	F	9417	9431	0	-1,020	3,270	0
780606	F	9417	9503	0	-1,020	3,270	0
780607	F	9417	9507	0	-1,020	3,270	0
780608	F	9417	9502	0	-1,020	3,270	0
780609	F	9417	9430	0	-1,020	3,270	0
780612	F	9417	9429	0	-1,020	3,270	0
780613	F	9417	9431	0	-1,020	3,270	0
780614	F	9417	9505	0	-1,020	3,270	0
780615	F	9417	9503	0	-1,020	3,270	0
780616	F	9417	9427	0	-1,020	3,270	0
780619	F	9417	9423	0	-1,020	3,270	0
780620	F	9417	9415	0	-1,020	3,270	0
780621	F	9417	9407	0	-1,020	3,270	0

RUN ENDED 08-07-1989 09:53:13

Next is the output file of the program. In this example, three market systems were run. The program allows you the option to add an additional market system, called "CASH (NON-INTEREST BEARING)". There are times, in certain portfolios, where treating cash as a market system in and of itself is beneficial (per capital asset pricing theory). For instance, an optimal portfolio may have you allocate 10% of your capital to cash. This is not at all unusual.

The output report first shows you the dates that the system was run over. The dates the system selects are the latest start date and the earliest end date of all the systems used. Thus, only the time periods where all market systems were running are used. As can be seen, this way your input files need not start and end on exactly the same dates. Next, the report displays the number the program has assigned to each market system, as well as the amount you input for the system to use to trade one contract (1k). This is usually the optimal f factor in dollars, but the program lets you input any amount you want.

One of the constraints that this program allows for is maximum percentage commitments to any one market system. For the purposes of this report we set this to 50%. Therefore, combinations that would result in a market system getting a percentage commitment greater than 50% are not calculated. This amount is overridden if for a given number of markets there wouldn't be any portfolios. For example, even if you use a percentage commitment less than 100%, the program will always run the passes where there is only one market system. The same is true if you specify maximum percentage commitments less than 50%—the system will run all of the combinations of two market systems.

Now we go into the main body of the output report. Across the top are the numbers (1 to 4 in this example) corresponding to the different market systems. Next are the calculation columns, which will be discussed shortly. Running down along the left-hand side of the report are the different portfolio numbers for the different combinations that can be created. Let's take portfolio 8 for example, "50% SYSTEM A HEAT_ OIL 1k per $2210" and "50% SYSTEM Z DMARKS 1k per $2820". What this means is: If you divided your account so that 50% of your funds went to trading SYSTEM A HEAT_OIL, and you traded 1 contract for every $2,210 of that 50%, and you traded SYSTEM Z DMARKS 1 contract per every $2,820 of that 50% of your equity, then the results off to the right show how you would have fared. (Note that the program assumes you can trade fractional contracts, and they are adjusted on a daily basis as the account equity also changes on a daily basis). The system will now make this combination of market systems for each day in the run and will compute a daily HPR that is the net of the combination.

Now, we turn to the output results columns. The "avg hpr" is the arithmetic average of the daily HPRs of the combined market systems, and "std dev" is simply the population standard deviation of the daily HPRs. These two figures can be plotted on an X–Y graph to obtain the familiar modern portfolio theory graph. Average HPR is the return axis (Y axis) of the graph; standard deviation is the risk (X) axis. Next is the "drawdown", expressed as a percent of account equity. For portfolio number 8, this is 47.69%. In other words, if you were trading portfolio 8, at one point you would have had only 52.31% of your account equity left from the previous high mark. The final, and perhaps most important, column is the "geomean" (actually this is the estimated geomean), calculated from the arithmetic average of the daily HPRs and the population standard deviation, in their correct mathematical relation to each other.

Near the bottom of the report, the linear correlation coefficients between the daily HPRs of all market systems are listed. A value greater than + .3 is generally a very high correlation, indicating two market systems that should not be traded together. The lower the correlation coefficient the better the combination is. Rarely is a combination less than − .1.

At the end of the report is a section titled "BEST PORTFOLIOS". Here, we take the best portfolios for combinations of 1 market system, 2 market systems, and so on, based on two measures: the highest geometric means, and the lowest drawdowns (for those market systems that do not include cash).

If you work with this program you will notice another interesting aspect, one that the output results will bear out over and over: There isn't any benefit to diversifying into more than 3, 4, or sometimes 5 uncorrelated market systems. In fact, you will notice that around 4, 5, or sometimes 6 markets the performances actually start to deteriorate! This is proof that it's generally not how much you diversify but into what that counts.

Output File for DIV.C Program

FOR THE FOLLOWING MARKET SYSTEMS:

Data used is from 831010 to 890309

1 = SYSTEM A TBONDS   1k per $1901
2 = SYSTEM A HEAT_OIL   1k per $2210
3 = SYSTEM Z DMARKS   1k per $2820
4 = CASH (NON-INTEREST BEARING)

	1	2	3	4	avg hpr	std dev	drawdown	geomean
1	100%	0%	0%	0%	1.0250	0.1495	87.86%	1.0141
2	0%	100%	0%	0%	1.0054	0.0643	83.52%	1.0034
3	0%	0%	100%	0%	1.0091	0.1012	88.57%	1.0040
4	0%	0%	0%	100%	1.0000	0.0000	0.00%	1.0000
5	50%	50%	0%	0%	1.0152	0.0826	65.42%	1.0119
6	50%	0%	50%	0%	1.0171	0.0905	62.72%	1.0130
7	50%	0%	0%	50%	1.0125	0.0747	56.17%	1.0098
8	0%	50%	50%	0%	1.0073	0.0598	47.69%	1.0055
9	0%	50%	0%	50%	1.0027	0.0322	53.13%	1.0022
10	0%	0%	50%	50%	1.0045	0.0506	55.57%	1.0033
11	50%	40%	10%	0%	1.0156	0.0807	62.74%	1.0124
12	50%	30%	20%	0%	1.0160	0.0806	62.41%	1.0127
13	50%	20%	30%	0%	1.0163	0.0823	62.18%	1.0130
14	50%	10%	40%	0%	1.0167	0.0857	62.35%	1.0131
15	40%	50%	10%	0%	1.0136	0.0698	58.71%	1.0112
16	40%	40%	20%	0%	1.0140	0.0692	56.91%	1.0116
17	40%	30%	30%	0%	1.0144	0.0706	56.61%	1.0119
18	40%	20%	40%	0%	1.0147	0.0740	56.43%	1.0120
19	40%	10%	50%	0%	1.0151	0.0790	56.55%	1.0120
.	.	.	.	.	.	.	.	.
.	.	.	.	.	.	.	.	.
.	.	.	.	.	.	.	.	.

CORRELATION COEFFICIENTS:

+0.0426   SYSTEM A TBONDS
            SYSTEM A HEAT_OIL

+0.0066   SYSTEM A TBONDS
            SYSTEM Z DMARKS

−0.0071   SYSTEM A HEAT_OIL
            SYSTEM Z DMARKS

```
_____BEST PORTFOLIOS_____

Based on Highest Geometric Means:
# Mkts         Portfolio #        Geomean
   1               1              1.0141
   2               6              1.0130
   3              14              1.0131
   4              86              1.0126

Based on Lowest Drawdowns (without including cash):
# Mkts         Portfolio #        Drawdown
   1               2               83.52%
   2               8               47.69%
   3              27               41.53%
```

Finally, here is the code to the program. A few notes are in order. The program was compiled on the Microsoft C compiler version 5.0 using the large library for the IBM PC under PC or MS-DOS 2.0 or higher. As a result, no array may consume more than 64K. Therefore, the manifest constants "MAXMKTS" and "MAXDAYS" cannot be so high as to cause a problem with an array exceeding 64K. "MAXMKTS" is the number of market systems you are going to read in for any one run. "MAXDAYS" is the maximum number of days in any one input file. Unfortunately, the program could not be written in BASIC in a format similar to the one shown here in C, due to the numerous limitations of BASIC.

Note that the program uses the calendar functions described in Appendix D. Also note that all weekdays are used to figure HPRs from, whether or not there is a holiday on that weekday. This is necessary since not all exchanges have holidays on the same dates. When there is no data from the input file for a given weekday, the program assumes an HPR of 1.00 for that market system for that day. This is mathematically correct, since there is no equity change for that market system for that day.

The function **combos()** figures all the possible combinations of different market systems and the function **whatpcnts()** figures all the different percentage combinations that can be created for each combination passed to it by **combos()**. Whatpcnts() calls **getfolio()** once the combination and percent allocations are in place for each combination, and **getfolio()** does the calculations for the net HPRs of each combination.

This program is included for two reasons. The first is so that you may alter it to suit your particular needs. The second and more important reason is so that you may study the program to better understand the process described in the text.

```
    DIV.C Program (in C)

/* div.c a program to find the efficient frontier and geometric optimals */

#include <stdio.h>
#include <graph.h>
#include <dos.h>
```

```
#include <conio.h>
#include <string.h>
#include <math.h>          /*     *** note ****        */
#include <ctype.h>         /*    MAXMKTS * MAXDAYS     */
#define MAXMKTS 9          /*    must be < 16000       */
#define MAXDAYS 1600       /*  for hpr[][] to be <=64k */

static unsigned       howmany, howfew, nmbrmkts = 0;
static float    f[MAXMKTS+1];
static float    hpr[MAXMKTS+1][MAXDAYS+1];
static unsigned long    sdate[MAXMKTS+1], edate[MAXMKTS+1];
static unsigned       elem[MAXMKTS+1];
static float    amts[MAXMKTS+1];
static float    mpa;  ·
static int      usecash = 0;
char mkts[MAXMKTS+1][80];
char mktsys[MAXMKTS+1][50];
unsigned long tojul(unsigned long), toyymmdd(unsigned long);
unsigned dayofweek(unsigned long), nocols;
char *commaout(char *);
int yorn();
static char     outfl[50];
FILE *in;
struct bestg {
     unsigned  f1olnmbr[MAXMKTS+1];
     unsigned  f2olnmbr[MAXMKTS+1];
     float     gmn[MAXMKTS+1];
     float     lodraw[MAXMKTS+1];
} summa;

main()
{
     void gitvarbls(void), findhprs(void), combos(void), esum(void);

     fcloseall();
     gitvarbls();
     findhprs();
     combos();
     esum();
     exit(0);
}
void combos()
{
     unsigned a, x, b, w, z, y, nmbrdown, flag, minmkts = 0;
     void whatpcnts();
     float      pcnts;

     fcloseall();
     for (x = 0; x < MAXMKTS + 2; x++) {
          summa.f1olnmbr[x] = 0;
          summa.f2olnmbr[x] = 0;
          summa.gmn[x] = 0.0;
          summa.lodraw[x] = 1000.0;
     }
     summa.lodraw[0] = 0.0;
     flushall();
     printf("\n\n");
     printf("Specify Output File: ");
     scanf("%s", outfl);
     printf("\n\nSpecify Percentage Increments for Combining Market-Systems ");
     pcnts = 0.0;          /* reqd to get fp routines working correctly */
     scanf("%f", &pcnts);
     in = fopen( outfl, "w" );
     printf("\n\n\n\n\n");
     fprintf(in, "FOR THE FOLLOWING MARKET SYSTEMS:\n\n");
     fprintf(in, "Data used is from %lu to %lu\n\n", sdate[0], edate[0]);
     for (x = 1; x <= nmbrmkts - usecash; x++)
          fprintf(in, "%u = %s 1k per $%-7.0f\n", x, mktsys[x], f[x]);
     if (usecash)
          fprintf(in, "%u = CASH (NON-INTEREST BEARING) \n\n", nmbrmkts);
     fprintf(in, "\n      ");
     for (x = 1; x <= nmbrmkts; x++)
          fprintf(in, "%6u", x);
     fprintf(in, "  avg hpr   std dev    drawdown   geomean");
     minmkts = howfew;
```

```
        for (flag = 0; flag < 2; flag++) {
            if (flag == 1) {
                minmkts = 1;
                fprintf(in, "\n\nCORRELATION COEFFICIENTS:\n");
                printf("\n\nNow Calculating Correlation Coefficients.........");
            }
            for (x = minmkts; x <= howmany; x++) {
                for (a = 1; a <= nmbrmkts; a++) {
                    elem[a] = 0;
                    amts[a] = 0.0;
                }
                if (x == 1) {
                    for (a = 1; a <= nmbrmkts; a++) {
                        elem[1] = a;
                        whatpcnts(pcnts, flag);
                    }
                } else {
                    b = 1;
                    do {
                        w = 1;
                        for (a = b; a <= (x + b - 1); a++) {
                            elem[w] = a;
                            w++;
                        }
                        z = x;
                        nmbrdown = 0;
                        while (z > 1) {
                            for (y = (x + b - 1); y <= (nmbrmkts
                                                - nmbrdown); y++) {
                                elem[z] = y;
                                whatpcnts(pcnts, flag);
                            }
                            /* the combination is now recorded       */
                            /* e.g. elem[1]=1,elem[2]=2..elem[nmbmkts] */
                            /* now you need to set the %'s            */
                            z--;
                            nmbrdown++;
                        }
                        b++;
                    } while ((x + b - 1) <= nmbrmkts);
                }
            }
        }
    }
}


void whatpcnts(p, f)
float      p;
unsigned int   f;
{
    void corrcof(void);
    void getfolio(int);
    int  x, farright, k;
    float     mx, tempindex;

    for (x = nmbrmkts; x > 1; x--) {
        /* find how many elements u r pesently working with */
        if (elem[x] == 0)
            farright = x - 1;
    }
    if (elem[nmbrmkts] > 0)
        farright = nmbrmkts;
    mx = 1.0 - (p * (float)(farright - 1.0));
    if (f == 1) {
        if (farright == 2)
            corrcof();
        return;
    }
    amts[1] = mx;                     /* now initialize amounts */
    if (farright == 1) {
        getfolio(farright);
    } else if (farright == 2) {
        amts[2] = p;
        do {
```

```
                   if (amts[1] > .005 && amts[2] > .005)
                       getfolio(farright);
                   amts[1] -= p;
                   amts[2] += p;
             } while (amts[1] >= 0.0);
       } else {
             for (x = 1; x <= nmbrmkts; x++) {
                   if ((x <= farright) && ((1.0 / farright) <= mpa))
                       amts[x] = mpa;
                   if ((x <= farright) && ((1.0 / farright) > mpa))
                       amts[x] = 1.0 - p;
                   if (x > farright)
                       amts[x] = 0.0;
             }
             while (amts[1] > 0.0) {
                   tempindex = 0.0;
                   for (x = 1; x <= farright; x++)
                       tempindex += amts[x];
                   k = 1;
                   for (x = 1; x <= farright; x++) {
                       if (amts[x] < .00001)
                           k = 0;
                   }
                   if ((tempindex > 1.0 - ( p - .00001))
                           && (tempindex < 1.0 + ( p - .00001)) && (k))
                       getfolio(farright);
                   amts[farright] -= p;
                   for (x = farright; x > 1; x--) {
                       if (amts[x] <= 0.0) {
                           amts[x-1] -= p;
                           if ((1.0 / farright) <= mpa)
                               amts[x] = mpa;
                           if ((1.0 / farright) > mpa)
                               amts[x] = 1.0 - p;
                       }
                   }
             }
       }
}


void esum()
{
      int  x;

      fprintf(in, "\n\n\n\n_____BEST PORTFOLIOS_____\n");
      printf("\n\nNow Calculating Best Portfolios......................");
      fprintf(in, "\n\nBased on Highest Geometric Means:");
      fprintf(in, "\n# Mkts        Portfolio #        Geomean");
      for (x = howfew; x < howmany + 1; x++)
            fprintf(in, "\n%3d           %7u              %7.4f", x,
                    summa.f1olnmbr[x-1], summa.gmn[x-1]);
      if (!usecash)
            fprintf(in, "\n\nBased on Lowest Drawdowns:");
      fprintf(in, "\n# Mkts        Portfolio #        Drawdown");
      for (x = howfew; x < howmany + 1; x++)
            if (summa.lodraw[x-1] < 999.0)
                fprintf(in, "\n%3d           %7u              %7.2f%%", x,
                        summa.f2olnmbr[x-1], summa.lodraw[x-1]);
      fcloseall();
}


void getfolio(farright)
int  farright;
{
      unsigned  x, y, z;
      float     avg, sd, geom, sx;
      double    cum, max, ddown;
      static unsigned       foliono = 0;
      int  blowup = 0;

      foliono++;
      for (x = 1; x <= nocols; x++)
            hpr[0][x] = 0.0;
```

```
for (x = 1; x <= nocols; x++) {
    for (y = 1; y <= farright; y++) {
        z = elem[y];
        hpr[0][x] += (hpr[z][x] * amts[y]);
    }
    if (hpr[0][x] <= 0.0)
        blowup = 1;
}
if (blowup) {
    avg = 0.0;
    sd = 999.0;
    ddown = 1.0;
    geom = 0.0;
}
if (!blowup) {
    avg = 0.0;
    ddown = 0.0;
    max = 0.0;
    cum = 1.0;
    for (x = 1; x <= nocols; x++) {
        cum *= ((double) hpr[0][x]);
        if (cum > max)
            max = cum;                      /* ddown is % retracement  */
        if (max > 0) {                      /* therefore ddown=>100% is */
            if ((1.0 - (cum / max)) > ddown) /* a bust. If=40% means   */
                ddown = 1.0 - (cum / max);   /* the a/c had 60% left    */
            if (ddown > 1.0)
                ddown = 1.0;
        }
        avg += hpr[0][x];
    }
    avg = avg / ((float) nocols);
    sx = 0.0;
    for (x = 1; x <= nocols; x++)
        sx += ((hpr[0][x] - avg) * (hpr[0][x] - avg));
    sd = (float)(sqrt(sx / nocols));
}
_settextposition(23, 1); /* print near the bottom of the screen */
printf("Now Processing Portfolio Combination Number %u", foliono);
fprintf(in, "\n%5u", foliono);
_settextposition(24, 1); /* print this at the bottom of the screen */
x = 1;
y = 1;
while (y <= nmbrmkts) {
    if (elem[x] == y) {
        fprintf(in, "%5.0f%%", (amts[x] * 100));
        if (y < 13)
            printf("%5.0f%%", (amts[x] * 100));
        x++;
    } else {
        fprintf(in, "    0%%");
        if (y < 13)
            printf("    0%%");
    }
    y++;
}
if (!blowup)
    geom = sqrt((avg * avg) - (sd * sd));
fprintf(in, "  %7.4f    %7.4f    %7.2f%%    %7.4f", avg, sd, ((double)
        (ddown * 100.0)), geom);
if (geom > summa.gmn[farright-1]) {
    summa.f1olnmbr[farright-1] = foliono;
    summa.gmn[farright-1] = geom;
}
if (summa.lodraw[0] == 0)
    summa.lodraw[0] = 1000.0;
if (((ddown * 100) < summa.lodraw[farright-1]) &&
        (elem[farright] <= nmbrmkts - usecash)) {
    summa.f2olnmbr[farright-1] = foliono;
    summa.lodraw[farright-1] = (ddown * 100);
}
}

void corrcof()
```

```
{
    int  x;
    double    fc2, fc3, fc4, xbar, ybar = 0.0;
    float     cof;

    if ((elem[2] == nmbrmkts) && (usecash))
        return; /* if cash is one of them then forget it */
    xbar = 0.0;
    ybar = 0.0;
    for (x = 1; x <= nocols; x++) {
        xbar += hpr[elem[1]][x];
        ybar += hpr[elem[2]][x];
    }
    xbar /= nocols;
    ybar /= nocols;
    fc2 = 0.0;
    fc3 = 0.0;
    fc4 = 0.0;
    for (x = 1; x <= nocols; x++) {
        fc2 += ((hpr[elem[2]][x] - ybar) * (hpr[elem[1]][x] - xbar));
        fc3 += ((hpr[elem[1]][x] - xbar) * (hpr[elem[1]][x] - xbar));
        fc4 += ((hpr[elem[2]][x] - ybar) * (hpr[elem[2]][x] - ybar));
    }
    if (fc3 < 0)
        fc3 *= -1.0;
    if (fc4 < 0)
        fc4 *= -1.0;
    cof = (float)(fc2 / (sqrt(fc3) * sqrt(fc4)));
    fprintf(in, "\n\n%+6.4f     %s\n              %s", cof, mktsys[elem[1]],
            mktsys[elem[2]]);
}


void findhprs()
{
    int  x, y, z; /* x is what mkt, y is what day */

    z = nmbrmkts;
    if (usecash) {
        z = nmbrmkts - 1;
        for (y = 0; y <= nocols; y++) /*set cash hpr's to 1.0 */
            hpr[nmbrmkts][y] = 1.0;
    }
    for (x = 1; x <= z; x++) {
        hpr[x][0] = f[x];
        for (y = 1; y <= nocols; y++) {
            hpr[x][y] = ((hpr[x][y] / f[x]) + 1.0);
        }
        hpr[x][0] = 0.0;
    }
}


void gitvarbls()
{
    int  x;
    unsigned  y, u, eflag;
    FILE * datafile;
    char blk1[80], blk2[50], blk3[50];
    char owcrlf(char *);
    void dates(void);
    float     q, h;
    char p[25], i[25];

    printf("\n\n\nNumber of Market Systems You Wish to Investigate ? ");
    scanf("%u", &nmbrmkts);
    if (nmbrmkts > MAXMKTS)
        nmbrmkts = MAXMKTS;
    if (nmbrmkts < MAXMKTS) {
        printf("\n\nUse Cash as Another Market System ? ");
        usecash = yorn();
    }
    printf("\n\n\nMinimum Number of Markets Systems Per Combination? ");
    scanf("%u", &howfew);
```

```
    if ((howfew > (nmbrmkts + usecash)) || (howfew <= 0))
        howfew = 1;
    printf("\n\nMaximum Number of Markets Systems Per Combination? ");
    scanf("%u", &howmany);
    if ((howmany > (nmbrmkts + usecash)) || (howmany <= 0))
        howmany = nmbrmkts;
    mpa = 0.0;
    printf("\n\nMaximum Percentage Allotment Per Market System ? ");
    scanf("%f", &mpa);
    if (mpa > 1)
        mpa /= 100.0;
    if (mpa <= 0)
        mpa = 1;
    for (x = 1; x <= nmbrmkts; x++) {
        printf("\n\nLocation of File Number %d: ", x);
        scanf("%s", mkts[x]);
        printf("\nDollars to Apply Towards Each Contract $");
        f[x] = 0.0; /* reqd to get fp routines working correctly */
        scanf("%f", &f[x]);
    }
    fcloseall();
    for (x = 1; x <= nmbrmkts; x++) {
        fcloseall();
        printf("\n\nPlease make the file %s available and hit any key...",
                mkts[x]);
        getch();
        datafile = fopen( mkts[x], "r" );
        fgets(blk1, 80, datafile);
        fgets(blk2, 50, datafile);
        fgets(blk3, 50, datafile);
        strcat(mktsys[x], blk2);
        strcat(mktsys[x], blk3);
        fgets(blk1, 80, datafile);
        fgets(blk1, 80, datafile);
        fscanf(datafile, "%s", blk1);
        fscanf(datafile, "%s", blk1);
        fscanf(datafile, "%lu", &sdate[x]);
        fscanf(datafile, "%s", blk1);
        fscanf(datafile, "%s", blk1);
        fscanf(datafile, "%lu", &edate[x]);
        fclose(datafile);
        owcrlf(mktsys[x]);
    }
    fcloseall();
    dates(); /* now find latest start and earliest end dates set up array */
    for (x = 1; x <= nmbrmkts; x++) {
        u = 1;
        fcloseall();
        for (y = 0; y <= MAXDAYS; y++)
            hpr[x][y] = 0.0;
        printf("\n\nPlease make the file %s available and hit any key...",
                mkts[x]);
        getch();
        datafile = fopen( mkts[x], "r" );
        for (y = 1; y <= 12; y++)
            fgets(blk1, 80, datafile); /* read the first 12 blank lines */
        eflag = 0;
        do {
            fscanf(datafile, "%f", &q);
            if ((unsigned long)(q) == edate[0])
                eflag = 1;
            while (hpr[0][u] < q)  /* if date read, q, is>1st day in array */
                u++;
            fscanf(datafile, "%s", p);
            fscanf(datafile, "%s", p);
            fscanf(datafile, "%s", p);
            fscanf(datafile, "%s", p);
            fscanf(datafile, "%s", p);
            fscanf(datafile, "%s", p);
            fscanf(datafile, "%s", p);
            strcpy(i, commaout(p));
            if (q == hpr[0][u]) {
                hpr[x][u] = atof(i);
                u++;
```

```
                    }
                    if (eflag == 1)
                        eflag = 2;
            } while (eflag < 2 && *p != EOF && q != 0.0 );
            fclose(datafile);
    }
    if (usecash)
        nmbrmkts++;
}


void dates()
{
    unsigned long  xdate;
    unsigned  d, u, x;

    sdate[0] = 0;
    edate[0] = 999999;
    u = 1;
    for (x = 1; x <= nmbrmkts; x++) {
        if (sdate[x] > sdate[0])
            sdate[0] = sdate[x];
        if (edate[x] < edate[0])
            edate[0] = edate[x];
    }
    sdate[0] = tojul(sdate[0]);
    xdate = sdate[0];
    edate[0] = tojul(edate[0]);
    while (xdate <= edate[0]) {
        d = dayofweek(xdate);
        if (d > 0 && d < 6) {
            hpr[0][u] = (float)(toyymmdd(xdate));
            u++;
        }
        xdate++;
    }
    edate[0] = toyymmdd(edate[0]);
    sdate[0] = toyymmdd(sdate[0]);
    nocols = u;
}


unsigned  dayofweek(x)
unsigned long  (x);
{
    x++;
    return((unsigned int)(x % 7));
}


unsigned long  tojul(x) /* converts yymmdd format to julian */
unsigned long  (x);
{
    float      day, month, year, igreg, julday, ja, jy, jm;

    igreg = (float)(15 + 31 * (10 + 12 * 1582));
                            /* Gregorian Calendar Adopted October 15, 1582 */
    year = (float)((int)(x / 10000));
    month = (float)((int)((x / 100) - ((x / 10000) * 100)));
    day = (float)((int)(x - (year * 10000) - (month * 100)));
    year += 1900.0;
    if (year < 0.0)
        year++;
    if (month > 2.0) {
        jy = year;
        jm = month + 1.0;
    } else {
        jy = year - 1.0;
        jm = month + 13.0;
    }
    julday = (float)((unsigned long)(365.25 * jy));
    julday += ((float)((unsigned long)(30.6001 * jm)));
    julday += ((float)(day + 1720995));
    if ((day + 31 * (month + 12 * year)) >= igreg) {
        ja = (float)((unsigned long)(.01 * jy));
```

```
            julday += (2.0 - ja);
            julday += (.25 * ja);
     }
     return((unsigned long)(julday));
}
unsigned long  toyymmdd(x)
unsigned long  x;
{
     long igreg, jalpha, ja, jb, jc, jd, je, id, mm, yy, q;

     igreg = 2299161;
     if (x >= igreg) {
          jalpha = (((x - 1867216) - .25) / 36524.25);
          q = (.25 * jalpha);
          ja = x + 1 + jalpha - q;
     } else {
          ja = x;
     }
     jb = ja + 1524;
     jc = 6680 + ((jb - 2439870) - 122.1) / 365.25;
     q = .25 * jc;
     jd = 365 * jc + q;
     je = (jb - jd) / 30.6001;
     q = (30.6001 * je);
     id = jb - jd - q;
     mm = je - 1;        .
     if (mm > 12)
          mm = mm - 12;
     yy = jc - 4715;
     if (mm > 2)
          yy--;
     if (yy <= 0)
          yy--;
     yy = yy - 1900;
     return((unsigned long)((yy * 10000) + (mm * 100) + id));
}


char *commaout(str)
/* cnvts string to a format that can be atof'd, atol'd by getting the junk out*/
char str[14];
{
     char intarr[14]; /* store input string - up to 13 characters */
     int  ch;
     int  ind = 0; /* array index */
     int  u = 0;

     while ((ch = str[u]) != NULL) {
          if (ch == '-' || ch == '.' || isdigit(ch)) {
               intarr[ind] = ch;
               ind++;
          }
          u++;
     }
     intarr[ind] = NULL;
     strcpy(str, intarr);
}
char owcrlf(str)   /* converts cr and lf to spaces */
char str[160];
{
     int  a, b;

     a = 1;
     b = strlen(str);
     while (a <= b) {
          if (str[a] == '\012' || str[a] == '\015')
               str[a] = '\040';
          a++;
     }
     str[a] = NULL;
     str[a++] = NULL;
}


int  yorn ()
```

```
{
    int   x = 0;

    printf("  ( Y or N ) ");
    do {
        x = getch();
    } while (x != 'N' && x != 'n' && x != 'y' && x != 'Y');
    printf("%c", x);
    if (x == 'N' || x == 'n')
        return(0);
    if (x == 'Y' || x == 'y')
        return(1);
}
```

Important Notes on Using the DIV.C Program and Optimal Portfolios

It is quite possible that the sum of the percentage allocations exceed 100% for the portfolio that would result in the greatest geometric growth. Consider, for instance, two market systems, A and B, that are identical in every respect except that there is a negative correlation (r < 0) between them. Assume that the optimal f, in dollars, for each of these market systems is $5,000. Suppose the optimal portfolio (based on highest geomean) shows to be that portfolio that allocated 50% to each of the two market systems. This would mean that you should trade 1 contract for every $10,000 in equity for market system A and likewise for B. However, it can be shown that, when there is negative correlation, the optimal account growth is actually obtained by trading 1 contract for an amount less than $10,000 in equity for market system A and/or market system B. In other words, when there is negative correlation, you can have the sum of percentage allocations exceed 100%. Further, it is possible, although not too likely, that the individual percentage allocations to the market systems exceed 100% individually.

It is interesting to consider what happens when the correlation between two market systems approaches −1.00. When such an event occurs the amount by which to finance trades for the market systems tends to approach an infinitely small amount. This is so since the portfolio, the net result of the market systems, tends to never suffer a losing day (since an amount lost by a market system on a given day is offset by the same amount won by a different market system in the portfolio that day). Therefore, with diversification it is possible to have the optimal portfolio allocate a smaller f factor in dollars to a given market system than trading that market system alone would.

To accommodate this, you can divide the optimal f in dollars for each market system by the number of market systems you are running the program on. In our example, rather than inputting $5,000 as the optimal f for market system A, we would input $2,500 (dividing $5,000, the optimal f, by 2, the number of market systems we are going to run). Likewise for market system B. Now when the program determines the optimal geomean portfolio as being the one that allocates 50% to A and 50% to B, it means that you should trade 1 contract for every $5,000 in equity for market system A ($2,500/.5) and likewise for B.

If you decide to employ this method of using the program, you simply divide the optimal f in dollars for each market system by the total number of market systems you are planning on running. Also, you *must* make sure to use cash as another market system. Suppose in our previous example the program showed that the optimal growth is obtained at 50% in market system A and 40% in market system B. In other words, you should trade 1 contract for every $5,000 in equity for market system A and 1 contract for every $6,250 for B ($2,500/.4). If we were using cash as another market system, this combination would be run (showing the optimal portfolio as having the remaining 10% in cash). If we were not using cash as another market system, this combination wouldn't be run.

The reason the program doesn't allow for percentage allocations in excess of 100% is that these correlations are not set in stone. Should the correlations of the market systems all change to +1.00 between themselves, you will still be at the peak of the f curve (of the composite portfolio) by using the program with the actual optimal f values as input. However, be aware that the percentage allocations of the portfolio which would have resulted in the greatest geometric growth in the past can be in excess of 100%, and this program can accommodate this as described here.

APPENDIX G

Converting from a Z Score to a Confidence Limit

Chapter 1 presented a small table to convert from a Z score to a confidence limit at selected values. Since tables are awkward to work with from a programming standpoint, I am presenting a formula that will give you the confidence limit for a given Z score.

Confidence Limit = 1 − (2 * ((X * .31938153) − (Y * .356563782) + (X * Y * 1.781477937) − (Y * Y * 1.821255978) + (Y * Y * X * 1.330274429)) * (1/((EXP(Z * Z) * 6.283185307)^(1/2))))

where: X = 1.0/((ABS(Z) * .2316419) + 1.0)

Y = X^2

Z = The Z score you are converting from.

EXP() = The exponential function.

ABS() = The absolute value function.

This will give you the confidence limit for the so-called "two-tailed" test. To convert this to a confidence limit for a "one-tailed" test:

Confidence Limit = 1 − ((1-A)/2)

where: A = The "two-tailed" confidence limit.

APPENDIX H

How the Dispersion of Outcomes Affects Geometric Growth

This discussion will use a gambling illustration for the sake of simplicity. Let's consider two systems: System A, which wins 10% of the time and has a 28 to 1 win/loss ratio, and System B, which wins 70% of the time and has a 1 to 1 win/loss ratio. Our mathematical expectation, per unit bet, for A is 1.9 and for B is .4. Therefore we can say that for every unit bet System A will return, on average, 4.75 times as much as System B. But let's examine this under fixed fractional trading. We can find our optimal fs here by dividing the mathematical expectations by the win/loss ratios. This gives us an optimal f of .0678 for A and .4 for B. The geometric means for each system at their optimal f levels are then:

A = 1.044176755
B = 1.0857629

System	% Wins	Win:Loss	ME	f	Geomean
A	.1	28:1	1.9	.0678	1.0441768
B	.7	1:1	.4	.4	1.0857629

As you can see, System B, although less than one quarter the mathematical expectation of A, makes almost twice as much per bet (returning 8.57629% of your entire stake per bet on average when reinvesting at the optimal f levels) as does A (returning 4.4176755% of your entire stake per bet on average when reinvesting at the optimal f levels).

Now, assuming a 50% drawdown on equity will require a 100% gain to recoup, then:

> 1.044177 to the power of X is equal to 2.0 at approximately X equals 16.5, or more than 16 trades to recoup from a 50% drawdown for System A. Contrast this to System B where 1.0857629 to the power of X is equal to 2.0 at approximately X equals 9, or 9 trades for System B to recoup from a 50% drawdown.

What's going on here? Is this because System B has a higher percentage of winning trades? The reason B is outperforming A has to do with the dispersion of outcomes and its effect on the growth function. Most people have the mistaken impression that the growth function, the TWR, is:

$$TWR = (1 + R)^{\wedge}N$$

where: R = The interest rate per period, e.g., 7% = .07.
        N = The number of periods.

Since 1 + R is the same thing as an HPR, we can say that most people have the mistaken impression that the growth function, the TWR, is:

$$TWR = HPR^{\wedge}N$$

This function is true only when the return (i.e., the HPR) is constant, which is not the case in trading.

The real growth function in trading (or any event where the HPR is not constant) is the multiplicative product of the HPRs. Assume we are trading coffee. Our optimal f is one contract for every $21,000 in equity, and we have two trades—a loss of $210 and a gain of $210—for HPRs of .99 and 1.01, respectively. In this example our TWR would be:

$$TWR = 1.01 * .99$$
$$= .9999$$

An insight can be gained by using the estimated geometric mean to the power of N to estimate the TWR. This will very closely approximate this "multiplicative" growth function, the actual TWR:

$$\text{Estimated TWR} = (((HPR^{\wedge}2) - (SD^{\wedge}2))^{\wedge}(1/2))^{\wedge}N$$

or

$$\text{Estimated TWR} = (((HPR^{\wedge}2) - V)^{\wedge}(1/2))^{\wedge}N$$

where: N = The number of periods.

HPR = The mean HPR.

SD = The population standard deviation in HPRs.

V = The population variance in HPRs.

The insight gained is that we can see here, mathematically, the tradeoff between an increase in the arithmetic average trade (the HPR) and the variance in the HPRs. Hence the reason the 70% 1:1 system did better than the 10% 28:1 system!

Our goal should be to maximize the coefficient of this function; to maximize:

$$((HPR^2) - V)^{(1/2)}$$

Expressed literally, "To maximize *the square root of the quantity HPR squared minus the population variance in HPRs*."

The exponent of the estimated TWR, N, will take care of itself. That is, increasing N is not a problem because we can increase the number of markets we are following, trade more short-term types of systems, and so on.

However, these statistical measures of dispersion—variance and standard deviation (V and SD, respectively)—are difficult for most nonstatisticians to envision. What many people therefore use in lieu of these measures is known as the mean absolute deviation (which we'll call M). Essentially, to find M you simply take the average absolute value of the difference of each data point to an average of the data points.

$$M = \frac{\sum abs\,(X_i - \overline{X})}{N}$$

In a bell-shaped distribution (as is almost always the case with the distribution of P&Ls from a trading system) the mean absolute deviation equals about .8 of the standard deviation (in a normal distribution, it is .7979). Therefore, we can say:

$$M = .8 * SD \text{ and } SD = 1.25 * M$$

We will denote the arithmetic average HPR with the variable A and the geometric average HPR with the variable G. The estimated geometric mean can therefore be expressed as:

$$G = ((A^2) - V)^{(1/2)}$$

From this equation, we can obtain:

$$G^2 = ((A^2) - V)$$

Now, substituting the standard deviation squared for the variance, we obtain:

$$G^2 = ((A^2) - (SD^2))$$

From this equation we can isolate each variable, as well as isolating zero to obtain the fundamental relationships among the arithmetic mean, geometric mean, and dispersion, expressed as SD^2 here:

$$(A^2) - (G^2) - (SD^2) = 0$$

$$G^2 = (A^2) - (SD^2)$$

$$SD^2 = (A^2) - (G^2)$$

$$A^2 = (G^2) + (SD^2)$$

In these equations, the value SD^2 can also be written as V or as $(1.25 * M)^2$.

This brings us to the point where we can envision exactly what the relationships are. Notice that the last of these equations is the familiar Pythagorean theorem, the hypotenuse of a right angle triangle squared equals the sum of the squares of its sides. But here, the hypotenuse is A, and we want to maximize one of the legs, G.

In maximizing G, any increase in D (the dispersion leg, equal to SD or $V^{(1/2)}$ or $1.25 * M$) will require an offsetting increase in A. When D equals zero, then A equals G, thus conforming to the misconstrued growth function $TWR = (1 + R)^N$. Actually, when D equals zero, then A equals G is true per $G^2 = (A^2) - (SD^2)$.

So, in terms of their relative effect on G, we can state that an increase in A^2 is equal to a decrease of the same amount in $(1.25 * M)^2$.

$$A^2 = -((1.25 * M)^2)$$

To see this, consider when A goes from 1.1 to 1.2:

A	SD	M	G	A^2	SD^2 = (1.25 * M)^2
1.1	.1	.08	1.095445	1.21	.01
1.2	.4899	.39192	1.095445	1.44	.24
				.23 =	.23

When $A = 1.1$, we are given an SD of .1. When $A = 1.2$, to get an equivalent G, SD must equal .4899 per $SD^2 = (A^2) - (G^2)$. Since $M = .8 * SD$, then $M = .3919$. If we square the values and take the difference, they are both equal to .23, as predicted by $A^2 = -((1.25 * M)^2)$

Consider the following:

A	SD	M	G	A^2	SD^2 = (1.25 * M)^2
1.1	.25	.2	1.071214	1.21	.0625
1.2	.5408	.4327	1.071214	1.44	.2925
				.23 =	.23

Notice that in the previous example where we started with lower dispersion values (SD or M) how much proportionally greater an increase was required to yield the same G as opposed to this latter example. Thus, we can state that *the more you reduce your dispersion the better, with each reduction providing greater and greater benefit.* It is an exponential function, with a limit at the dispersion equal to zero, where G is then equal to A.

Hence, contrary to most people's misconception, in fixed fractional trading, taking a loss of $500 per contract is *more than twice as beneficial* as would be the case if the loss were $1,000!

Most people are concerned with arithmetic return (A) and believe that there are two facets that make up this return in trading. They believe that the percentage of winning trades and the ratio of average win to average loss are what matter. Perhaps that is why mathematical expectation (average trade) tends to be very highly regarded. However, the dispersion of outcomes is unaccounted for.

If a trader is trading on a fixed fractional basis, then the objective is to maximize G, not necessarily A. In maximizing G, the trader should realize that the standard deviation, SD, affects G in directly the same proportion as it does A, according to the Pythagorean theorem! Thus, a reduction in the standard deviation (SD) of one's trades is equivalent to an equal increase in the arithmetic average HPR (A), and vice versa!

Bibliography and Suggested Reading

Balsara, Nauzer J. *Money Management Discipline in Commodities Trading*, John Wiley & Sons, Inc., New York, 1990.

Cohen, Jerome B., Zinbarg, Edward D., and Zeikel, Arthur. *Investment Analysis and Portfolio Management*, Richard D. Irwin, Inc., Homewood, Illinois, 1977.

Epstein, Richard A. *The Theory of Gambling and Statistical Logic*, Academic Press, New York, 1977.

Gehm, Fred. *Commodity Market Money Management*, Ronald Press, John Wiley & Sons, New York, 1983.

Griffin, P. *The Theory of Blackjack*, Gamblers Press, Las Vegas, Nevada, 1981.

Kelly, J. L., Jr. "A New Interpretation of Information Rate," *Bell System Technical Journal*, pp. 917–926, July 1956.

Knuth, Donald E. *The Art of Computer Programming*, Addison-Wesley, Reading, Massachusetts, 1981.

Latane, Henry, and Tuttle, Donald. "Criteria for Portfolio Building," *Journal of Finance* 22, pp. 362–363, September 1967.

MacMillan, Lawrence. *Options as a Strategic Investment*, New York Institute of Finance, New York.

Markowitz, Dr. Harry. *Portfolio Selection—Efficient Diversification of Investments*, Yale University Press, New Haven, Connecticut, 1959.

Newman, James R. *The World of Mathematics*, Simon & Schuster, New York, 1956.

Pasachoff, Jay M. *Contemporary Astronomy*, W. B. Saunders Company, Philadelphia, 1977.

Pascual, Mike. *Bankroll Control: The Mathematics of Money Management*, Reno, Nevada, 1987. (Available from the author for $30. The subject matter deals with finding the optimal f values for simultaneous wagers. Mike Pascual has mathematically solved these problems and is the sole source for these original solutions. Interested readers should write Mike Pascual, 150 North Center #219, Reno, Nevada 89501.)

Press, William H., Flannery, Brian P., Teukolsky, Saul A., and Vetterling, William T. *Numerical Recipes: The Art of Scientific Computing*, Cambridge University Press, New York, 1986.

Shannon, C. E. "A Mathematical Theory of Communication," *Bell System Technical Journal*, pp. 379–423, 623–656, October 1948.

Skinner, Michael. Easy Money, *Omni Magazine*, pp. 42–45, 48, 115–116, May 1989.

Thorp, Edward O. *Beat the Dealer*, Vintage Books, Random House, Inc., New York, 1966.

Thorp, Edward O. *The Mathematics of Gambling*, Gambling Times, Inc., Hollywood, California, 1984.

Wentworth, R. C. "Utility, Survival, and Time: Decision Strategies under Favorable Uncertainty," April 1989. (This paper is available at cost directly from the author. Interested readers should write Dr. R. C. Wentworth, 8072 Broadway Terrace, Oakland, California 94611.)

Wiley, Dean. *Understanding Gambling Systems*, Gambler's Book Club, Las Vegas, Nevada, 1975.

Williams, Larry R. *The Definitive Guide to Futures Trading, Vols. I and II*, Windsor Books, Brightwaters, New York, 1988.

Wilson, Allan. *The Casino Gambler's Guide*, Harper & Row, New York, 1965.

Ziemba, William T. "A Betting Simulation: The Mathematics of Gambling and Investment," *Gambling Times*, pp. 46–47, 80, June 1987.

Ziemba, William T. "Betting Systems: Money Management, the Mathematics of Gambling and Investment," *Gambling Times*, pp. 77, 80, May 1987.

Index